HIPPOCRENE LANGUAGE STUDIES

SPANISH GRAMMAR

HIPPOCRENE BOOKS
New York

Hippocrene paperback edition, 1991.

Second printing, 1993.

For information, contact:
HIPPOCRENE BOOKS, INC.
171 Madison Avenue
New York, NY 10016

Printed in the United States of America.

TABLE OF CONTENTS

LESSON I
<table>
<tr><td></td><td>Page</td></tr>
</table>

The alphabet 1
Diphthongs 6
Syllabication 8
Accentuation 9
Punctuation 10

LESSON II

Parts of Speech 11
    Nouns 11
    Pronouns 12
    Adjectives 13
    Articles 13
    Verbs 14
    Adverbs 14
    Prepositions 15
    Use of preposition "of" to replace adjectival nouns 16
    Conjunctions 17
    Interjections 17

LESSON III

The Spanish sentence 18
    Word order 18
    Negative sentences 18
    The personal "A" 19

LESSON IV

Possession of nouns 20
Possessive adjectives 20
Possessive pronouns 21
Demonstrative adjectives and pronouns 23

LESSON V

Present indicative tense (regular verbs) 25
"Tomar" and "llevar" 27

LESSON VI

Present indicative tense of irregular verbs 30
"Saber" and "conocer" 30
"Tener" and "traer" 31
Radical changing verbs 31
Interrogative words 33

LESSON VII

Page

Uses of "ser" and "estar" 36
Present participles 37
Progressive action 37

LESSON VIII

"Tener" and "haber" 40
Present perfect tense 40
Irregular past participles 40
Idiomatic use of "hay" 41
Idiomatic use of "tener" 41

LESSON IX

Direct object pronouns 43
Indirect object pronouns 46

LESSON X

Governing verbs 50
Pseudo-governing verbs 51

LESSON XI

Polite command of regular verbs 53
Polite command of irregular verbs 53
Polite command of radical changing verbs 54
Familiar command of regular verbs 56
Familiar command of irregular verbs 56
Familiar command of radical changing verbs 57

LESSON XII

Preterite indicative tense 59
Special uses of certain verbs in the preterite tense ("saber" and
    "querer") 61
Difference between "salir" and "dejar" 62

LESSON XIII

Uses of "por" and "para" 64
Special construction of verbs with prepositions 65

LESSON XIV

Imperfect indicative tense 68
Past progressive tense 69
Requirement of the imperfect tense with certain verbs 69
Pluperfect (past perfect) indicative tense 70
Idiomatic use of "había" 70

Lesson XV

	Page
Numbers	72
Cardinal numbers	72
Ordinal numbers	73
Time expressions	74
Calendar divisions	75

Lesson XVI

Passive voice	78
Idiomatic uses of some verbs	80
"Hacer"	80
Verbs of perception ("ver" and "oír")	82
"Gustar" and "faltar"	83

Lesson XVII

Future indicative tense	86
Irregular verbs of the future indicative tense	86
Conditional tense	88
Conditional tense of irregular verbs	88
Conditional perfect tense	89

Lesson XVIII

Reflexive verbs	91
Reflexive pronouns after prepositions	92
Reciprocal verbs	92
Reflexive substitute for passive voice	93

Lesson XIX

Expressions of comparison	95
Absolute superlative	97
Comparison of equality	98
"Sino"—How used	98
"Only"—How expressed	98

Lesson XX

Subjunctive mood	101
Present subjunctive	101
Present progressive subjunctive	102
Present perfect subjunctive	102
Imperfect subjunctive	102
Past progressive subjunctive	103
Pluperfect subjunctive	103
Uses of the subjunctive	103
After verbs of causing	103
Expressions of feeling or emotion	105
Expressions of doubt or denial	106
Impersonal expressions	106
After relative pronouns	107
After conjunctive expressions	108
In conditions contrary to fact	109

Lesson XXI

	Page
Word study	111
Words similar in English and Spanish	114
States of Mexico and their abbreviations	125
Occupations	126

Appendix

Acceptable translations for exercises contained in the text	127
Useful expressions	142
Practice material	145
Spanish names	**149**
Regular verbs	**152**
Orthographical changing verbs	157
Irregular verbs	159
Radical changing verbs	165
Verb list, English-Spanish	166
Verb list, Spanish-English	171
English-Spanish vocabulary	**176**
Spanish-English vocabulary	**197**

THE ALPHABET

The Spanish alphabet consists of the same letters as the English alphabet and these four additional characters: CH, LL, Ñ, and RR.

A Closely resembles "A" in "father."

alto—high   mayo—May
allá—there   allí—there
aquí—here   antes—before

B The "B" and "V" are pronounced exactly alike in Spanish. At the beginning of a breath group; that is, after a pause in speech, or the beginning of a sentence, and after the letters "M" or "N" they are pronounced about like the "B" in "book."

bonito—pretty   hombre—man
bajo—low   ambos—both
bien—well   hambre—hunger

At all other times the "B" and "V" are pronounced about like the "V" in "level."

hablar—to speak   libro—book
haber—to have   libra—pound
abril—April   libre—free

C Soft like the "S" in "see" before "E" and "I."

centavo—cent   cincuenta—fifty
cerca—near   civil—civil
cinco—five   cicatriz—scar

Hard like "C" in "country" at all other times.

caballo—horse   comer—to eat
calle—street   color—color
casa—house   cuando—when

CH Like the "CH" in "church" at all times. This is the first of the Spanish characters that differs from the English. It is found in the dictionary immediately following the "C" and not as in English.

mucho—much, a lot,   chico—small
 a great deal
muchacho—boy   choque—wreck
chiste—joke   marchar—to march

D At the beginning of a breath group and after "L" and "N" it is pronounced about as it is in English with the tongue against the upper front teeth.

donde—where	indio—Indian
dar—to give	mandar—to send
el día—the day	doy—I give

Following other letters about like the "TH" in "they."

madre—mother	cuidado—care
padre—father	ciudad[1]—city
lado—side	usted[1]—you

E Has two sounds in Spanish. In open syllables (syllables in which it is the final letter) about like the English long "A"; but without the diphthongal sound often made in English.

leche—milk	enero—January
café—coffee, brown	leña—firewood

In closed syllables (one in which another letter follows) about like the English "E" in "bet."

ser—to be	el—the
estar—to be	en—in, on, at
comer—to eat	entrar—to enter

F About as in English.

falta—fault	flor—flower
falso—false	fe—faith
fecha—date	favor—favor

G Before the vowels "A," "O," and "U" and all the consonants like the "G" in "go."

ganar—to earn	gustar—to like
gasolina—gasoline	guante—glove
gota—drop	grande—large

Before "E" and "I" the "G" is pronounced like the "H" in "house."

gente—people	giro—draft
agente—agent	gigante—giant

In order to retain the "G" sound of "go" before "E" or "I," it is necessary to insert "U" after the "G," and the "U" is silent.

guía—guide	guerrero—warrior
guerra—war	Guillermo—William

---

[1] Many Spanish-speaking people fail to pronounce distinctly the final "D" of a word, saying rather **"ciudá"** and **"usté."**

If it is desired to retain the "U" sound following "G" before "E" or "I," place the dieresis (two dots) over the "U."

averigüé—I ascertained   vergüenza—shame

H This letter is silent[2] in Spanish.

humano—human   hasta—until
hermoso—beautiful   húmedo—humid
huelga—strike (work)   huevo—egg
hueso—bone   almohada—pillow

I Like the "I" in the English word "machine."

idea—idea   lindo—pretty
idioma—language   comida—dinner
iglesia—church   isla—island

J This letter is strongly aspirated like the "H" in the English word "house."

juez—judge   jueves—Thursday
juro—I swear   jardín—garden
junio—June   reloj[3]—watch

K This letter is found only in foreign words and is pronounced in the same manner as it is in the foreign word.

L About as it is in English with the tongue nearly flat and the tip close to the front teeth.

lago—lake   leer—to read
lana—wool   lejos—far
lápiz—pencil   lugar—place

LL This is the second of the Spanish characters that differs from the English. It is considered as a single symbol and not as a double letter. It is found in the dictionary directly after the "L." On the Mexican Border this letter is pronounced like the English consonant "Y."

ella—she   llegar—to arrive
llave—key   lluvia—rain
llevar—to carry   llegada—arrival

---

[2] This letter is very slightly aspirated before the diphthong "UE"; however, in many instances the aspiration is so slight that it is almost imperceptible.

[3] Many Spanish-speaking persons pronounce this word "reló," and in some instances it will be found so written.

M   As in English.

mapa—map	más—more
martes—Tuesday	mes—month
marzo—March	marido—husband

N   As in English.

nada—nothing	nombre—name
nadie—nobody	noche—night
nunca—never	anoche—last night

Ñ   This is the third of the Spanish characters that differs from the English, and it is found after the "N" in the dictionary. It has the same value of the "NY" of "canyon."

montaña—mountain	compañía—company
niño—child	albañil—mason
leña—firewood	mañana—tomorrow

O   In open syllables like the "O" in "obey."

ocho—eight	oro—gold
oficina—office	permiso—permission
ojo—eye	recibo—receipt

In closed syllables like the "O" in "order."

son—they are	con—with
señor—sir	sombrero—hat
vapor—ship	por—by, through, for

P   About as in English.

peso—peso	puerto—port
pagar—to pay	para—for, in order to
puerta—door	pelo—hair

Q   This letter is always followed by "U" and in turn by either "E" or "I," and the "U" is always silent. The "QU" has the value of the English "K."

querer—to want, to wish	quien—who
quince—fifteen	quebrar—to break
¿qué?—What?	quemar—to burn

R   This letter is slightly trilled in Spanish. At the beginning of a word it is very strongly trilled.

pero—but	razón—reason
primero—first	renta—rent
parte—part	tener—to have

RR This is the last of the Spanish characters that differs from the English letters. It is found after the letter "R" in the dictionary. It is very strongly trilled.

perro—dog
perra—female dog
hierro—iron

carro—car
herrero—blacksmith
cigarro—cigarette

S About like the "S" in the English word "sister."

bastante—enough
buscar—to look for
casa—house

contestar—to answer
cosa—thing
bosque—forest

The "S" preceding "D" or "M" has a buzzing sound.

desde—since, from

mismo—same

T As in English.

tarde—late
tez—complexion
taza—cup

triste—sad
turista—tourist
también—also, too

U As a vowel like the "OO" of "moon."

último—last
un—one, a, an
usar—to use

único—only
luna—moon
sujeto—subject

For "U" as a consonant, see diphthongs.

V See "B."

voy—I am going
viaje—trip
invierno—winter

evidencia—evidence
jueves—Thursday
enviar—to send

W This letter appears only in foreign words and is pronounced as it is in the foreign word in which it appears.

X This letter has the value of the English "GS" between vowels.

exacto—exact
exactamente—exactly

examinar—to examine
examen—examination

It is pronounced like the English "S" before consonants. Some people pronounce the "X" before a consonant in Spanish as it is pronounced in English.

explicar—to explain
extranjero—alien, foreigner

extensión—extension
expreso—express

Y Standing alone it means "and" and is pronounced like the English long "E."

As a consonant it is pronounced like the "Y" in "Yuma."

yo—I
ya—already

yerno—son-in-law
leyó—he read

See diphthongs for its use in diphthongs.

Z Has the same value as "C" before "E" or "I."

zapato—shoe
zapatero—shoemaker
zapatería—shoeshop

comenzar—to begin
empezar—to begin
vez—time (numerically)

This letter rarely appears before "E" or "I" in Spanish. In conjugating verbs the "Z" is changed to "C" before "E." There are no conjugations where the letter "I" follows "Z."

DIPHTHONGS

Diphthongs in Spanish are formed by the following combinations of vowels in one syllable: a weak plus a strong vowel, a strong plus a weak vowel, or two weak vowels. The strong vowels are "A," "E," and "O"; the weak ones are "I," "U," and "Y." Two strong vowels cannot appear in the same syllable. In order to retain the full value of a weak vowel when it appears in combination with a strong vowel, it is necessary to place the written accent over the weak vowel. This results in two syllables and breaks up the diphthong.

AI or **AY**—About like the "Y" in "rye."

aire—air
hay—there is, there are

traigo—I bring
tráigame—bring me

EI or **EY**—About like the "EY" in "they."

rey—king
reina—queen

seis—six
veinte—twenty

OI or **OY**—About like the "OY" in "boy."

doy—I give
voy—I am going
oigo—I hear

soy—I am
hoy—today
estoy—I am

AU—About like the "OW" in "cow."

cautivo—captive
autor—author

aunque—although
causa—cause

EU—An "E" plus "U" sound as in

Europa—Europe   reumatismo—rheumatism

In the following groups the "U" and "I" preceding other vowels are often considered as semiconsonants and have the value of "W" and "Y" respectively.

UA

¿cuánto?—how much?   cuatro—four
¿cuándo?—when?   cuarto—room, fourth

UE

puerta—door   nuevo—new
puente—bridge   cuerpo—body

UO

cuota—quota or share

IA

hacia—toward   farmacia—pharmacy
estudia—he studies   Alemania—Germany

IE

pierna—leg   tiempo—time (length)
diente—tooth   viejo—old

IO

adiós—goodbye   precio—price
palacio—palace   recibió—he received

IU

triunfo—triumph   ciudadano—citizen
ciudad—city   ciudadanía—citizenship

UI

cuidado—care   ruido—noise

In all of the foregoing diphthongs the stress of the voice falls on the strong vowel when the syllable is stressed. In the case of two weak vowels, the stress is on the second of the two when the syllable is stressed.

"UE" or "UI" following "Q" or "G" are not diphthongs, the "U" being silent.

SYLLABICATION

In dividing words into syllables the following principles should be observed:

A consonant goes with the following vowel.

a-mi-go   e-ne-ro   ma-ña-na

Two strong vowels are separated.

le-o   ca-er   lí-ne-a   le-e

Two consonants coming between vowels are usually separated.

cin-co   pron-to   her-ma-no   par-te

The letters "CH," "LL," and "RR" are considered as one letter and are never separated.

mu-cha-cho   ca-lle   ci-ga-rro   pe-rro

A consonant followed by "R" or "L" is not separated from the "R" or "L" except "RL," "SL," "TL," "SR," and "NR."

ha-blar   li-bro   en-trar   hom-bre

but:

is-la   per-la   at-las   char-la

The letters of a diphthong or triphthong are not separated.

jui-cio   puer-ta   hue-ro

If the weak vowel of a diphthong or triphthong is accented, or the first vowel when both are weak, the accent mark is placed over said vowel to show that there is no longer a diphthong or triphthong.

dí-a   le-í-do   flú-i-do

The last of more than two consonants coming between vowels goes with the following vowel.

cons-tan-te   pers-pec-ti-va   ins-tan-te

A prefix forms a separate syllable.

ex-pre-sar   con-se-guir

ACCENTUATION

Words ending in a vowel or "N" or "S" receive the stress of the voice regularly on the next to the last syllable. In the following list, the words are divided into syllables, and the syllable receiving the stress is underlined.

<u>ju</u> lio—July
a <u>mi</u> go—friend
<u>fe</u> cha—date

<u>u</u> no—one, a
tra <u>ba</u> jo—work
di <u>ne</u> ro—money

Words ending in a consonant other than "N" or "S" receive the stress of the voice regularly on the last syllable.

ve <u>nir</u>—to come
mu <u>jer</u>—woman
pa <u>pel</u>—paper

ca <u>lor</u>—heat
co <u>lor</u>—color
de se <u>ar</u>—to desire

Words stressed contrary to the two foregoing rules bear the written accent over the vowel of the syllable to be stressed.

lec <u>ción</u>—lesson
<u>fá</u> cil—easy
di <u>fí</u> cil—difficult

<u>ár</u> bo les—trees
a <u>quí</u>—here
<u>jó</u> ve nes—youths

Certain words bear the written accent in order to distinguish them from other words otherwise spelled alike and pronounced alike, but having an entirely different meaning.

él—he	el—the	dé—give	de—of, from
sí—yes	si—if	mí—me	mi—my
tú—you	tu—your	té—tea	te—you

The written accent is used to distinguish the interrogative or exclamatory from the relative use of pronouns and adverbs.

¿cuánto?—how much?
cuanto—how much
¿cuándo?—when?
cuando—when

¿cómo?—how?
como—like, as, how
¿quién?—who?
quien—who

The written accent over the weak vowel of a weak plus strong or strong plus weak combination breaks up the diphthong and results in two separate syllables.

creído—cre í do   leído—le í do   país—pa ís

PUNCTUATION

Punctuation is the same in Spanish as in English with the following exceptions:

A question has an inverted question mark (¿) at the beginning of the question as well as the regular question mark (?) at the end.

¿ (En) dónde está Juan?	Where is Juan?
¿Cómo está Vd.?	How are you?

An exclamation has the inverted exclamation mark (¡) at the beginning of the interjection as well as the regular exclamation mark (!) at the end.

¡Qué bonito!	How pretty!
¡Qué lástima!	What a pity!

In quotations a dash (—) is generally used to indicate a change of speaker instead of quotation marks.

Juan dijo:—Yo no voy. —Ni yo tampoco. —respondió Ana.
Juan said: "I am not going." "Nor I neither," responded Ana.

The days of the week and the months of the year are not capitalized unless at the beginning of a sentence.

Hoy es lunes.	Today is Monday.
Es el dos de mayo.	It is the second of May.

The pronoun "yo" (I) is not capitalized, except at the beginning of a sentence.

An adjective of nationality is not capitalized. Some authors capitalize adjectives of nationality used as nouns while others do not.

Yo hablo español.	I speak Spanish.
Hablo con un francés. ⎫	I am speaking to
Le hablo a un Francés.⎭	a Frenchman.

The following abbreviations are capitalized.

usted—Vd.	señor—Sr.
ustedes—Vds.	señora—Sra.
señorita—Srta.	

Lesson II

PARTS OF SPEECH

There are eight parts of speech in Spanish as well as in English: nouns, pronouns, adjectives, verbs, adverbs, prepositions, conjunctions, and interjections.

NOUNS

A noun is the name of a person, place, or thing. A proper noun is the name of a particular person, place, or thing.

John—**Juan**	Mary—**María**
Charles—**Carlos**	Anna—**Ana**
Henry—**Enrique**	Louise—**Luisa**
Paul—**Pablo**	El Paso—**El Paso**
Mexico—**México**	Texas—**Texas**

A common noun is a common name for persons, places, or things that are of the same class or kind.

boy—**muchacho**	town—**pueblo**
year—**año**	book—**libro**
week—**semana**	passport—**pasaporte**
river—**río**	month—**mes**
visa—**visa**	bridge—**puente**

In English there are three genders: masculine, feminine, and neuter. In Spanish all nouns are masculine or feminine, there being no neuter. Generally nouns ending in "O" are masculine, and nouns ending in "A" are feminine. Names of male beings are masculine, and names of female beings are feminine.

the boy—**el muchacho**	the brother—**el hermano**
the girl—**la muchacha**	the sister—**la hermana**
the state—**el estado**	the money—**el dinero**
the pen—**la pluma**	the silver—**la plata**
the gold—**el oro**	the table—**la mesa**

There are several exceptions to the above, such as:

the hand—**la mano**   the map—**el mapa**   the day—**el día**

Nouns not ending in "O" or "A" should be memorized with the definite article.

the paper—**el papel**	the pencil—**el lápiz**
the month—**el mes**	the foot—**el pie**

The following endings are generally feminine or masculine respectively:

Generally feminine: **ción, dad, tad, umbre, tud**
Generally masculine: **ón, el, al, ente, ador, or**

Nouns ending in a vowel form their plurals by adding "S," and those ending in a consonant form their plurals by adding "ES." Those ending in "Z" change the "Z" to "C" before adding "ES."

hijo—son	hijos—sons
mesa—table	mesas—tables
papel—paper	papeles—papers
doctor—doctor	doctores—doctors
luz—light	luces—lights
lápiz—pencil	lápices—pencils

The masculine plural of nouns and of adjectives used as nouns may include both male and female beings when they denote rank or relation: **"Los niños,"**—the children, the boy and the girl, the boys and the girls, or the boys. Should there be any ambiguity in meaning, the noun may be repeated: **"El niño y la niña."**

los abuelos—the grandparents	los niños—the children
los padres—the parents	los hermanos—the brothers & sisters
los alumnos—the students	los tíos—the uncle & aunt
los viejos—the old (people)	los pobres—the poor (people)
los jóvenes—the young (people)	los ricos—the rich (people)

PRONOUNS

A pronoun is a word that takes the place of, or is used instead of a noun. Listed below are the English and Spanish subject pronouns with the persons and numbers:

1st person singular—I (yo)	1st person plural—we (nosotros)
2nd person singular—you (tú)	2nd person plural[1]—you (vosotros)
3rd person singular—he (él)	3rd person plural—they (ellos)
3rd person singular—she (ella)	3rd person plural—they (ellas)
3rd person singular—you (Vd.)	3rd person plural—you (Vds.)

In Spanish there are two ways of saying "you" in the singular. **"Tú"** is called the familiar form and is used in speaking to members of one's family, intimate friends, servants, and animals. This form is used with the second person form of the verb. **"Usted"** and its plural **"Ustedes"** are called the formal or polite form. **"Vd."** and **"Vds."** are the abbreviations for **"Usted"** and **"Ustedes."** In writing they may be written in the abbreviated form or written completely. This form is derived from "vuestra merced" and "vuestras mercedes" meaning "your grace." This form is used only with the third person of the verb. The plural form of "you" is always **"Vds."**

---

[1] Since the 2nd person plural is seldom, if ever, used in the average conversation, it will be omitted throughout this book, except in the appendix.

ADJECTIVES

An adjective is a word that modifies (limits or describes) a noun or a pronoun.

alto—tall	viejo—old
nuevo—new	azul—blue
pocos—few	mucho—much

Adjectives agree in gender and number with the noun or pronoun that they modify.

Adjectives form their plurals in the same manner as nouns. If they end in a vowel, form plurals by adding "S"; if they end in a consonant, form plurals by adding "ES"; if they end in "Z," change the "Z" to "C" and add "ES."

Adjectives ending in "O" in the masculine change the "O" to "A" to form the feminine. Other adjectives are the same for both genders. Exception: Adjectives of nationality ending in a consonant in the masculine singular add "A" to form the feminine.

Masculine			*Feminine*	
Singular	*Plural*		*Singular*	*Plural*
blanco	blancos	(white)	blanca	blancas
alto	altos	(tall)	alta	altas
grande	grandes	(large)	grande	grandes
español	españoles	(Spanish)	española	españolas
inglés	ingleses	(English)	inglesa	inglesas
mexicano	mexicanos	(Mexican)	mexicana	mexicanas

Limiting adjectives precede the noun they modify; descriptive adjectives generally follow the noun they modify.

many books	muchos libros
many red books	muchos libros rojos
our house	nuestra casa
our large house	nuestra casa grande
ten horses	diez caballos
ten black horses	diez caballos negros

ARTICLES

The articles in Spanish are adjectives and, as such, precede the noun they modify and agree with it in number and gender. The singular is as follows:

	Masculine	*Feminine*
Definite	el—the	la—the
Indefinite	un—a, an	una—a, an

In the plural, the definite article has the following forms, agreeing with the nouns which they accompany (there are no plural indefinite articles):

Masculine	*Feminine*
los—the	las—the

Note: "Unos" and "unas" meaning "some" are not considered to be indefinite articles.

Masculine nouns require a masculine article; feminine nouns require a feminine article:

el hombre—the man	la muchacha—the girl
los hombres—the men	las muchachas—the girls
un pasaporte—a passport	una mesa—a table

Exception: Feminine nouns beginning with stressed "a" or "ha" take "el" in the singular instead of "la," when the article immediately precedes. "El" here is of different origin from the masculine article of the same form and its use does not by any means change the gender of the noun, thus:

el agua—the water	el hacha—the axe
el acta de nacimiento	the birth certificate

but:

las aguas—the waters	las hachas—the axes
las actas de nacimiento	the birth certificates

The definite article in Spanish generally has the same uses as the English. The leading difference being that Spanish employs the article before any noun used in a general sense or when nouns represent abstractions:

El hombre es mortal.	Man is mortal.
El tiempo es precioso.	Time is precious.

VERBS

A verb is a word that shows action, being, or state of being.

John writes a letter.	"action"
John is a boy.	"being"
John is sick.	"state of being"

ADVERBS

An adverb is a word that modifies a verb, an adjective, or another adverb. It answers: where (place), how (manner), and when (time).

cerca—near	aquí—here	bien—well	más—more
lejos—far	allí—there	muy—very	así—thus
temprano—early	tarde—late	nunca—never	entonces—then

Él habla bien.	He speaks well.	(Modifies a verb)
Ella es muy bonita.	She is very pretty.	(Modifies an adj.)
Ellos hablan muy bien.	They speak very well.	(Modifies an adverb)

Adverbs are often formed by adding **"mente"** to the feminine singular form of the adjective.

Adjective	*Adverb*
lenta (slow)	lentamente (slowly)
rápida (rapid)	rápidamente (rapidly)
feliz (happy)	felizmente (happily)
triste (sad)	tristemente (sadly)

Many times an adverbial phrase is used instead of the adverb.

Adverb	*Adverbial phrase*	*Translation*
finalmente	al fin, por fin	finally, at last
ciertamente	por cierto	certainly
claramente	con claridad	clearly
fácilmente	con facilidad	easily

When two or more adverbs occur in a series, only the last receives the termination **"mente"**; the other(s) assuming the form they would have if **"mente"** were to be added:

Él habla lenta y claramente.   He speaks slowly and clearly.

PREPOSITIONS

A preposition is a word that shows the relation of a noun or pronoun following it to some other word in the sentence.

de—from, of	sobre—on, over	sin—without
en—on, in, at (location)	por—by, through, for	con—with
a—at (time), to	desde—since, from	para—for, in order to

The prepositional pronouns are the same as the subject pronouns with the exception of the first and second persons singular.

Singular	*Plural*
mí—me	nosotros(as)—us
ti—you	
él—him, it	ellos—them
ella—her, it	ellas—them
Vd.—you	Vds.—you

When used after the preposition **"con,"** the first and second persons singular become **"conmigo"** (with me) and **"contigo"** (with you) respectively.

Este libro es para Vd.   This book is for you.
Ella no estudia conmigo.   She does not study with me.
María no está con él.   Maria is not with him.
¿Va Juan contigo?   Is Juan going with you?

In Spanish, the masculine singular definite article "el" contracts with the prepositions "a" and "de" respectively.

> "a" plus "el" equals "al"—to the
> "de" plus "el" equals "del"—from the, of the

This contraction does not occur with the feminine definite articles "la" or "las" nor with the masculine plural definite article "los." The word "él" meaning "he" does not contract with the above prepositions.

Certain Spanish nouns call for a definite article not normally used in English when they are governed by the prepositions "a," "de," or "en" respectively:

al pueblo, a la iglesia	to town, to church
a la escuela, a la clase	to school, to class
a la cárcel, al trabajo	to jail, to work
del pueblo, de la iglesia	from town, from church
de la escuela, de la clase	from school, from class
de la cárcel, del trabajo	from jail, from work
en el pueblo, en la iglesia	in town, in (at) church
en la escuela, en la clase	in (at) school, in class
en la cárcel, en el trabajo	in jail, at work

The word "casa" generally meaning "house," unaccompanied by any article, and preceded by a preposition, has the meaning of "home."

en casa—at home		en la casa—at the house
de casa—from home	BUT:	de la casa—from the house
a casa—home (to home)		a la casa—to the house

USE OF PREPOSITION "OF" TO REPLACE ADJECTIVAL NOUNS

In Spanish a noun is never used as an adjective to show the material of which a thing is made as in English. Instead, the object and material of which it is constructed are joined by the preposition "de."

English	*Spanish word order*	*Spanish translation*
the straw hat	the hat of straw	el sombrero de paja
the silk shirt	the shirt of silk	la camisa de seda
the wool suit	the suit of wool	el traje de lana

CONJUNCTIONS

A conjunction is a word that is used to join a word or group of words to a word or to a group of words.

y—and	porque—because	pero—but
si—if	aunque—although	o—or

El lápiz y la pluma están aquí.   The pencil and pen are here.
Tengo cinco o seis pesos.   I have five or six pesos.

INTERJECTIONS

An interjection is a word that expresses strong or sudden feeling.

¡Qué lástima!—What a pity!   ¡Qué bonito!—How pretty!

Lesson III

THE SPANISH SENTENCE

A sentence is a group of words expressing a complete thought. It has two parts; the subject (noun or pronoun) and its modifiers, and the predicate (verb) and its modifiers.

The subject is that part about which something is said, and the predicate tells that which is said about the subject. The subject is broken up into the subject word and its modifiers, and the predicate is broken up into the predicate word and its modifiers.

The black horse/runs a beautiful race. "The black horse" is the complete subject, "horse" being the subject word modified by the adjectives "the" and "black." "Runs a beautiful race" is the complete predicate, "runs" being the predicate word modified by the phrase "a beautiful race."

Generally, the word order of Spanish sentences is the same as that in English sentences, i.e., subject, verb, object. However, in a question, Spanish usually places the subject after the verb. The auxiliary verb "do" is not translated from English into Spanish.

WORD ORDER

English sentence	Spanish word order	Spanish translation
Do you speak Spanish?	Speak you Spanish?	¿Habla Vd. español?
Do you eat here?	Eat you here?	¿Come Vd. aquí?
Do you work today?	Work you today?	¿Trabaja Vd. hoy?

The same is true of the auxiliary (helping) verb "to be" except when used to form the passive voice or the progressive tenses.

English sentence	Spanish word order	Spanish translation
Are you going to town?	Go you to town?	¿Va Vd. al pueblo?
Is he working here?	Works he here?	¿Trabaja él aquí?

If an interrogative word is used in the question, generally the interrogative word is placed in the same position as in the English sentence.

Why do you speak Spanish?	¿Por qué habla Vd. español?
When are you going to town?	¿Cuándo va Vd. al pueblo?

NEGATIVE SENTENCES

Negative sentences in Spanish are formed by placing the negative word immediately before the verb.

The expression "¿no es verdad?" (frequently shortened to "¿verdad?" or merely to "¿no?") is used inquiringly with an expectation of assent, where in English we repeat the auxiliary verb; thus:

> Ustedes cruzan todos los días, ¿no es verdad?
> You cross every day, don't you?
>
> Ellos estudian en la Academia, ¿no?
> They are studying at the Academy, aren't they?

"No" is associated with other negative words which come after it, and do not as in English, counteract the negation, but rather strengthen it:

> No compro ninguna casa. I am not buying any house.
> No como nada. I do not eat anything.

If any negative word is used with "no" it must be placed after the verb, otherwise it must take the place of "no," immediately before the verb:

> Él no come nunca aquí. He never eats here.
> Él nunca come aquí. He never eats here.

THE PERSONAL "A"

Another important difference between the English and the Spanish sentence construction is the Spanish usage of the personal "a" to introduce a direct object noun referring to a definite person or persons.

> María lleva a los niños Maria is taking (is carrying)
>   a la escuela. the children to school.

Since the direct object noun "the children" is referring to definite persons, it is necessary to introduce it by the preposition "a." If "niños" (or any other direct object noun) is not referring to a definite person or persons but rather to children in general, the construction would be:

> María lleva niños a la Maria takes children to
>   escuela. school.

If the direct object noun is not referring to persons at all, then there is no "a" used:

> María lleva muchos libros. Maria is taking (is carrying)
>   a lot of books.

Lesson IV

POSSESSION OF NOUNS

The possession of nouns corresponding to the English " 's" or "s' " (apostrophe s, or s apostrophe) is expressed in Spanish by the use of the preposition **"de"** placed before the possessor.

The girl's book.	The book of the girl.	El libro de la muchacha.
Mary's pencils.	The pencils of Mary.	Los lápices de Mary.
The boys' home.	The home of the boys.	La casa de los muchachos.

POSSESSIVE ADJECTIVES

Singular	*Plural*
mi—my	mis—my
tu—your[1]	tus—your
su—his	sus—his
su—her	sus—her
su—your[1]	sus—your
nuestro(a)—our	nuestros(as)—our
su—their	sus—their
su—their	sus—their
su—your[1]	sus—your

In Spanish the possessive adjectives agree in gender and number with the thing possessed and not with the possessor.

mi sombrero—my hat	mis sombreros—my hats
mi pluma—my pen	mis plumas—my pens
nuestra casa—our house	nuestras casas—our houses
nuestro tío—our uncle	nuestros tíos—our uncles
su primo—your cousin	sus primos—your cousins
su prima—your cousin	sus primas—your cousins

The possessive adjectives precede the noun and are repeated before each noun.

Carlos tiene mi libro y mi pluma.	Carlos has my book and pen.
Nuestra pluma y nuestro lápiz están en la mesa.	Our pen and pencil are on the table.

Since **"su"** and **"sus"** can have so many meanings, in order to prevent ambiguity, it is often necessary to use the preposition **"de"** and the proper prepositional pronoun after the object possessed. When the prepositional pronoun is used for clearness, the

---

[1] The possessive adjectives corresponding to the English possessive pronoun "your" are expressed in three ways as listed above. **"Tu"** is the familiar form and **"su"** is the polite form.

definite article is generally substituted for the possessive adjective. Either form is correct, but the use of the definite article is preferable:

Su casa.	Your house.
La casa de Vd.	Your house.
Sus libros.	His books.
Los libros de él.	His books.
Su tía.	Their aunt.
La tía de ellos.	Their aunt.
Sus tías.	His aunts.
Las tías de él.	His aunts.

In the first two sentences below, the possessor has already been given in the sentence and no ambiguity exists. In the third sentence, "John" has the book of "ella," another person; therefore, it is necessary to explain the sentence further with the prepositional phrase "de ella."

John tiene su libro.	John has his book.
Ella tiene su pluma.	She has her pen.
John tiene el libro de ella.	John has her book.

POSSESSIVE PRONOUNS

Singular	Plural	Singular	Plural	English
el mío	los míos	la mía	las mías	mine
el tuyo	los tuyos	la tuya	las tuyas	yours
el suyo	los suyos	la suya	las suyas	his
el suyo	los suyos	la suya	las suyas	hers
el suyo	los suyos	la suya	las suyas	yours
el nuestro	los nuestros	la nuestra	las nuestras	ours
el suyo	los suyos	la suya	las suyas	theirs
el suyo	los suyos	la suya	las suyas	theirs
el suyo	los suyos	la suya	las suyas	yours

A possessive pronoun agrees with the noun for which it stands in gender and number.

In the following sentences the word "libro" has been replaced by the possessive pronoun. "Libro" is masculine singular; therefore, the masculine singular possessive pronoun has replaced it.

¿En dónde está su libro?	Where is your book?
El mío está aquí.	Mine is here.
El suyo (El de él) es verde.	His is green.
El nuestro es grande.	Ours is large.

In the following sentences the word **"pluma"** is feminine singular and is replaced by the feminine singular possessive pronoun.

Esta pluma es verde.	This pen is green.
La mía no es blanca.	Mine is not white.
La suya (La de él) es negra.	His is black.
La nuestra es grande.	Ours is large.

In the following sentences the word **"libros"** is masculine plural and is replaced by the masculine plural possessive pronoun.

¿En dónde están sus libros?	Where are your books?
Los míos están aquí.	Mine are here.
Los suyos (Los de él) son rojos.	His are red.
Los nuestros son azules.	Ours are blue.

In the following sentences the word **"plumas"** is feminine plural and is replaced by the feminine plural possessive pronoun.

Estas plumas son verdes.	These pens are green.
Las mías son blancas.	Mine are white.
Las suyas (Las de él) son negras.	His are black.
Las nuestras son grandes.	Ours are large.

In order to prevent ambiguity, instead of **"el suyo"** use **"el de él," "el de ella," "el de Vd.,"** etc. Instead of **"la suya"** use **"la de él," "la de ella," "la de Vd.,"** etc. Instead of **"los suyos"** use **"los de él," "los de ella," "los de Vd.,"** etc. Instead of **"las suyas"** use **"las de él," "las de ella," "las de Vd.,"** etc.

Tengo el suyo. = {
Tengo el de él.—I have his.
Tengo el de ella.—I have hers.
Tengo el de Vd.—I have yours.
Tengo el de ellos.—I have theirs.
Tengo el de ellas.—I have theirs.
Tengo el de Vds.—I have yours.
}

In order to prevent the repetition of the noun, the following construction may be used:

Mi pluma y la pluma de Juan.	My pen and Juan's pen.
Mi pluma y la de Juan.	My pen and Juan's.
Su lápiz y el lápiz de María.	Your pencil and Maria's pencil.
Su lápiz y el de María.	Your pencil and Maria's.

Immediately following the verb **"ser"** the definite article may be omitted. However, it may be used for emphasis.

Este libro es el suyo.	This book is yours. (emphasis)
Este libro es suyo.	This book is yours.
Esta pluma es la suya.	This pen is his. (emphasis)
Esta pluma es suya.	This pen is his.
La pluma es la de él.	The pen is his. (emphasis)
La pluma es de él.	The pen is his.
La pluma es la de Juan.	The pen is Juan's. (emphasis)
La pluma es de Juan.	The pen is Juan's.

The possessive pronoun is sometimes used after a noun and is usually translated "of mine," "of his," etc., or "my" is used in an exclamation.

Un amigo mío vive aquí.	A friend of mine lives here.
¡Hijo mío! ¡Qué alto es Vd.!	My son! How tall you are!

DEMONSTRATIVE ADJECTIVES AND PRONOUNS

	Singular				Plural		
Masculine	English	Feminine			Masculine	English	Feminine
este	this	esta	near speaker		estos	these	estas
ese	that	esa	near spoken to		esos	those	esas
aquel	that	aquella	at a distance		aquellos	those	aquellas

The demonstrative adjective precedes the noun that it modifies and agrees with it in number and gender.

esta pluma	this pen	estas plumas	these pens
este libro	this book	estos libros	these books
esa carta	that letter	esas cartas	those letters
ese libro	that book	esos libros	those books
aquella pluma	that pen	aquellas plumas	those pens
aquel libro	that book	aquellos libros	those books

When the demonstratives stand alone, they take the place of the object pointed out and bear the written accent mark over the vowel of the proper syllable. When they stand alone they are demonstrative pronouns. The pronouns agree in number and gender with the nouns whose place they take.

Éste es mi libro.	This is my book.
Ése es (el) mío.	That is mine.
Éstas son de mi padre.	These are my father's.
¿De quién es éste?	Whose is this?

The neuter pronouns **"esto," "eso,"** and **"aquello"** have no written accent mark and are used when the thing for which they stand is a statement, idea, or something indefinite or unknown.

¿Qué es esto?	What is this?
Eso no es verdad.	That is not true.
¡Eso es!	That's it!
No quiero pensar en aquello.	I don't want to think of that.

LESSON V

PRESENT INDICATIVE TENSE OF REGULAR VERBS

In Spanish, verbs are conjugated to show mood, tense, person, and number. Most verbs are conjugated after a regular pattern. Verbs that do not follow the pattern are said to be irregular and must be committed to memory. Even these irregular verbs are not irregular in all tenses.

The present indicative tense in Spanish means that the time spoken of is present and indicates or points out a thing as material or existing. It may be used to make a statement or to ask a question, either affirmatively or negatively.

> 1st conjugation—**habl-AR**—to speak
> 2nd conjugation—**vend-ER**—to sell
> 3rd conjugation—**viv-IR**—to live

The infinitive is the key word that is used to form all conjugations and tenses. The present indicative tense is formed by dropping the infinitive endings "AR," "ER," and "IR," and to the remainder, which is the stem, attaching the proper endings. From the infinitive of all regular "AR" verbs, of which **"hablar"** is an example, the "AR" ending is dropped, and to the remainder **"habl,"** which is the stem, are attached the following endings: o, as, a, amos, an.

yo	hablo	1st person singular	The person speaking	I
tú	hablas	2nd person singular	The person spoken to	you
él	habla	3rd person singular	The person spoken of	he
ella	habla	3rd person singular	The person spoken of	she
Vd.	habla	3rd person singular	The person spoken to	you
nosotros(as)	hablamos	1st person plural	The persons speaking	we
ellos	hablan	3rd person plural	The persons spoken of	they
ellas	hablan	3rd person plural	The persons spoken of	they
Vds.	hablan	3rd person plural	The persons spoken to	you

From the infinitive of all regular "ER" verbs, of which **"vender"** is an example, the "ER" ending is dropped and to the remainder, **"vend,"** which is the stem, are attached the following endings: o, es, e, emos, en.

yo	vendo	nosotros(as)	vendemos
tú	vendes		
él	vende	ellos	venden
ella	vende	ellas	venden
Vd.	vende	Vds.	venden

From the infinitive of all regular "IR" verbs, of which **"vivir"** is an example, the "IR" ending is dropped and to the remainder, **"viv,"** which is the stem, are attached the following endings: o, es, e, imos, en.

yo	viv**o**	nosotros(as)	viv**imos**
tú	viv**es**		
él	viv**e**	ellos	viv**en**
ella	viv**e**	ellas	viv**en**
Vd.	viv**e**	Vds.	viv**en**

The present indicative of these verbs translates in the following ways in English:

Yo hablo.	I speak. I do speak. I am speaking.
¿Hablo yo?	Do I speak? Am I speaking?
Yo no hablo.	I do not speak. I am not speaking.
¿No hablo yo?	Do I not speak? Am I not speaking?
Tú hablas.	You speak. You do speak. You are speaking.
¿Hablas tú?	Do you speak? Are you speaking?
Tú no hablas.	You do not speak. You are not speaking.
¿No hablas tú?	Do you not speak? Are you not speaking?
Él habla.	He speaks. He does speak. He is speaking.
¿Habla él?	Does he speak? Is he speaking?
Él no habla.	He does not speak. He is not speaking.
¿No habla él?	Does he not speak? Is he not speaking?
Ella habla.	She speaks. She does speak. She is speaking.
¿Habla ella?	Does she speak? Is she speaking?
Ella no habla.	She does not speak. She is not speaking.
¿No habla ella?	Does she not speak? Is she not speaking?
Vd. habla.	You speak. You do speak. You are speaking.
¿Habla Vd.?	Do you speak? Are you speaking?
Vd. no habla.	You do not speak. You are not speaking.
¿No habla Vd.?	Do you not speak? Are you not speaking?

The plural forms are used in the same manner as above. Notice that the negative **"no"** immediately precedes the verbs.

Following are a few regular verbs that are conjugated in the present indicative tense by following the key given in this lesson.

1st Conjugation (AR)

acabar—to finish	gastar—to spend
aconsejar—to advise	llamar—to call
arrestar—to arrest	llegar—to arrive
ayudar—to help	llevar—to carry, to take
comprar—to buy	olvidar—to forget
contestar—to answer	pagar—to pay
cortar—to cut	pasar—to pass
deportar—to deport	pesar—to weigh
desear—to wish, to desire	sacar—to take out
dudar—to doubt	solicitar—to solicit
entrar—to enter	terminar—to finish
esperar—to wait for	tomar—to drink, to take
estudiar—to study	trabajar—to work
ganar—to earn, to win	usar—to use

2nd Conjugation (ER)

aprender—to learn	comer—to eat
beber—to drink	deber—to owe

vender—to sell

3rd Conjugation (IR)

abrir—to open	recibir—to receive
escribir—to write	residir—to reside

vivir—to live

"TOMAR" AND "LLEVAR"

The verbs **"tomar"** and **"llevar"** both meaning "to take" are never used interchangeably. Both are regular verbs.

Uses of **"Tomar"**

To take a public conveyance:

Tomo el autobús hoy.	I am taking the bus today.
Sergio toma el avión.	Sergio is taking the airplane.
Tomamos un taxi al pueblo.	We are taking a taxi to town.

To eat or drink something:

Susana toma café.	Susana drinks coffee.
Antonio toma un refresco.	Antonio is drinking a soft drink.
Ese hombre toma mucho.	That man drinks a lot.
Tomamos la medicina a las ocho.	We take the medicine at eight.

To grasp or take hold of:

Él toma el lápiz de la mesa.	He takes the pencil from the table.

To take a seat:

La señora toma un asiento.	The lady takes a seat.

Uses of "Llevar"

To transport a person or thing from one location to another:

Ellos llevan el algodón a la otra labor.	They are taking the cotton to the other field.
Llevamos los extranjeros al corralón.	We take the aliens to the detention camp.

To carry or to take with oneself:

Él lleva su pasaporte en su cartera.	He carries his passport in his billfold.
Llevamos mucho dinero.	We are carrying a lot of money.

To wear:

El hombre lleva una camisa negra.	The man is wearing a black shirt.

VOCABULARY

el muchacho—the boy
la señora—the lady, the woman
la madre—the mother
el doctor—the doctor
la enfermera—the nurse
el abogado—the lawyer
el autobús—the bus
el taxi—the taxi
el carro—the car
el tren—the train
la lección—the lesson
el pasaporte—the passport
la visa—the visa
la tarjeta—the card
la pistola—the pistol
el lápiz—the pencil
el dinero—the money
el agua—the water
México—Mexico

el español—Spanish
la ciudad—the city
el día—the day
el mes—the month
el año—the year
dos—two
falso—false
cada—each, every
mucho—a lot of, much, a great deal of
azul—blue
bastante—enough
hoy—today
mañana—tomorrow
siempre—always
temprano—early
nunca—never, not ever
ilegalmente—illegally
de día—by day, in the daytime

EXERCISE

1. The boy buys a pencil.
2. Does she live in El Paso?
3. We study a lot.
4. Do we write the lessons every day?
5. Is he working today?
6. Is he taking the bus tomorrow?
7. Alberto is taking the book to his room.
8. I always take a taxi.
9. He and Pepe earn enough money.
10. Luis and María do not earn a lot of money.
11. We do not speak Spanish.
12. He is taking out his visa today.
13. Simon arrives early every day.
14. Do you drive your boss's car?
15. They are waiting for the train.
16. He does not drink much water.
17. They (f) work a great deal.
18. Does this lady owe a lot of money?
19. The boy's mother passes through (por) this city every month.
20. That doctor's nurse lives in that blue house.
21. Are those lawyers buying these two cars?

LESSON VI

PRESENT INDICATIVE TENSE OF IRREGULAR VERBS

Caber—to contain, to fit	quepo	cabes	cabe	cabemos	caben
Caer—to fall	caigo	caes	cae	caemos	caen
Dar—to give	doy	das	da	damos	dan
Decir—to say, to tell	digo	dices	dice	decimos	dicen
Estar—to be	estoy	estás	está	estamos	están
Haber—to have (auxiliary)	he	has	ha	hemos	han
Hacer—to do, to make	hago	haces	hace	hacemos	hacen
Ir—to go	voy	vas	va	vamos	van
Oír—to hear	oigo	oyes	oye	oímos	oyen
Poner—to put, to place	pongo	pones	pone	ponemos	ponen
Saber—to know	sé	sabes	sabe	sabemos	saben
Salir—to leave, to depart	salgo	sales	sale	salimos	salen
Ser—to be	soy	eres	es	somos	son
Tener—to have (possession)	tengo	tienes	tiene	tenemos	tienen
Traer—to bring	traigo	traes	trae	traemos	traen
Valer—to be worth	valgo	vales	vale	valemos	valen
Venir—to come	vengo	vienes	viene	venimos	vienen
Ver—to see	veo	ves	ve	vemos	ven

"SABER" AND "CONOCER"

Although **"saber"** and **"conocer"** both mean "to know," they are not interchangeable. **"Saber"** means to know through having learned mentally, while **"conocer"** means to be acquainted with.

Yo sé la lección.	I know the lesson.
¿Sabe Vd. leer español?	Do you know how to read Spanish?
Yo conozco al contra-bandista.	I know the smuggler.
Él conoce a mi papá.	He knows my father.
¿Conoce Vd. a México?[1]	Do you know Mexico?

---

[1] The personal "a" may be used with geographical names.

"TENER" AND "TRAER"

The verb **"tener"** means "to have" showing possession "traer" meaning "to bring" has a special meaning when it is in place of the English verb "to have." When **"traer"** is used for "to have," it implies "on the person" or "in his belonging or belongings."

¿Tiene Vd. un pasaporte?	Do you have a passport?
¿Trae Vd. un pasaporte?	Do you have a passport? (on you)
Yo traigo mis papeles en mi maleta.	I have my papers in my suitcase.
Ella tiene tres hermanos.	She has three brothers.

RADICAL CHANGING VERBS

There are three classes of radical changing verbs. The root vowel (the vowel of the syllable coming immediately before the infinitive ending) makes certain changes.

FIRST CLASSIFICATION

Radical changing verbs of the first classification include verbs of the first (ar) conjugation and the second (er) conjugation. The root vowel "o" changes to "ue" and the root vowel "e" to "ie" when the stress falls on that syllable. This change takes place in four places: 1st, 2nd, and 3rd persons singular, and 3rd person plural of the present indicative tense.

First Conjugation

Pensar		Recordar	
pienso	pensamos	recuerdo	recordamos
piensas		recuerdas	
piensa	piensan	recuerda	recuerdan

Other first conjugation verbs:

cerrar—to close	encontrar—to meet, encounter
comenzar—to begin	empezar—to begin
confesar—to confess	pensar—to think
contar—to count, to relate	mostrar—to show
costar—to cost	negar—to deny
despertar—to awaken	probar—to prove
encerrar—to enclose, to lock up	regar—to irrigate

Second Conjugation

Entender		Poder	
entiendo	entendemos	puedo	podemos
entiendes		puedes	
entiende	entienden	puede	pueden

Other second conjugation verbs:

devolver—to give back
llover—to rain
perder—to lose
querer—to want
volver—to return

SECOND CLASSIFICATION

Radical changing verbs of the second classication have verbs of the third (ir) conjugation. The root vowel "o" changes to "ue" and the root vowel "e" changes to "ie" in the same places as do radical changing verbs of the first classification.

Third Conjugation

Mentir		Dormir	
miento	mentimos	duermo	dormimos
mientes		duermes	
miente	mienten	duerme	duermen

Other third conjugation verbs:

consentir—to consent
morir—to die
preferir—to prefer
referir—to refer
sentir—to feel

THIRD CLASSIFICATION

Radical changing verbs of the third classification have only verbs of the third (ir) conjugation, and in the root or stem, the vowel is "e." This classification differs from the second classification in that the root vowel "e" changes to "i" when the stress is on the stem of the verb.

Third Conjugation

Pedir		Conseguir	
pido	pedimos	consigo	conseguimos
pides		consigues	
pide	piden	consigue	consiguen

Other third conjugation verbs:

medir—to measure
repetir—to repeat
seguir—to follow, continue

INTERROGATIVE WORDS

"¿Cuál (es)?" meaning "which?" refers to persons or things, and is used to select or choose one or more than one from a larger group.

¿Cuál de los libros es (el) suyo?	Which (one) of the books is yours?
¿Cuáles de los libros son (los) suyos?	Which (ones) of the books are yours?
¿Cuál es su hermano?	Which (one) is your brother?
¿Cuáles son sus hermanos?	Which (ones) are your brothers?

"¿Cuál?" meaning "what?" is used before "ser," except when a definition is asked for, in which case "¿qué?" is used.

¿Cuál es la focha (de hoy)?	What is the date?
¿Cuál es su ocupación?	What is your occupation?
¿Cuál es su nacionalidad?	What is your nationality?
¿Qué es gramática?	What is grammar? (definition)
¿Qué es esto?	What is this? (explanation)

At all other times, except in idioms, the English interrogative "what?" is rendered by "¿qué?" in Spanish.

¿Qué come Vd.?	What are you eating?
¿Qué estudia María?	What is Maria studying?
¿Qué escribe Alberto?	What is Alberto writing?

"¿Quién?" or "quiénes?" meaning "who?" or "whom?" refers to persons only.

¿Quién estudia con Antonio?	Who is studying with Antonio?
¿Quién tiene mi libro?	Who has my book?
¿Con quiénes vive Vd.?	With whom do you live?
¿De quién habla ella?	Of whom is she speaking?

"¿De quién?" or "¿de quiénes" meaning "whose?" is always followed immediately by the verb when used as an interrogative.

¿De quién es esta tarjeta?	Whose card is this?
¿De quién es este carro?	Whose car is this?
¿De quién es esa pluma?	Whose pen is that?
¿De quién es ese libro?	Whose book is that?

NOTICE: When this interrogative word is not used with the verb "to be" (ser), it has the following Spanish sentence construction:
Object/ Interrogative Word/ Verb/ Subject

¿El carro/ de quién/ maneja/ él?   Whose car does he drive?

¿El reloj/ de quién/ trae/ Vd.?   Whose watch do you have?

"¿Cuánto(a)?" meaning "how much" and "¿cuántos(as)?" meaning "how many?" are used as pronouns or as adjectives.

¿Cuánto cuesta el libro?   How much does the book cost?

¿Cuánto dinero gana Vd.?   How much money do you earn?

¿Cuántos van al pueblo?   How many are going to town?

¿Cuántas personas trabajan aquí?   How many persons work here?

VOCABULARY

la señorita—Miss, the young lady
el señor—Mr., Sir, the man
el pariente—the relative
la gente—the people
el esposo—the husband
los padres—the parents
el oficial—the officer, the official
el mayordomo—the foreman
el documento—the document
la fe de bautismo—the baptismal certificate
el acta de nacimiento—the birth certificate
el papel—the paper
la ley—the law
el problema—the problem
la cosa—the thing
el nombre—the name
la cortada—the cut, cut scar

el lunar—the mole
la mano—the hand
la ocupación—the occupation
la ayuda—the help
la ciudadanía—the citizenship
los Estados Unidos—the United States
la semana—the week
la semana que viene—next week
el año que viene—next year
legal—legal
derecho—right, straight
nuevo—new
siete—seven
muy bien—very well
sí—yes
porque—because
con—with

EXERCISE

1. Whose card do you have?
2. How many relatives do you have?
3. What do you have (on you)?
4. Do you have cuts or moles?
5. Yes sir, I have a cut scar on my right hand.[2]
6. A week has seven days.
7. Is she going with us next week?
8. I don't have my brother's documents.
9. This man has my things.
10. This girl comes and goes every day.
11. Does she have a husband?
12. Why do you want a visa?
13. The foreman is asking for help.
14. These men do not know anything (nada).
15. Manuel does not know the officer's name.
16. Why do you always lie?
17. They do not understand the problem.
18. Mrs. Silva[3] knows the Spanish lessons very well.

---

[2] The definite article instead of the possessive is used with parts of the body and articles of clothing.

[3] A proper name modified by a title requires the definite article immediately before the title except in direct address.

La señorita López está enferma.	Miss Lopez is sick.
El señor García no está aquí.	Mr. Garcia is not here.
But: Buenos días, señor Valdez.	Good morning, Mr. Valdez.

Lesson VII

"SER" AND "ESTAR"

The verbs "**ser**" and "**estar**" both meaning "to be," are irregular in the present indicative tense. These verbs are never used interchangeably without altering the meaning of the sentence.

Ser		*Estar*	
soy	somos	estoy	estamos
eres		estás	
es	son	está	están

"Estar" is used:

To show location or position (place where a person or thing is, temporarily or permanently).

El libro está en la mesa.	The book is on the table.
Juárez está en México.	Juarez is in Mexico.
¿ En dónde está Benito?	Where is Benito?

To express a condition that is accidental or temporary.

La mujer está enferma.	The woman is sick.
El agua está fría.	The water is cold.
La muchacha está pálida.	The girl is pale.

With a past participle to express a resultant state. The past participle is used as an adjective and as such, agrees in gender and number with the subject of the sentence.

El libro está bien escrito.	The book is well written
La mujer está sentada.	The woman is seated.
La puerta está cerrada.	The door is closed.

With a present participle to express progressive action. (Progressive action will be discussed later in this lesson.)

"Ser" is used at all other times. Generally **"ser"** expresses a state or condition that is natural or inherent and essentially lasting rather than accidental or occasional. Such conditions may show: age, character, financial status, appearance, origin, ownership, material of which a thing is made, occupation, nationality, time expressions, impersonal expressions. It is always used before a predicate noun or pronoun.

Mi tío es viejo.	My uncle is old. (age)
Ella es una mujer buena.	She is a good woman. (character)
Él es rico.	He is rich. (financial status)
Olga es muy bonita.	Olga is, very pretty. (appearance)
Yo soy de México.	I am from Mexico. (origin)

El libro es de Simón.	The book is Simon's. (possession)
El anillo es de oro.	The ring is gold. (material)
Él es médico[1].	He is a doctor. (occupation)
Él es un buen médico.	He is a good doctor. (predicate noun)
Hoy es miércoles.	Today is Wednesday. (time)
Son las dos y media.	It is two-thirty. (time)
Ellos son mexicanos.	They are Mexicans. (nationality)
¿De qué color es el libro?	What color is the book? (appearance)
Es imposible hacerlo.	It is impossible to do it. (impersonal expression)
Es él.	It is he. (predicate pronoun)

PRESENT PARTICIPLES

The present participle of a verb is formed by adding "ando" to the stem of "AR" verbs and "iendo" to the stem of "ER" and "IR" verbs. The English present participle ends in "ing."

Habl(ar)—hablando—speaking
Com(er)—comiendo—eating
Viv(ir)—viviendo—living

There are very few verbs which have any irregularities in the present participle. These irregularities occur in the stem of the verb, so these verbs are considered stem changing; all are third conjugation verbs.

Decir—diciendo—saying, telling
Mentir—mintiendo—lying
Pedir—pidiendo—asking for
Morir—muriendo—dying
Seguir—siguiendo—following, continuing

PROGRESSIVE ACTION

Progressive action is a word for word translation of the verb. The present progressive is used for a portrayal of an action in progress. Most uses of the progressive in Spanish emphasize what is going on at that moment. The present tense of the verb "estar" is used before the present participle of a verb to express progressive action in the present time.

Estar trabajando—to be working

Yo estoy trabajando—I am working

---

[1] The indefinite article is omitted before an unmodified predicate noun in the Spanish sentence.

38

Tú estás trabajando—You are working
Él está trabajando—He is working
Ella está trabajando—She is working
Usted está trabajando—You are working

Nosotros estamos trabajando—We are working
Ellos están trabajando—They are working (M)
Ellas están trabajando—They are working (F)
Ustedes están trabajando—You are working

NOTICE: The present participle remains constantly the same for all persons. The present participle will be the same for all persons in all tenses. Only the conjugation of the verb "estar" will change to agree with the subject.

The verbs **"ir," "andar,"** and **"seguir"** are also often used with the present participle for an even stronger progressive meaning. These forms give the idea of "keeping on," "continuing," or "progressing."

Pedro va comiendo por el camino.	Pedro keeps on (continues) eating along the road.
Víctor sigue caminando.	Victor continues walking.
Gabriel anda trabajando en la labor.	Gabriel is working in the field (out in the field).

"IR," "VENIR," "SALIR," and generally other verbs of motion, should not be used in the progressive.

VOCABULARY

el **presidente**—the president
el **hijo**—the son
el **sobrino**—the nephew
el **primo**—the cousin
el **padre**—the father, the priest
el **hermano**—the brother
el **trabajador**—the worker, the laborer
el **cuñado**—the brother-in-law
el **ciudadano**—the citizen
la **tienda**—the store
la **fábrica**—the factory
los **pantalones**—the pants, the trousers
el **saco**—the coat
la **camioneta**—the small truck (pickup), station wagon
la **verdad**—the truth
el **color**—the color
el **sábado**—Saturday
al **pueblo**—to town

bonito—pretty
mojado—wet
grande—large, big
alto—high, tall
mexicano—Mexican
enfermo—sick, ill
viejo—old
esta noche—tonight
aquí—here
allí—there
ahora—now
ahorita—right now
muy—very
por—per, through, by, for
de—from, of
pero—but
y—and
mentir—to lie
valer—to be worth
¿**qué tan lejos?**—how far?

EXERCISE

1. Are you a Mexican citizen?
2. This house is very big.
3. Who is the president of Mexico?
4. Where is Rogelio working now?
5. They are always sick.
6. Miss Garcia is not pretty, because she is very old.
7. Your nephew is from Mexico, but what is he doing here?
8. Yes sir, they are from Puebla.
9. These are Pedro's pants.
10. Miss Cabaza is not very tall.
11. Our papers are wet.
12. This boy is that woman's son.
13. My father and brother are in California, but they are from Mexico.
14. You are lying right now.
15. The man's brother-in-law is not here.
16. How far is the store from your house?
17. You are not telling the truth..
18. How much are you earning per month?
19. What time is it?[2]
20. How much is your station wagon worth?
21. My cousin is from Mexico, and he is working in a factory there.
22. Today is Saturday, and we are going to town tonight.
23. Mr. Moreno is a good worker, but he is always sick.
24. (Of) What color is your new coat?

---

[2] The pronoun "it" is not translated into Spanish when it is used as the subject of the English sentence. This also is true when "it" is used as the predicate nominative in English.

Lesson VIII

"TENER" AND "HABER"

The verbs **"tener"** and **"haber,"** both meaning "to have," are irregular in the present indicative tense.

Tener		*Haber*	
tengo	tenemos	he	hemos
tienes		has	
tiene	tienen	ha	han

"Tener" means "to have" showing possession and is not to be used interchangeably with **"haber,"** which means "to have" as an auxiliary verb in forming the compound tenses.

PRESENT PERFECT TENSE

The present perfect indicative tense (called "perfect" by many grammarians) is formed by placing the present tense of the auxiliary verb **"haber"** immediately in front of the past participle of the main verb. No word can come between the auxiliary verb and the past participle.

The past participle of regular verbs is formed by adding **"ado"** to the stem of verbs of the first conjugation and **"ido"** to the stem of verbs of the second and third conjugations.

Tom(ar)—tom<u>ado</u>
Com(er)—com<u>ido</u>
Viv(ir)—viv<u>ido</u>

Tomar	*Comer*	*Vivir*
he tomado	he comido	he vivido
has tomado	has comido	has vivido
ha tomado	ha comido	ha vivido
hemos tomado	hemos comido	hemos vivido
han tomado	han comido	han vivido

He tomado un examen hoy.	I have taken an exam today.
Hemos comido mucho.	We have eaten a lot.
Ella ha vivido aquí por mucho tiempo.	She has lived here for a long time.

Irregular Past Participles

Infinitive	*Past Participle*
abrir—to open	abierto—open(ed)
cubrir—to cover	cubierto—covered
decir—to say, to tell	dicho—said, told
escribir—to write	escrito—written

Infinitive	*Past Participle*
hacer—to do, to make	**hecho**—done, made
morir—to die	**muerto**—dead, died
poner—to put, to place	**puesto**—put, placed
romper—to tear	**roto**—torn
volver—to return	**vuelto**—returned
ver—to see	**visto**—seen

The following past participles require a written accent over the "i".

caer—to fall	**caído**—fallen
creer—to believe	**creído**—believed
leer—to read	**leído**—read
oír—to hear	**oído**—heard
traer—to bring	**traído**—brought

IDIOMATIC USE OF "HAY"

The phrases "there is," "there are," "is there?," and "are there?" are translated by the single Spanish word **"hay"** or **"¿hay?."**

No hay nadie en el cuarto.	There is nobody in the room.
¿Hay mucha gente allí?	Are there many people there?
¿Hay patrulleros en ese lugar?	Are there any patrolmen at that place?

IDIOMATIC USE OF "TENER"

"Tener" is commonly used to indicate age.

¿Cuántos años tiene Vd.?	How old are you?
Tengo veinte años.	I am twenty years old.

"Tener" is used with a personal subject in the following idioms:

tener (mucho) calor—to be (very) warm
tener cuidado—to be careful
tener la culpa—to be at fault, to be guilty
tener (mucho) frío—to be (very) cold
tener (mucha) hambre—to be (very) hungry
tener (mucha) sed—to be (very) thirsty
tener miedo—to be afraid
tener sueño—to be sleepy
tener razón—to be right
no tener razón—to be wrong

VOCABULARY

el extranjero—the alien
el amigo—the friend
el papá—the father
la esposa—the wife
la calle—the street
la cicatriz—the scar
el avión—the airplane
la mesa—the table
la silla—the chair
el cuarto—the room
la puerta—the door
el libro—the book
la tinta—the ink

el sombrero—the hat
el rancho—the ranch
el país—the country
la línea—the line
alguien—somebody, someone
verde—green
tres—three
doce—twelve
antes—before
alguna vez—ever
varias veces—several times
por mucho tiempo—for a long
   time

EXERCISE

1. There is a book on the table.
2. Are you very sleepy?
3. Why have you lied?
4. There are twelve chairs in the room.
5. How is your wife?
6. I have not seen that man before.
7. Where is the letter? There it is!
8. We have brought our documents today.
9. We haven't opened the door.
10. His friend does not have money.
11. Has he seen Pedro's scar?
12. I have taken the car to town.
13. What have you done today?
14. They have gone to town several times.
15. Are there men on that ranch?
16. Somebody has put the ink on the table.
17. Have you ever been in Chicago?
18. How many times have you returned to this country?
19. Does your boss have a green airplane?
20. He is very careful when he crosses the street.
21. I am very hungry and very thirsty, because I have not eaten
    anything (nada) for a long time.

Lesson IX

DIRECT OBJECT PRONOUNS

The direct object (noun or pronoun) of a sentence is the complement or "completer" of a verb of action. It receives the action of the verb directly; that is, the direct object is acted upon by the subject. It answers "what" when it is referring to things. For example:

John throws the ball.
    What does John throw?   Answer: the ball; therefore, ball is the direct object noun.

Mary loses the pencils.
    What does Mary lose?   Answer: the pencils; therefore, pencils is the direct object noun.

Pablo reads the lesson.
    What does Pablo read?   Answer: the lesson; therefore, lesson is the direct object noun.

All the direct objects underlined have been nouns. When a pronoun is substituted for each noun, the sentences read:

John throws it.
Mary loses them.
Pablo reads it.

The above underlined words are direct object pronouns. In a normal conversation one does not repeat the noun after it has already been established; in other words, one does not say: John throws the ball. John throws the ball fast. John throws the ball to first base. Instead, one says: John throws the ball. He throws it fast. He throws it to first base. Because of this normal trend in conversation, object pronouns are very important both in English and in Spanish. Since hardly anything is neuter in Spanish, we have to substitute object pronouns that agree both in number and gender with the noun they are replacing. Spanish direct object pronouns for things are:

lo—it (masculine)   los—them (masculine)
la—it (feminine)   las—them (feminine)

In English, when converting the noun into a pronoun the position of the direct object is not affected.

John throws it. subject/ verb/ direct object pronoun/

John throws the ball. subject/ verb/ direct object noun/

In Spanish, a direct object noun has the same position as in English.

John tira la <u>pelota</u>. subject/ verb/ direct object noun/

This is not so when a direct object pronoun is used in the Spanish sentence. The rules for the position of object pronouns in the Spanish sentence are:

Immediately before a conjugated verb.

John <u>la</u> tira.   John throws it.

Immediately before a governing verb or attached to the infinitive that accompanies the governing verb. (Will be discussed later.)

Immediately before the conjugated form of the verb **"haber"** when dealing with the perfect tenses.

John <u>la</u> ha tirado.   John has thrown it.

Immediately before the conjugated form of the verb "estar" or attached to the present participle when dealing with the progressive tenses.

John <u>la</u> está tirando.   John is throwing it.

or

John está tirándo<u>la.</u>   John is throwing it.

Attached to positive commands, but before negative commands. (Will be discussed later.)

The direct object can also be referring to a person or persons. It still receives the action of the verb, but in this case the direct object answers "whom".

Jane sees John.
    Whom does Jane see?   Answer: <u>John</u>; therefore, <u>John</u> is the direct object noun.

Mary sees the men.
    Whom does Mary see?   Answer: the <u>men</u>; therefore, <u>men</u> is the direct object noun.

John sees the woman.
    Whom does John see?   Answer: the <u>woman</u>; therefore, <u>woman</u> is the direct object noun.

In Spanish, whenever the direct object is a definite person noun, it is introduced by the personal "a":

Jane ve a John.   Jane sees John.
Mary ve a los hombres.   Mary sees the men.
John ve a la mujer.   John sees the woman.

If pronouns are substituted for the direct object nouns, the sentences will read:

Jane sees <u>him.</u>
Mary sees <u>them.</u>
John sees <u>her.</u>

The English direct object pronouns for people and their Spanish equivalents are:

Singular	Plural
me—me	nos—us
te—you (familiar)	
le, lo—him	les, los—them (m)
la—her	las—them (f)
le, lo (m), la (f)—you	les, los (m), las (f)—you

The position of object pronouns for persons is the same as that for things. If ambiguity exists when direct object pronouns in the third person are used, they may be explained further by the use of the prepositional pronoun.

Jane le ve (a él).	Jane sees him.
Mary les ve (a ellos).	Mary sees them.
John la ve (a ella).	John sees her.

VOCABULARY

la regla—the rule
la comida—the food
la cuenta—the bill
·el lado—the side
el bolsillo—the purse
la iglesia—the church
la oficina—the office
las armas—the guns, weapons
los abuelos—the grandparents
el domingo—Sunday
caro—expensive
barato—cheap
legal—legal
otro—other, another

ya—already, yet
también—also, too
todavía—still, not yet
en casa—at home
a menudo—often
casi—almost
una vez—once, one time
de vez en cuando—from time to time
en el otro lado—on the other side
pasar de contrabando—to smuggle
buscar—to look for, seek
visitar—to visit
aprender—to learn

EXERCISE NO. 1

1. Josefa has my legal papers. She has them in her purse.
2. He has not seen your pistol. Do you have it with you?
3. We buy our food in that store. It is not very expensive there.
4. Miguel is selling his house. He is selling it cheap.
5. Do you understand the rules? Yes, I have already learned them.
6. I have the guns at home. My wife has already seen them.

9. He has crossed the river before. He crosses it every week.
10. Have you seen Felipe? No, I haven't seen him yet.
11. Have you (pl) seen my wife? Yes, we see her at the store from time to time.
12. We see Gabriel and his sister every week. We see them in church every Sunday.
13. Timoteo visits his grandparents often. He visits them once a week.
14. Does he know you very well? No, he doesn't know me very well.
15. Have you paid the bill? Yes, I have already paid it.

INDIRECT OBJECT PRONOUNS

Indirect object nouns or pronouns name the person or persons to or for whom the subject gives or does something. It receives the action of the verb indirectly. It may be a prepositional phrase in English, but in Spanish it is always considered the indirect object. The indirect object answers "to whom" or "for whom."

Martha gives John a camera.
or
Martha gives a camera to John.　　　　Answer: to <u>John</u>; therefore, <u>John</u> is
　　To whom does Martha give　　　　　　　　the indirect object.
　　a camera?

She makes Jane a dress.
or
She makes a dress for Jane.　　　　　Answer: for <u>Jane</u>; therefore, <u>Jane</u>
　　For whom does she make　　　　　　　　is the indirect object.
　　a dress?

If a pronoun is substituted for each of the indirect object nouns above, the sentences will read:

Martha gives <u>him</u> a camera.　　　　She makes <u>her</u> a dress.
or　　　　　　　　　　　　　　　　or
Martha gives a camera　　　　　　　　She makes a dress <u>for her.</u>
　　<u>to him.</u>

The English indirect object pronouns and their Spanish equivalents are:

Singular	*Plural*
me—me	**nos**—us
te—you (familiar)	
le—him, her, you	**les**—them, you

Since "**le**" may mean "you," "him," or "her," the speaker may want to explain further by adding "**a Vd.**," "**a él**," or "**a ella**" respectively. "**Les**" may be clarified by "**a Vds.**," "**a ellos**," or "**a ellas.**"

Martha **le** da una cámara **a él.**	Martha gives him a camera.
Ella **le** hace un vestido **a ella.**	She makes her a dress.

The position of indirect object pronouns in the Spanish sentence is the same as direct object pronouns.

An indirect object noun is often anticipated by the use of the indirect object pronoun. Although the indirect object pronoun is not always required, it is better Spanish to use it. The indirect object noun in Spanish is always introduced by the personal "**a.**"

Él **le** paga a José muy poco.	He pays Jose very little.
Luis **le** ha dado a María su anillo.	Luis has given Maria his ring.
Yo **le** he escrito a mi esposa hoy.	I have written to my wife today.

The following verbs almost invariably take indirect objects:

ayudar—to help	**escribir**—to write
comprar—to buy	**robar**—to steal
dar—to give	**pagar**—to pay
deber—to owe	**pedir**—to ask for
decir—to say, to tell	**pedir prestado**—to borrow

"**Comprar**," "**pedir prestado**,"[1] and "**robar**" require an object pronoun and a personal "**a**" before their objects. The preposition "from" is not translated into Spanish.

Yo **le** compro el diario **a** Pepe.	I buy the newspaper from Pepe.
Él **le** pide prestado el carro a Mike.	He borrows the car from Mike.
Él **le** roba dinero a su padre.	He steals money from his father.

---

[1] "**Prestado**" agrees with the thing borrowed in gender and number.

VOCABULARY

el **comerciante**—the merchant
la **cuñada**—the sister-in-law
el **compañero**—the companion
el **zapatero**—the shoemaker
el **diario**—the newspaper
el **periódico**—the newspaper
la **información**—the information
el **radio**—the radio
el **cinto**—the belt

la **bicicleta**—the bicycle
el **ganado**—the cattle
algo—something, anything
alguna cosa—something, anything
correcto—correct
tocante a—about (concerning)
leer—to read
robar—to steal

EXERCISE NO. 2

1. He is giving me his correct name.
2. She is reading the newspaper to us.
3. Have you written Mary this week?
4. We are buying the belts from Mr. Jones.
5. Osvaldo is selling his bicycle to Pepe.
6. Have you asked him for money?
7. Haven't you (pl) asked the consul for a permit?
8. Why don't you borrow the radio from Martin?
9. He is borrowing $5.00 from his sister-in-law.
10. He has stolen many things from that merchant.
11. Has he stolen anything from you?
12. He is telling the officer the truth.
13. I am asking them for more information about (concerning) their companions.
14. He is buying the cattle from Mr. Aguilar.
15. They have given the officer a lot of information.
16. He has never helped us before.
17. Have you paid the shoemaker the bill?

When a sentence contains a direct and indirect object **pronoun,** they may not be split in the Spanish sentence and the **indirect** always precedes the direct.

John ya *me* lo ha pagado.	John has already paid *it to me.*
Mary *nos* lo ha vendido.	Mary has sold *it to us.*

For the sake of sound, when both object pronouns begin **with** the letter "l," the indirect object pronoun, whether singular **or** plural, becomes "se" in the Spanish sentence.

1. Juan *le* lo da. = Juan *se* lo da.— Juan gives *it to him.*

2. Mary *les* los vende. = Mary *se* los vende.— Mary sells *them to them.*

EXERCISE NO. 3

1. Why is he showing it to us?
2. We are sending them to them.
3. Andres has asked us for it (f).
4. Guillermo is paying them (f) to me now.
5. We have crossed it with him many times.
6. He is buying it from him for (por) $10.00.
7. Who is selling it (f) for us?
8. Why don't you ask him for them (f)?
9. He has stolen it from the merchant.
10. They have already given it to them.
11. Have you sent it (f) to Susana?
12. Has he borrowed it from Miss Peña?
13. Jaime has told it to me many times.
14. I have already bought it from Mr. Garza.
15. Who sends them (f) to you?

Lesson X

GOVERNING VERBS

"**Ir a**" with an infinitive has the same meaning of intention which is expressed by "going to do something," in English. It forms a future expression with its starting point either at the present or at a past time, according to the tense assumed by "**ir.**"

Luis va a mandármelo[1] mañana.	Luis is going to send it to me tomorrow.
or	
Luis me lo[1] va a mandar mañana.	
¿Va a sacarlo Vd. hoy?	Are you going to take it out today?
or	
¿Lo va a sacar Vd. hoy?	

"**Tener que**" denotes obligation or necessity to perform the action expressed by the following infinitive. "**Tener que**" plus infinitive translates "have to or must do something" in English.

Yo tengo que ir al pueblo hoy.	I have to go to town today.
¿Tiene Vd. que hacerlo ahorita?	Do you have to do it right now?
or	
¿Lo tiene que hacer Vd. ahorita?	

"**Querer**" plus infinitive means "to want or to wish to do something."

Simón quiere trabajar aquí.	Simon wants to work here.
¿Quiere Vd. sacar un pasaporte?	Do you want to take out a passport?

"**Poder**" is a true auxiliary and it corresponds to the English "be able," and expresses physical power or ability, generally represented in English by the defective verb "can."

Yo no puedo hacerlo ahorita.	I can not do it right now.
or	
Yo no lo puedo hacer ahorita.	
¿Puede Vd. trabajar ocho horas al día?	Can you work eight hours a day?

---

[1] Object pronouns (direct or indirect or both) can either be attached to the infinitive or be placed immediately before the conjugated governing verb. If two object pronouns are attached to the infinitive, a written accent is required on the original stress of the infinitive.

"Pensar" plus infinitive means "to intend or to plan to do something."

Antonio <u>piensa</u> venir acá
el año que viene.

Antonio plans (intends) to
come here next year.

"Saber" before an infinitive denotes knowledge or mental ability. **"Saber"** in English as a governing verb means "to know how to do something." "How" should not be translated into Spanish.

Yo <u>sé</u> hacer esa clase de
trabajo.

I know how to do that type of
work.

Ellos ya <u>saben</u> leer.

They already know how to read.

"Deber (de)" placed as an auxiliary verb before an infinitive expresses the ideas of duty, obligation or undefined necessity which are represented in English by the defective verbals, "ought" or "should."

Benito <u>debe (de)</u> comprarlo
pronto.

Benito should buy it soon.

Nosotros <u>debemos</u> estudiar
más.

We ought to study more.

"Tratar de" plus infinitive means "to try or to attempt to do something."

Ellos <u>han tratado</u> de brincar la línea muchas veces.

They have tried (attempted) to
jump the line many times.

"Acabar de," preceding an infinitive, usually expresses an action completed in the immediate past or an action completed in conjunction with another event. The time expressed depends upon the tense used. **"Acabar de"** in the present tense expresses an action just completed while the imperfect tense denotes a past action completed in conjunction with another event.

Ricardo <u>acaba</u> de llegar.

Ricardo has just arrived.

¿<u>Acaban</u> ellos <u>de</u> salir?

Have they just left?

PSEUDO-GOVERNING VERBS

The following verbs when followed by an infinitive are considered pseudo-governing verbs. Care should be taken in reference to the position of object pronouns with these verbs. A pronoun may depend either upon the infinitive or the preceding verb, according to the meaning intended, in which case each pronoun accompanies the verb to which it belongs.

aprender a—to learn
ayudar a—to help
comenzar a (ie)—to start, to begin
dejar—to let, to allow
dejar de—to stop, to cease doing something
enseñar a—to teach
venir a—to come

VOCABULARY

el cónsul—the consul
el tractor—the tractor
la tarde—the afternoon
el lugar—the place
la cita—the appointment, the date
mañana por la mañana—tomorrow morning
mañana por la noche—tomorrow night

otra vez—again
lo más pronto posible—as soon as possible
sin—without
como—as
firmar—to sign
hallar—to find
manejar—to drive

EXERCISE

1. Do you know how to drive a tractor?
2. Is he going to work tomorrow morning?
3. We can't go this afternoon.
4. We have to sign this paper as soon as possible.
5. Do you (pl) know how to read and write?
6. She wants to be with her husband as soon as possible.
7. They plan to return tomorrow night.
8. Have you just returned from Mexico?
9. I ought to pay him today.
10. You should buy it from him.
11. You have to leave this place right now.
12. How has Antonio been able to find work in the United States?
13. What is he going to do tonight?
14. I have tried to do it before.
15. They have just entered, but haven't been able to find work.
16. To whom does he plan to give it?
17. We have just arrived in this city.
18. Don't you know that you can not take it with you?
19. Do they allow you to see the consul without an appointment?
20. Does Jorge start to work (working) very early?
21. Why have you stopped working as a nurse?

LESSON XI

POLITE COMMAND OF REGULAR VERBS

The polite command of regular verbs' is obtained by using the stem of the first person singular of the present indicative tense and adding the following endings:

For "ar" verbs, add:

"e"—singular
"en"—plural

For "er" and "ir" verbs, add:

"a"—singular
"an"—plural

Infinitive	Present tense, 1st person Singular	Stem	Command Singular	Plural
llevar	yo llevo	llev	lleve Vd.	lleven Vds.
aprender	yo aprendo	aprend	aprenda Vd.	aprendan Vds.
abrir	yo abro	abr	abra Vd.	abran Vds.

"Vd." and "Vds." are used respectively as the subject of the command. They may be omitted. The negative word "no" is placed before the affirmative command to make it a polite negative command. Object pronouns (direct, indirect, or both) are attached to affirmative commands and are placed immediately before a negative command. If an object pronoun is attached to a multi-syllable command, a written accent is required on the original stress of the command.

Lléveselo Vd.	Take it to him.
No se lo lleve Vd.	Don't take it to him.
Apréndala bien.	Learn it well.
No la aprenda bien.	Don't learn it well.
Abran Vds. sus libros.	Open your books.
No abran Vds. sus libros.	Don't open your books.

POLITE COMMAND OF IRREGULAR VERBS

The polite command of irregular verbs is obtained by using the stem of the first person singular of the present indicative tense and adding the same vowel endings as for the formation of commands of regular verbs.

Infinitive	Present tense, 1st person Singular	Stem	Command Singular	Plural
tener	yo tengo	teng	tenga Vd.	tengan Vds.
hacer	yo hago	hag	haga Vd.	hagan Vds.
poner	yo pongo	pong	ponga Vd.	pongan Vds.
traer	yo traigo	traig	traiga Vd.	traigan Vds.

Infinitive	Present tense, 1st person singular	Stem	Command Singular	Plural
ver	yo veo	ve	vea Vd.	vean Vds.
decir	yo digo	dig	diga Vd.	digan Vds.
venir	yo vengo	veng	venga Vd.	vengan Vds.
salir	yo salgo	salg	salga Vd.	salgan Vds.
oír	yo oigo	oig	oiga Vd.	oigan Vds.

POLITE COMMAND OF RADICAL CHANGING VERBS

The polite command of radical changing verbs is obtained by applying the same rule as for the formation of commands for regular and irregular verbs.

Infinitive	Present tense, 1st person Singular	Stem	Command Singular	Plural
cerrar	yo cierro	cierr	cierre Vd.	cierren Vds.
entender	yo entiendo	entiend	entienda Vd.	entiendan Vds.
mentir	yo miento	mient	mienta Vd.	mientan Vds.

In order to retain the "k" sound in any verb ending in "car" (brincar, sacar, buscar, etc.), change the "c" to "qu" before adding "e" or "en".

brinque Vd.	brinquen Vds.
saque Vd.	saquen Vds.
busque Vd.	busquen Vds.

In order to retain the hard "g" sound in any verb ending in "gar" (pagar, llegar, rogar, etc.), change the "g" to "gu" before adding "e" or "en".

pague Vd.	paguen Vds.
llegue Vd.	lleguen Vds.
ruegue Vd.	rueguen Vds.

The following verbs do not follow the above rules and should be memorized:

	Singular	Plural
estar—to be	esté Vd.	estén Vds.
dar—to give	dé Vd.	den Vds.
ir—to go	vaya Vd.	vayan Vds.
ser—to be	sea Vd.	sean Vds.
saber—to know	sepa Vd.	sepan Vds.

With commands come new verbs. Following is a good starting list.

Aflojar	to relax, to loosen
Alzar	to raise, to lift
Apear	to get out of (car, bus, etc.), to get down
Apurarse	to hurry (up), to hasten
Bajar (se) (de)	to get out of (car, bus, etc.), to get down, to climb down
Deletrear	to spell
Enseñar	to teach, to show
Firmar	to sign
Pararse	to stop, to stand (up)
Seguir	to follow, to pursue
Soltar	to relax, to release, to untie, to let go, to free (radical changing verb)
Subir (se) (a)	to get into (car, bus, etc.), to climb up

Following is a group of commands that may be helpful to the beginner. Some are given with reflexive pronouns which will be explained later.

Enséñeme su pasaporte	Show me your passport.
Alce las manos	Raise your hands.
Súbase al carro	Get in the car.
Bájese del carro	Get out of the car.
Apéese del tren	Get out of the train.
Sígame	Follow me.
Párese	Stop. or Stand up.
Alto	Stop.
Suelte la mano	Relax your hand.
Afloje la mano	Relax your hand.
Dígame la verdad	Tell me the truth.
Enséñeme la vereda	Show me the trail.
Ponga sus cosas en la mesa	Put your things on the table.
Apúrese	Hurry up.
Ándele	Hurry up.
Deletréeme su nombre	Spell your name for me.
Tráigalo	Bring it.
Pídale al cónsul una visa	Ask the consul for a visa.
Dígame otra vez	Tell me again.
Cómprelo	Buy it.
Venga acá	Come here.
Vaya allá	Go over there.
Búsquelo	Look for it.
Déme la navaja	Give me the knife.
Vaya a la oficina	Go to the office.
Váyase	Go away.
Esté aquí mañana	Be here tomorrow.
Dígame el nombre de su patrón	Tell me your boss's name.
Hágalo ahorita	Do it right now.

Inclínese contra la pared	Lean against the wall.
Párese contra la pared	Stand against the wall.
Firme su nombre aquí	Sign your name here.
Repita, por favor	Repeat, please.
Hable en voz más alta	Speak louder.
Quítese el sombrero	Take off your hat.
Perdóneme	Excuse me. **or** Pardon me.
Siéntese	Sit down.
Voltéese	Turn around.
Hable más despacio	Speak slower.
Mire hacia la pared	Look towards the wall.

FAMILIAR COMMAND OF REGULAR VERBS

The familiar command of regular verbs is obtained from the third person singular of the present indicative tense as it is. The subject "tú" is generally omitted.

Contesta tú la carta.	Answer the letter.
Aprende tú la lección.	Learn the lesson.
Abre la puerta.	Open the door.

The negative familiar command is obtained by adding an "s" to the polite singular command.

No contestes la carta.	Don't answer the letter.
No aprendas la lección.	Don't learn the lesson.
No abras la puerta.	Don't open the door.

FAMILIAR COMMAND OF IRREGULAR VERBS

Some familiar commands of irregular verbs do not follow a rule and should be learned separately. The negative familiar command of these verbs is obtained by adding an "s" to the polite singular command. (Subject pronouns are generally not used with familiar commands.)

decir—to say, tell	di	no digas
hacer—to do, make	haz	no hagas
ir—to go	ve	no vayas
poner—to put, place	pon	no pongas
salir—to leave, depart	sal	no salgas
ser—to be	sé	no seas
tener—to have	ten	no tengas
venir—to come	ven	no vengas

FAMILIAR COMMAND OF RADICAL CHANGING VERBS

The familiar command of radical changing verbs is obtained by using the third person singular of the present indicative tense.

Infinitive	Present tense, 3rd person Singular	Familiar Command
cerrar	él cierra	cierra
entender	él entiende	entiende
mentir	él miente	miente

The negative familiar command of radical changing verbs is obtained by adding an "s" to the polite singular command.

No cierres la puerta.	Don't close the door.
No pidas eso.	Don't ask for that.
No mientas tanto.	Don't lie so much.

VOCABULARY

el camino—the road
la pluma—the pen
la caja—the box
la asignatura—the assignment
la cartera—the billfold
amarillo—yellow
primero—first
juntos—together
temprano—early

luego—then
hasta—until
tan rápido—so fast
el cheque—the check
cerrar—to close
correr—to run
esperar—to wait for
subirse a—to get in; climb
abrir—to open

EXERCISE

1. Show me the road.
2. Wait until tomorrow.
3. Help us do the assignment.
4. Don't run so fast.
5. Don't close the door.
6. Tell us the truth.
7. Give it to them.
8. Take us early in your car.
9. Pay us with a check.
10. Let me see your billfold.
11. Get in the car.
12. Don't cross together.

13. Do this first and then open the box.
14. Tell her that her husband is lying.
15. Don't pay him yet.
16. Go home and bring us those documents.
17. Come to the office tomorrow and help me.
18. Bring me his yellow pen, please.
19. Be here early tomorrow.
20. Get a visa as soon as possible.

LESSON XII

PRETERITE INDICATIVE TENSE

The preterite indicative tense is used to express a definitely completed past action. It is called by some grammarians the past absolute, past definite, or historical past. The preterite indicative tense simply calls attention to completed action in past time.

To conjugate verbs in the preterite indicative tense, attach the following endings to the stem of the verbs:

> For "ar" verbs: é, aste, ó, amos, aron
> For "er" verbs: í, iste, ió, imos, ieron
> For "ir" verbs: í, iste, ió, imos, ieron

Hablar	*Comer*	*Recibir*
hablé	comí	recibí
hablaste	comiste	recibiste
habló	comió	recibió
hablamos	comimos	recibimos
hablaron	comieron	recibieron

All regular verbs in the preterite tense bear a written accent over the last vowel in the first and third persons singular. The preterite is used anytime a definite past action is expressed. A specific time does not have to be mentioned.

¿Cuántos documentos vendió Vd.?	How many documents did you sell?
¿(En) dónde compró Vd. eso?	Where did you buy that?
Yo hablé con él ayer.	I talked to him yesterday.

There are seventeen verbs that are irregular in the preterite indicative tense. It is an easy tense to learn in that fourteen of these verbs, although possessing irregular stems, take the same irregular preterite endings as follow: "e," "iste," "o," "imos," "ieron."

NOTICE: These endings carry no written accents. In these fourteen verbs, those ending in "j" drop the "i" of the "ieron" ending: "condujeron," "dijeron," "trajeron." In the third person singular, of "hacer" the "c" changes to "z" to retain the original soft "c" sound.

Infinitive	*Irregular Stem*	*Conjugation*
andar	anduv	anduve, anduviste, anduvo, anduvimos, anduvieron
estar	estuv	estuve, estuviste, estuvo, estuvimos, estuvieron

Infinitive	Irregular Stem	Conjugation
haber	hub	hube, hubiste, hubo, hubimos, hubieron
hacer	hic	hice, hiciste, hizo, hicimos, hicieron
poder	pud	pude, pudiste, pudo, pudimos, pudieron
poner	pus	puse, pusiste, puso, pusimos, pusieron
tener	tuv	tuve, tuviste, tuvo, tuvimos, tuvieron
venir	vin	vine, viniste, vino, vinimos, vinieron
querer	quis	quise, quisiste, quiso, quisimos, quisieron
saber	sup	supe, supiste, supo, supimos, supieron
traer	traj	traje, trajiste, trajo, trajimos, trajeron
decir	dij	dije, dijiste, dijo, dijimos, dijeron
conducir	conduj	conduje, condujiste, condujo, condujimos, condujeron
caber	cup	cupe, cupiste, cupo, cupimos, cupieron

"Ser" and "ir" are conjugated alike in the preterite indicative tense.

Ser—to be	Ir—to go
fuí	fuí
fuiste	fuiste
fué	fué
fuimos	fuimos
fueron	fueron

"Dar" is conjugated like a regular "er" verb in the preterite tense but without the written accents: **di, diste, dio, dimos, dieron.**

Any verb of the second and third conjugation whose stem ends in a vowel changes the unaccented "i" between vowels to "y" as an unaccented "i" may not appear between vowels in Spanish:

Leer—to read .... leí, leíste, leyó, leímos, leyeron
Caer—to fall .... caí, caíste, cayó, caímos, cayeron
Oír—to hear .... oí, oíste, oyó, oímos, oyeron
Creer—to believe .... creí, creíste, creyó, creímos, creyeron

Many verbs appear to be irregular in the preterite, but are only orthographically (spelling) so. The change in spelling is made in order to retain the sound of the final consonant of the stem of the verb. Infinitives ending in **"car"** change the "c" to "qu" before "e" in the first person singular in order to retain the "k" sound. Infinitives ending in **"gar"** change the "g" to "gu" in the first person singular in order to retain the hard "g" sound.

brincar—to jump	brinqué, brincaste, brincó, brinca-mos, brincaron
buscar—to look for	busqué, buscaste, buscó, buscamos, buscaron
tocar—to touch	toqué, tocaste, tocó, tocamos, toca-ron
sacar—to take out	saqué, sacaste, sacó, sacamos, sacaron
llegar—to arrive	llegué, llegaste, llegó, llegamos, llegaron
pagar—to pay	pagué, pagaste, pagó, pagamos, pagaron
rogar—to beg	rogué, rogaste, rogó, rogamos, rogaron
pegar—to hit	pegué, pegaste, pegó, pegamos, pegaron

Radical changing verbs of the second and third classifications make certain changes in the stem of the verb in the preterite tense. The "o" of the stem changes to "u" in the third persons singular and plural. The "e" of the stem changes to "i" in the third persons singular and plural.

mentir—to lie		dormir—to sleep	
mentí	mentimos	dormí	dormimos
mentiste		dormiste	
mintió	mintieron	durmió	durmieron

The following verbs undergo the same changes mentioned above in the preterite tense:

consentir—to consent	referir—to refer
divertir—to amuse	repetir—to repeat
medir—to measure	seguir—to follow
morir—to die	sentir—to feel
pedir—to ask for	servir—to serve
preferir—to prefer	vestir—to dress

SPECIAL USES OF CERTAIN VERBS
IN THE PRETERITE TENSE

Certain verbs have entirely different meanings when they are used in the preterite tense.

"Saber" in the preterite tense means "did find out," or "found out."

¿Cómo supo Vd. eso?	How did you find that out?
Yo supe porque él me dijo.	I found out because he told me.

"No querer" in the preterite tense means "would not." (It should be used only with negative sentences indicating refusal.)

El cónsul no quiso darme una visa.	The consul would not give me a visa.
Ellos no quisieron hacerlo.	They would not do it.

DIFFERENCE BETWEEN SALIR AND DEJAR

In any tense, **"salir"** means to leave in the sense of departing from a place, whereas, **"dejar"** means to leave someone or something behind or abandoned.

Él salió de casa el mes pasado.	He left home last month.
¿A qué hora sale el tren?	(At) what time does the train leave?
¿(En) dónde dejó Vd. a su familia?	Where did you leave your family?
Yo los dejé en Reynosa.	I left them in Reynosa.

"Dejar" may also be used as a governing verb meaning "to allow," or "to let."

Ellos no nos dejaron entrar.	They did not allow us to enter.
Déjeme ayudarle.	Let me help you.
¿Le dejaron ellos cruzar?	Did they let you cross?

VOCABULARY

el padrastro—the stepfather
el criminal—the criminal
la maleta—the suitcase
la navaja—the knife
la botella—the bottle
la marijuana—the marijuana
el tequila—the tequila
el lado—the side
la milla—the mile

el desierto—the desert
la última vez—the last time
la primera vez—the first time
el mes pasado—last month
hace—ago
ayer—yesterday
ayer por la mañana—yesterday morning

EXERCISE

1. Anita did not come from Mexico with her stepfather.
2. Simon did not bring me my suitcase.
3. She said she did not tell the officer the truth.
4. How many years did your parents live in Sonora?
5. I couldn't do the work yesterday morning.
6. We didn't see the criminal.
7. Did he leave his passport with you?
8. The woman sent seven dollars to her daughter last month.

9. The legal papers did not cost her much.
10. He let me go because I told him the truth.
11. They left here with my uncle five days ago.
12. Why did you leave your wife at that place?
13. I didn't believe what[1] he said.
14. Did you ask him for any money?
15. He wouldn't give me the knife when I asked him for it.
16. At what time did he find out?
17. When was the last time you saw this man?
18. I worked in that factory for a long time.
19. How many bottles of tequila did you bring from Mexico?
20. How many miles did you walk through the desert?
21. What did you do when you arrived in Chicago?
22. He told me that he saw Mr. Moreno yesterday.

---

[1] Whenever "what" is not used as an interrogative word, but rather has the meaning of "that which", it is rendered in Spanish by the construction "lo que."

Lesson XIII

USES OF "POR" AND "PARA"

The prepositions **"por"** and **"para"** are employed in senses that have so great an apparent resemblance and are so frequently translated alike in English that it is necessary to study their uses carefully in order to know which one to use in Spanish. These prepositions each have their definite uses and cannot be interchanged without altering the meaning of a sentence.

"PARA" is used:

To show destination, purpose, or use. (For, to)

Él sale para Nueva York.	He is leaving for New York.
¿Para dónde va Vd.?	Where are you going?
El libro es para Vd.	The book is for you.
Estudio para aprender.	I study in order to learn.
Él estudia para médico.	He is studying to be a doctor.
Ella tiene un vaso para vino.	She has a wine glass.
Tengo veinte dólares para ropa.	I have twenty dollars for clothes.

To express a point in future time. (For, by)

La lección para mañana es fácil.	The lesson for tomorrow is easy.
Él tiene una cita para el lunes.	He has an appointment (date) for Monday.
Tenga el carro listo para esta tarde.	Have the car ready by this afternoon.

Whenever a conjugated verb is followed by an infinitive, or when an infinitive is standing alone in an English sentence, Spanish sometimes requires insertion of the preposition **"para"**. This is rendered in English by "in order to;" so a good rule of thumb is that if a conjugated verb is followed by an infinitive, or an infinitive stands alone in English, test to see if insertion of "in order to" would make sense in the English sentence. If "in order to" makes sense, and if it expresses a purpose, **"para"** must be used before the infinitive in Spanish.

Fuí para ver a mi hermana.	I went to see my sister.
Lo traje para cambiarlo.	I brought it to exchange it.
No pude venir con él.	I couldn't come with him. ("In order to" would not make sense here so no **"para"**.)

"POR" is used:

To denote an agent (see passive voice).

Él fué arrestado por el oficial.	He was arrested by the officer.
El libro fué escrito por un extranjero.	The book was written by a foreigner.

To express source (by, through, for, or along).

Él entró por la puerta.	He entered through the door.
Él va por el médico.	He is going for the doctor.
Lo hice por Vd.	I did it for you. (for your sake)
Trabajé por mi hermano.	I worked for my brother. (in his place)

To show reason or motive for an action.

Él fué arrestado por matar a un hombre.	He was arrested for killing a man.
Ella estuvo en la cárcel por robar.	She was in jail for stealing.

To express a unit of measure or number, and to express exchange.

Gano dos pesos por día.	I earn two pesos a day.
Cuestan quince centavos por libra.	They cost fifteen cents per pound.
Diez por ciento de los hombres fueron allá.	Ten per cent of the men went there.
Él pagó cinco dólares por el sombrero.	He paid five dollars for the hat.
Hemos dado el carro viejo por uno nuevo.	We have given the old car for a new one.

To express a period of time.

He trabajado aquí por dos meses.	I have worked here for two months.
Él ha vivido allí por mucho tiempo.	He has lived there for a long time.
Él estuvo aquí por cinco minutos.	He was here for five minutes.

SPECIAL CONSTRUCTION OF VERBS WITH PREPOSITIONS

After a preposition, whenever an "ing" form of a verb is used in English, in Spanish one must always use the full infinitive of the verb. Some of the more common prepositions that are followed by an infinitive in Spanish are:

Después de	After
Antes de	Before
Desde	Since
Sin	Without
Por	Through, for
Para	For, in order to
Al	On, upon
En vez de	Instead of

Después de cruzar el río, fuimos a un rancho grande.
After crossing the river, we went to a big ranch.

Le escribimos una carta al gobernador antes de venir.
We wrote a letter to the governor before coming.

Él no ha visto a su amigo desde prestarle el dinero.
He has not seen his friend since lending him the money.

Le despidieron del trabajo por hablar tanto.
They fired him from the job for talking so much.

Al salir del teatro, él fue arrestado.
On leaving the theater, he was arrested.

En vez de decir la verdad, él mintió más.
Instead of telling the truth, he lied more.

The preposition "by" **(por)** when followed by an "ing" is generally best expressed by omitting the "by" and using only the present participle in Spanish.

Él cruzó el río vadeando por los lugares bajos.
He crossed the river by wading through the low places.

Ella no ganó nada mintiendo.
She didn't gain anything by lying.

When a preposition is followed by a verb that has to be conjugated, **"que"** must be placed in front of the subject or the conjugated verb.

Después (de) que Antonio comió, salió para el centro.
After Antonio ate, he left for town.

Desde que (nosotros) llegamos, él no ha venido a esta casa.
Since we arrived, he has not come to this house.

Después (de) que María llegó, la señora nos dió las noticias.
After Maria arrived, the lady gave us the news.

VOCABULARY

la garita—sentry box (the entrance
gate—Mexican border)
el minero—the miner
la ofensa—the offense
el vaso—the drinking glass
la leche—the milk
la vaca—cow
el día de fiesta—the holiday
la plaza—the square
la montaña—the mountain
la carta—the letter
la mercancía—merchandise
el oeste—west
el hospital—the hospital
el centavo—the cent
el ejercicio—the exercise
la iglesia—the church
la plata—the silver

el pan—the bread
la máquina—the machine
el teléfono—the telephone
pequeño—small
solo—alone
hacia—towards
menos—less
el lunes por la mañana—Monday
morning
quebrar—to break
parar—to stop
cambiar—to change; exchange
voltear—to turn
andar—to walk
estar listo—to be ready

EXERCISE

1. Why did the officers arrest you?
2. They arrested me for a very small offense.
3. Eliseo has an appointment for Monday morning.
4. I need a glass for milk.
5. He ran towards the west when I saw him.
6. She wants to go home for the holidays.
7. I paid the rancher $100 for the cow.
8. The miners went to the mountains to look for silver.
9. He sold each one for five cents.
10. Do these exercises by (for) tomorrow.
11. He earns very little money doing this kind of work.
12. After he left the hospital, he started to work.
13. That lawyer can do a lot for you.
14. What is this machine for? It is for writing letters.
15. Upon arriving at the office, I called him by telephone.
16. Marta cannot go to the store without telling me.
17. You cannot walk through the park alone.
18. Instead of telling us the truth, she lied.
19. The officer stopped him because he started to run.
20. After exchanging his merchandise for money, he went to town.
21. He and his two friends always travel together.
22. Turn to the right where you see the church.
23. He broke the bottle without knowing it.

Lesson XIV

IMPERFECT INDICATIVE TENSE

In Spanish there are two past indicative tenses; the preterite indicative and the imperfect indicative. They are not used interchangeably. The latter is an added tense not found in English grammar. In Spanish it is called the co-preterite. To conjugate verbs in the imperfect indicative tense, the following endings are attached to the stem of the verb:

For "ar" verbs, add: aba, abas, aba, ábamos, aban
For "er" verbs, add: ía, ías, ía, íamos, ían
For "ir" verbs, add: ía, ías, ía, íamos, ían

Comprar—to buy	*Vender—to sell*	*Venir—to come*
compraba	vendía	venía
comprabas	vendías	venías
compraba	vendía	venía
comprábamos	vendíamos	veníamos
compraban	vendían	venían

There are only three verbs that are irregular in the imperfect indicative tense.

Ser—to be	era, eras, era, éramos, eran
Ver—to see	veía, veías, veía, veíamos, veían
Ir—to go	iba, ibas, iba, íbamos, iban

The imperfect indicative tense is used:

To express customary or habitual past action. This corresponds to the English "used" followed by an infinitive.

Yo comía allí cada día.	I used to eat there every day.
Él ganaba mucho dinero en México.	He used to earn a lot of money in Mexico.

To express an interrupted past action. In this case the interrupted action, that which was going on, is placed in the imperfect indicative, and the interrupting action, that which did the interrupting, is put in the preterite indicative. The imperfect action is generally expressed by the progressive imperfect (imperfect of **"estar"** plus the present participle of the main verb).

| Yo estaba estudiando cuando Carlos entró. | I was studying when Carlos entered |

To express two or more actions going along together. All of these actions will be put in the imperfect and either the simple imperfect or the progressive imperfect may be used. (Notice that the translation in these cases is "was" or "were" plus the present participle in English.)

Yo estaba trabajando (trabajaba), y ella estaba leyendo (leía).	I was working, and she was reading.
Enrique estaba jugando (jugaba) con su hijo, y su esposa estaba preparando (preparaba) la comida.	Enrique was playing with his son, and his wife was preparing dinner.

PAST PROGRESSIVE TENSE

The imperfect tense of the verb "estar" is used before the present participle of a verb to show progressive action in past time. This action may also be expressed by the imperfect tense of the main verb.

Ella estaba trabajando allí.	She was working there.
Juan estaba viviendo solo.	Juan was living alone.

AVOID USING "IR," "VENIR," "SALIR," AND OTHER VERBS OF MOTION IN THE PROGRESSIVE TENSES.

The verbs "ir," "andar," and "seguir" are also used with the present participle to express an even stronger progressive meaning. Of the three verbs, "ir" and "andar" are more commonly used.

Lo arrestaron porque andaba tomando.	They arrested him because he was drinking.
Ellos iban caminando por el camino.	They were walking along the road.
Ella seguía cantando.	She kept on singing.

REQUIREMENT OF THE IMPERFECT TENSE WITH CERTAIN VERBS

The imperfect tense expresses an action of indefinitely prolonged duration: Whatever the person was doing, used to do, or customarily did are the usual translations. Use the imperfect indicative tense to state whatever the person or persons (1) was or were, (2) had (possession), (3) knew, (4) wanted, (5) intended, (6) needed, or (7) owed.

Él no tenía dinero.	He didn't have any money.
No sabíamos eso.	We didn't know that.
No queríamos ir porque no teníamos dinero.	We didn't want to go because we didn't have any money.

¿Cuándo pensaba Vd. cruzar?	When did you intend to cross?
Yo sabía que él era mexicano.	I knew that he was a Mexican.
Él no me necesitaba.	He did not need me.

The imperfect is a very important tense with governing verbs. Adhering to the special uses of the imperfect tense, note that some of the governing verbs are usually used in the imperfect: "Ir a," "querer," "pensar," "saber," and "acabar de."

PLUPERFECT (PAST PERFECT) INDICATIVE TENSE

The pluperfect (by some grammarians called the past perfect) is formed by placing the imperfect tense of the auxiliary verb "haber" before the past participle of the main verb.

Yo había comido—I had eaten
Tú habías comido—You had eaten
Él había comido—He had eaten
Nosotros habíamos comido—We had eaten
Ellos habían comido—They had eaten

IDIOMATIC USE OF "HABÍA"

The third person singular of the imperfect indicative of the verb "haber" is used idiomatically meaning "there was" or "there were" or "was there?", "were there?".

| Había mucho algodón en el campo. | There was a lot of cotton in the field. |
| ¿Había mucha gente trabajando allí? | Were there many people working there? |

VOCABULARY

el estudiante—the student
el alumno—the student
el marido—the husband
el bracero—day laborer
la sala de clase—the classroom
el algodón—the cotton

el troque (slang)—the truck
la troca (slang)—the truck, pick-up
otro—another, other
estar enfermo—to be sick
pizcar—to pick (cotton, etc.)
localizar—to locate

EXERCISE

1. I had already bought the house when they arrived.
2. There was much (a lot of) cotton in the fields.
3. Had he gone to the office when you went to see him?

4. She did not come for the money because she had received a check.
5. You told me that you had worked for him before.
6. Did you know that the man was a smuggler?
7. Were there any contract laborers picking cotton?
8. I used to work for Mr. Kent, but now I am working on a big ranch.
9. What kind of work were you doing before coming to the United States?
10. He said that he wanted to come to San Antonio to work.
11. When I was working on that ranch, Enrique was there also.
12. Her husband had been working in Cotulla for many years.
13. They were walking along the road when I arrested them.
14. Who was driving the truck when you (pl) were going to California?
15. They intended to come to the United States, but couldn't because they didn't have any money.
16. Had you seen this man before?
    I was very sick yesterday.
17. There were many people without work when I left Mexico.
18. The student was doing the lesson when I entered the classroom.
19. His uncle needed other papers to take out a passport.
20. Did you know how to locate this man's house?
21. Did you know Elias when you were working there?

Lesson XV

NUMBERS

CARDINAL NUMBERS

cero	0	ochenta	80
uno, a	1	ochenta y ocho	88
dos	2	noventa	90
tres	3	noventa y nueve	99
cuatro	4	ciento (cien)	100
cinco	5	ciento uno	101
seis	6	doscientos, as	200
siete	7	doscientos dos	202
ocho	8	trescientos, as	300
nueve	9	trescientos tres	303
diez	10	cuatrocientos, as	400
once	11	cuatrocientos cuatro	404
doce	12	quinientos, as	500
trece	13	quinientos cinco	505
catorce	14	seiscientos, as	600
quince	15	seiscientos seis	606
diez y seis	16	setecientos, as	700
diez y siete	17	setecientos siete	707
diez y ocho	18	ochocientos, as	800
diez y nueve	19	ochocientos ocho	808
veinte	20	novecientos, as	900
veinte y uno	21	novecientos nueve	909
veinte y dos	22	mil	1,000
treinta	30	mil novecientos diez	1,910
treinta y tres	33	mil novecientos sesenta y seis	1,966
cuarenta	40	dos mil	2,000
cuarenta y cuatro	44	dos mil doscientos doce	2,212
cincuenta	50	seis mil	6,000
cincuenta y cinco	55	seis mil diez y seis	6,016
sesenta	60	ocho mil	8,000
sesenta y seis	66	ocho mil ciento ochenta y ocho	8,188
setenta	70	un millón	1,000,000
setenta y siete	77	un millón cien mil cien	1,100,100

The cardinal numbers, except "uno" and multiples of "ciento," are invariable. These two numbers agree with the noun that they modify in gender and number. "Ciento" used alone before a masculine or feminine noun drops the final syllable "to" and becomes "cien." "Uno" drops the "o" when used before a masculine noun and changes the "o" to "a" before a feminine noun.

cien hombres	one hundred men
cien mujeres	one hundred women
treinta y un libros	thirty-one books
doscientas una libras	two hundred one pounds

"Uno" is not used before "ciento or "mil."

mil ochocientos	1,800
ciento cinco	105

In English we may say "one hundred one" or "one hundred and one," "two hundred seventeen" or "two hundred and seventeen." In Spanish the conjunction is not used between hundred (thousand, million) and the next numeral in a series.

ciento quince	115
setecientos diez y ocho	718
doscientos cuarenta	240

Counting above one thousand is not done by hundreds as is sometimes done in English.

mil ochocientos treinta	1830 (eighteen-thirty)
mil quinientos catorce	1514 (fifteen-fourteen)

In Spanish the word "millón" is a noun and is followed by the preposition "de" before the object enumerated.

un millón de pesos	one million pesos
dos millones de libros	two million books

ORDINAL NUMBERS

primero—first	sexto—sixth
segundo—second	séptimo—seventh
tercero—third	octavo—eighth
cuarto—fourth	noveno—ninth
quinto—fifth	décimo—tenth

The ordinal numbers agree with the word they modify in number and gender. They are seldom used above ten. "Primero" and "tercero" drop the "o" when used before a masculine singular noun.

el primer piso	the first floor
los primeros días	the first days
el segundo hombre	the second man
la segunda mujer	the second woman
el tercer libro	the third book
las terceras copias	the third copies

The cardinal numbers are used with the days of the month except with the first day of the month.

El sábado es el primero de mayo.	Saturday is the first of May.
Nací el tres de mayo.	I was born the third of May.
El cinco de mayo es día de fiesta en México.	The fifth of May is a holiday in Mexico.

TIME EXPRESSIONS

The verb **"ser"** is always used in telling time. The verb agrees with the hour in number and person. The words **"hora"** (o'clock) and **"minutos"** (minutes) are understood. The number expressing the hour is preceded by the definite article, which agrees with the word **"hora"** (understood in Spanish) in number and gender. **"Media"** (half) is an adjective and **"cuarto"** (quarter) is a noun. From one o'clock to one fifty-nine the verb **"ser"** and article **"la"** will be singular. From two o'clock to twelve fifty-nine the verb **"ser"** and the article **"la"** will be plural. To express fractional time, the hour and the number of minutes past the hour are joined by the conjunction **"y."** In spoken Spanish the conjunction **"y"** is sometimes omitted.

¿Qué hora es?	What time is it?
Es la una.	It is 1:00 o'clock.
Es la una y cinco.	It is 1:05 o'clock.
Es la una quince.	It is 1:15 o'clock.
Es la una y media.	It is 1:30 o'clock.
Es la una treinta y cinco.	It is 1:35 o'clock.
Son las dos.	It is 2:00 o'clock.
Son las tres y cuarto.	It is 3:15 o'clock.
Son las siete y media.	It is 7:30 o'clock.
Son las doce diez y siete.	It is 12:17 o'clock.

In the spoken language, minutes beyond the half hour are often expressed by subtracting them from the following hour by use of the word **"menos"** (less, minus) or **"falta," "faltan"** (lacking). To express A.M., add **"de la mañana"** to the time expression. To express P.M., add **"de la tarde"** or **"de la noche,"** as appropriate, to the time expression. There are several ways of telling time. The beginner will do well to use one until completely familiar with it before attempting others.

Son las doce menos cinco.	It is 11:55 o'clock.
Faltan cinco para las doce.	It is 11:55 o'clock.
Falta un cuarto para las dos.	It is 1:45 o'clock.
Falta un minuto para la una.	It is 12:59 o'clock.
Es mediodía.	It is noon.
Son las doce del día.	It is 12:00 o'clock noon.
Es medianoche.	It is midnight.
Son las doce de la noche.	It is 12:00 o'clock midnight.
Son las cuatro en punto.	It is 4:00 o'clock sharp.
Son las tres de la mañana.	It is 3:00 A.M.
Es la una y media de la tarde.	It is 1:30 P.M.

Son las nueve veinte y cinco de la noche.	It is 9:25 P.M.
A las ocho y media de la noche.	At 8:30 P.M.
A la una cuarenta y cinco de la mañana.	At 1:45 A.M.

CALENDAR DIVISIONS

Months of the Year

enero	January
febrero	February
marzo	March
abril	April
mayo	May
junio	June
julio	July
agosto	August
septiembre	September
octubre	October
noviembre	November
diciembre	December

Days of the Week

el domingo	Sunday
el lunes	Monday
el martes	Tuesday
el miércoles	Wednesday
el jueves	Thursday
el viernes	Friday
el sábado	Saturday

Seasons of the Year

la primavera	spring
el verano	summer
el otoño	autumn
el invierno	winter

The months of the year, days of the week, and the seasons of the year are not capitalized in Spanish.

There are several ways of asking the date, month, or day of the month; however, the following expressions are most commonly used:

¿Cuál es la fecha (de hoy)?	What is the date?
¿A qué fecha estamos?	What is the date?
¿A qué mes estamos?	What month is this?
¿A qué día del mes estamos?	What day of the month is it?
¿Qué día del mes es hoy?	What day of the month is it?
¿A cuántos estamos?	What day of the month is it?

To answer, use the following pattern:

el (day) de (month) de (year)

el diez y seis de septiembre de mil ochocientos diez	Sept. 16, 1810
el cuatro de julio de mil setecientos setenta y seis	July 4, 1776
el doce de febrero de mil ochocientos nueve	Feb. 12, 1809
el once de noviembre de mil novecientos diez y nueve	Nov. 11, 1919
el doce de octubre de mil novecientos cuarenta y cinco	Oct. 12, 1945

The articles "el" or "los" are used with the days of the week, except when the days of the week are preceded by the adjectives "cada," "muchos," "pocos," by any number, or by the verb "ser".

The preposition "on" is not stated in Spanish before days of the week or dates.

"At" is translated as "a" when used with time.

Tengo una cita el sábado a las seis.	I have a date Saturday at six.
Hoy es domingo; mañana es lunes.	Today is Sunday; tomorrow is Monday.
Esté aquí a las tres en punto.	Be here at three o'clock sharp.
Salimos para Juárez a las cinco de la mañana.	We are leaving for Juarez at five in the morning.
Vamos al cine cada sábado.	We go to the movies every Saturday.
Él trabajó muchos domingos el año pasado.	He worked many Sundays last year.
No trabajamos los lunes.	We don't work on Mondays.
Hay cinco domingos en este mes.	There are five Sundays in this month.

VOCABULARY

los niños—the children
el cuerpo—the body
el verano—the summer
la sandía—the watermelon
vámonos—let's go
durante—during
quincena—fortnight

a mediodía—at noon
nacer—to be born
enterrar—to bury
sepultar—to bury
ir de compras—to go shopping
decidir—to decide
conocer—to meet, to become acquainted, to know

EXERCISE

1. Where did you bury the body?
2. Micaela was born February 13, 1930.
3. Yesterday was Saturday; today is Sunday.
4. We sold the last watermelon at 10:20 P.M.
5. I go shopping every Friday.
6. Our parents arrived at 4:40 P.M. Friday.
7. She decided to take the train Tuesday at 8:55 A.M.
8. The foreman paid us at 6:30 A.M. yesterday.
9. During the summer we leave for Michigan.
10. Did you see anyone last night at 11:30?
11. What do you do on Sundays?
12. We do not have to be here until 12:30 P.M.
13. I met him day before yesterday at noon.
14. The last time I went there was on Monday, May 27, 1943.
15. Let's go, because it is already very late.
16. The inspectors are going to deport him tomorrow morning.

17. Concha is 31 years old, but she still lives with her parents.
18. Felipe says that they pay him every fortnight.
19. He owes me about $351.00 dollars for seven months of work.
20. Today is a holiday, and we do not have to work.
21. He wants to see us at the bridge tonight at 10:45.
22. At what time does your cousin arrive here?
23. I lost the first passport that I took out.
24. It is 12:00 noon, November 30, 1966.
25. One hundred children were sick yesterday.

LESSON XVI

PASSIVE VOICE

In Spanish, as in English, there are two voices: active and passive. The subject of an active voice acts:

El muchacho tira la pelota.	The boy throws the ball.

The subject of a passive verb receives the action. It does not do anything.

La pelota fué tirada por el muchacho.	The ball was thrown by the boy.

The passive voice is formed in Spanish by some form of the verb "ser" plus the past participle of the main verb. The past participle must agree with the subject in number and gender. The agent (by whom the action is done) will always be introduced by the preposition "por."

El contrabandista fué arrestado por el oficial.	The smuggler was arrested by the officer.

The true passive voice is most often used (1) when the "agent" is expressed or (2) when the subject is a person; otherwise, the passive voice is generally avoided in Spanish by making it active.

El oficial arrestó al contra-bandista.	The smuggler was arrested by the officer. or The officer arrested the smuggler.

When no interest is shown in the performer of the action, the true passive voice is replaced in Spanish by the reflexive "se". This construction is explained in depth in Lesson XVIII.

A third substitute for the passive voice is the impersonal use of the third person plural of the active voice, especially if the passive subject is a living thing. This construction lays more stress on the action than does the more definite construction with the reflexive. It is especially used when the passive subject is a pronoun.

Lo detuvieron ayer.	He was detained yesterday.
Nos invitaron anoche.	We were invited last night.
Cerraron la tienda.	The store was closed (by someone).

"Ser" plus the past participle is used only for a happening or action, never for description. The latter is an apparent passive, and it indicates the state or condition of the subject as the result of the action. The apparent passive is formed by the auxiliary verb "estar" with a past participle that agrees in number and gender with the subject expressed or understood.

La puerta estaba abierta.	The door was open.
El carro estaba abandonado.	The car was abandoned.
La casa está destruida.	The house is destroyed.

NOTICE: The imperfect is more frequent in resultant conditions (description), while the preterite is more frequent in the passive and its equivalents.

The following summary may be helpful in determining the more usual Spanish equivalents of the English passive.

Resultant Condition: No action = "estar" plus past participle.

True Passive: Action performed with the agent expressed = "ser" plus past participle.

Impersonal Passive: Action performed but agent unnamed =
  (1) reflexive construction, especially in general statements of fact and if the subject is a thing;
  (2) third person plural active voice, especially if the action is stressed, and the passive subject is a living thing.

VOCABULARY

la revista—the magazine
la frontera—the border
la estación de—the . . . station
el viento—the wind
el país—the country
los muebles—the furniture
el edificio—the building
extranjero—foreign

el extranjero—foreigner
cerca (de)—close (to), near
después (de)—after
cerrar—to shut, close
terminar—to finish
acabar—to finish

EXERCISE NO. 1

1. He was arrested by the police in 1947.
2. We have been living in that place for a long time.
3. This house was sold last week.
4. It was sent from here on the fifteenth of May.
5. The train station was open when I left.
6. All the doors were shut by the high winds.
7. Their new furniture had been taken out of the room.
8. At what time does the bank close?
9. When they arrived, the doors and windows were shut.
10. He was tired because he had worked all night.
11. Horacio was sent to the market for (por) bread.
12. These buildings were finished last year.

IDIOMATIC USES OF SOME VERBS

There are some verbs in the Spanish language which have either a different construction or a variety of meanings and thus warrant special attention. Following are a few of these verbs.

"HACER"

The impersonal form of the verb "hacer" has two important uses: to deal with time and to express the state of the weather. In either case, only the third person singular, the infinitive, present participle, and the past participle are used. The object of "hacer" is either a measure of time or a noun expressing the state of the weather, and in either case to be rendered in English by the verb "to be" used impersonally or, in the case of time, by "ago."

The idiomatic use of "hacer" is the only possible translation for the word "ago." Whereas in English the construction is: length of time plus "ago;" the Spanish construction is some form of "hacer" plus the time measure.

Él llegó hace cinco minutos.	He arrived five minutes ago.
Lo ví hace seis años.	I saw him six years ago.
Ella murió hace cinco días.	She died five days ago.

When the clause containing "hacer" stands first and is followed by a clause containing a verb, the latter is connected with "hacer" by the conjunction "que" in which case "ago" would be equivalent and interchangeable with "since."

Hace cinco minutos que él llegó.	It is five minutes since he arrived. or He arrived five minutes ago.
Hace cinco días que ella murió.	It is five days since she died. or She died five days ago.

When the clause following "hacer" is expressed by a noun, it is introduced by the preposition "desde," meaning "since."

Hace muchos siglos desde el diluvio.	It is many centuries since the flood.
Mañana va a hacer un mes desde el último día de pago.	Tomorrow is going to be one month since last pay day.

Besides rendering the idea of "ago" or "since," "hacer" expresses the length of time between two points. The initial point is always past; the terminal point may be past, present or future. "Hacer" corresponds to the terminal point, and is past, present or future accordingly. English uses the perfect "have been," "had been," or "will have been" plus the preposition "for" followed by the length of time to express this idea. In Spanish the length of time will follow "hacer" and the perfect tense will be rendered by its corresponding simple tense.

Hace dos años que estudio español.	I have studied Spanish for two years. or I have been studying Spanish for two years.
Hace dos meses que vivo aquí.	I have lived here for two months. or I have been living here for two months.
Hacía tres meses que vivía allí.	I had been living there for three months.
Hacía dos años que estudiaba inglés.	I had been studying English for two years.

All the preceding English sentences may be rendered in Spanish by a word by word translation, but the "hace" construction is preferable.

He estudiado español por dos años. or He estado estudiando español por dos años.	I have studied Spanish for two years. or I have been studying Spanish for two years.
He vivido aquí por dos meses. or He estado viviendo aquí por dos meses.	I have lived here for two months. or I have been living here for two months.
Había estado viviendo allí por tres meses.	I had been living there for three months.
Había estado estudiando inglés por dos años.	I had been studying English for two years.

"HACER" APPLIED TO WEATHER

In speaking of the state of the weather, "hacer" takes as its object a noun expressing the phrase desired:

Hace mucho sol.	It is very sunny.
Ayer hacía mal tiempo.	Yesterday the weather was bad.
¿Qué tiempo hacía ayer?	What kind of weather was it yesterday?

In expressing temperature, the Spanish verb corresponding to the English "to be" varies according to what is its subject. In speaking of weather, the verb is "hacer"; of a person, or anything animate, "tener"; and of a thing, "ser" or "estar" according to whether the quality is inherent or accidental:

Hace mucho calor.	It is very hot.
Yo tengo mucho frío.	I am very cold.
El hielo es muy frío.	Ice is very cold.
El agua está muy fría.	The water is very cold.

"HACER" PLUS INFINITIVE

"Hacer" may be used as a verb of causing when it is followed by an infinitive, and, as such, it renders the English meaning of "to make someone (to) do something or to cause something to be done."

Le hice contestar las preguntas.	I made him answer the questions.
Hicieron marchar el carro.	They started the car.
El oficial lo hizo bajarse del carro.	The officer made him get out of the car.

VERBS OF PERCEPTION

In English, when the verbs "to see" or "to hear" are followed by the action seen or heard, the present participle is usually employed. In Spanish, however, these two verbs of perception are more commonly followed by the infinitive form of the action "seen" or "heard." The best construction is to place the infinitive immediately after the verb of perception.

Ella oyó llegar a los oficiales.	She heard the officers arriving.

When English uses an infinitive form following the verbs of perception, the infinitive is still used in Spanish.

María oyó entrar al ladron
Maria heard the burglar enter.

"GUSTAR" AND "FALTAR"

"Gustar," to please or give pleasure, is employed in connections where the English uses "like," for which there is no exact equivalent in Spanish. In order to use **"gustar"** for "to like," the English construction is reversed so that the English object becomes the Spanish subject and the English subject becomes the Spanish indirect object. The simplest way to view this is to think of "to like" as "to be pleasing."

> I like those houses.
> Those houses are pleasing to me.
> **Me gustan esas casas.**

> He likes Texas.
> Texas is pleasing to him.
> **Le gusta Texas.**

Notice that only the third person singular or plural is used to agree with the subject, and that the Spanish word order is similar to the English even though the function of the words has been reversed.

Since the English object becomes the Spanish subject, it is generally necessary to insert an article.[1] Since the English subject becomes the Spanish indirect object, it must be accompanied by its corresponding indirect object pronoun and be introduced by the personal *a* if it is a noun.

> Juan likes school.
> School is pleasing to Juan.
> **A Juan le gusta la escuela.**

> Marta doesn't like those dresses.
> Those dresses are not pleasing to Marta.
> **A Marta no le gustan esos vestidos.**

---

[1] A common noun which is the subject of a sentence is usually preceded by its corresponding article.

"Gustar" is also used when "to like" in English is expressing fondness for a certain action:

> We like to study.
> To study is pleasing to us.
> Nos gusta estudiar.

Under this situation, Spanish always uses the infinitive as the subject of the sentence, and the verb is always in the third person singular form.

"Gustar" is not generally applied to liking people. The closest idioms that can be used to express the idea of liking someone are "caer bien" for the affirmative, and "caer mal" for the negative. The same reversal of object and subject occurs with these idioms.

> I like that man. (personality-wise)
> That man is pleasing to me.
> Ese hombre me cae bien.   or   Me cae bien ese hombre.

> We don't like those students.
> Those students are not pleasing to us.
> Nos caen mal esos estudiantes.   or   Esos estudiantes nos caen mal.

"Faltar," to lack or to need, is like "gustar" in all respects. Although its mastery is not as important as that of the verb "gustar," since for all practical purposes "faltar" can be replaced by "necesitar," at least a passing knowledge of its use should be helpful in understanding it when it is used by others.

> He lacks five dollars to buy a ticket.
> Five dollars to buy a ticket is lacking to him.
> Le faltan cinco dólares para comprar un boleto.

> They still need to go to the drugstore.
> To go to the drugstore is still lacking to them.
> Todavía les falta ir a la botica (farmacia).

VOCABULARY

el buque—the boat
el taller—the shop
el día de pago—payday
la cueva—the cave
la droga—the drug
el refugiado—the refugee
la compañía—the company
la película—the movie, film
el restaurante—the restaurant
abandonado—abandoned
el curso—the course
la fichera (slang)—the "B"-girl

desde—since
¿qué tal?—how are you?
hacer viento—to be windy
ir de pesca—to go fishing
ir a la pesca—to go fishing
hacer sol—to be sunny
cancelar—to cancel; void
encontrar—to find
rendir—to give up; to surrender
regresar—to go back
pedir—to order (food or supplies)

EXERCISE NO. 2

1. It was very windy when the boat entered the port.
2. We like to go fishing when it is sunny.
3. His passport was voided three weeks ago.
4. She was found in an abandoned house about five hours ago.
5. I have not seen him for five years.
6. Mario had worked in that shop for eight or nine months.
7. Seven days have gone by since my last payday.
8. The cave was very cold and wet.
9. We made him give us the drugs he was smuggling.
10. They can make us give up our local cards.
11. Did you (pl) see the smuggler talking to them?
12. We saw him drinking beer with that woman.
13. The "B" girl could not hear her boss coming.
14. Those refugees do not like to work in the fields.
15. She did not like the United States, so she went back to her country.
16. I have never liked his company.
17. How did you like the movie?
18. Eloisa likes to eat in that restaurant.
19. She always likes to order the same thing.
20. He lacks nine days finishing this course.

Lesson XVII

FUTURE INDICATIVE TENSE

The future indicative tense of regular verbs is formed by adding the following endings to the whole infinitive for all three conjugations:

é, ás, á, emos, án

Hablar—to speak

hablaré—I will or shall speak
hablarás—You will or shall speak
hablará—He will or shall speak
hablaremos—We will or shall speak
hablarán—They will or shall speak

Comer—to eat

comeré—I will or shall eat
comerás—You will or shall eat
comerá—He will or shall eat
comeremos—We will or shall eat
comerán—They will or shall eat

Vivir—to live

viviré—I will or shall live
vivirás—You will or shall live
vivirá—He will or shall live
viviremos—We will or shall live
vivirán—They will or shall live

IRREGULAR VERBS OF THE FUTURE INDICATIVE TENSE

The twelve verbs listed below are the basic irregular verbs of the future indicative tense. In five the vowel of the infinitive endings is deleted (caber, haber, poder, querer, saber), and in five the vowel of the infinitive endings is changed to "d" before attaching the regular endings (poner = pondr, salir = saldr, tener = tendr, valer = valdr, venir = vendr). In two, "decir" and "hacer," the letters "ec" and "ce," respectively, are deleted from the infinitive.

Caber—cabré, cabrás, cabrá, cabremos, cabrán
Haber—habré, habrás, habrá, habremos, habrán
Poder—podré, podrás, podrá, podremos, podrán
Querer—querré, querrás, querrá, querremos, querrán
Saber—sabré, sabrás, sabrá, sabremos, sabrán
Poner—pondré, pondrás, pondrá, pondremos, pondrán
Salir—saldré, saldrás, saldrá, saldremos, saldrán
Tener—tendré, tendrás, tendrá, tendremos, tendrán
Valer—valdré, valdrás, valdrá, valdremos, valdrán
Venir—vendré, vendrás, vendrá, vendremos, vendrán
Decir—diré, dirás, dirá, diremos, dirán
Hacer—haré, harás, hará, haremos, harán

In addition to its regular use to express future time, the future tense may be used instead of the present indicative to express probability or conjecture.

Juan no está aquí; estará malo.	Juan is not here; he is probably sick.
Él gasta mucho dinero; será rico.	He spends a lot of money; he must be rich.

"Habrá" is used impersonally meaning "there will be" or "there shall be."

Creo que habrá mucha gente aquí mañana.	I think there will be many people here tomorrow.

The present indicative tense of the verb "ir" + "a" preceding an infinitive is frequently used in Spanish to replace the future tense.

Voy a comer a las doce.	I am going to eat at twelve.
Comeré a las doce.	I shall eat at twelve.
Voy a estudiar esta noche.	I am going to study tonight.
Estudiaré esta noche.	I shall study tonight.

By comparing the preceding examples, it is readily seen that the English and Spanish usage for the future and the verb "to go" in the present indicative plus an infinitive express about the same idea.

VOCABULARY

el inspector—the inspector
el jornalero—the laborer
el correo—the post office
la estafeta—the post office
el permiso—the permit
la ventana—the window
la hora—the hour
la cosecha—the harvest
el campo—the field
la labor—the field
el maíz—the corn
la madrugada—the wee hours of the morning, dawn

antes—before
entonces—then
pasado mañana—day after tomorrow
mañana por la tarde—tomorrow afternoon
a la noche—tonight
probablemente—probably
como a—at about
¿a qué hora?—at what time?
brincar—to jump

EXERCISE NO. 1

1. Tomorrow morning I shall go to the post office.
2. When will you go to town?
3. I am going to see Luis tomorrow morning.
4. Tomorrow is a holiday, and all the stores will be closed.

5. Ricardo will leave here day after tomorrow.
6. You will have to come back as soon as possible.
7. At what time will they open the window?
8. He will be here at about nine o'clock.
9. Will you be home tonight at six?
10. No, I have to go to church at that hour, but I will be there at eight.
11. If you see the inspector, tell him that I will come[1] to his house tonight.
12. Will there be a lot of cotton in the fields this year?
13. He will have to sell the corn as soon as possible.
14. They plan to see the foreman tomorrow afternoon.
15. Why will they jump at that place?
16. His friends will try to enter in the wee hours of the morning.

CONDITIONAL TENSE

The conditional indicative tense (generally translated by "would"[2]) is formed by adding the following endings to the whole infinitive for all three conjugations:

ía, ías, ía, íamos, ían

Dar—to give	*Ver*—to see	*Ir*—to go
daría—I would give	**vería**—I would see	**iría**—I would go
darías—You would give	**verías**—You would see	**irías**—You would go
daría—He would give	**vería**—He would see	**iría**—He would go
daríamos—We would give	**veríamos**—We would see	**iríamos**—We would go
darían—They would give	**verían**—They would see	**irían**—They would go

CONDITIONAL TENSE—IRREGULAR VERBS

The same twelve verbs that are irregular in the future tense are also irregular in the conditional indicative tense. The irregular stem for the future tense is the same stem used for the con-

---

[1] The native speaker will generally say "I will go to his house."
[2] Remember that when "would not" expresses a refusal, it is still translated by the preterite tense of **"querer."**

dítional tense. The endings are the same as for the regular verbs in the conditional tense.

```
Caber—cabría, cabrías, cabría, cabríamos, cabrían
Haber—habría, habrías, habría, habríamos, habrían
Poder—podría, podrías, podría, podríamos, podrían
Querer—querría, querrías, querría, querríamos, querrían
Saber—sabría, sabrías, sabría, sabríamos, sabrían
Poner— pondría, pondrías, pondría, pondríamos, pondrían
Salir—saldría, saldrías, saldría, saldríamos, saldrían
Tener—tendría, tendrías, tendría, tendríamos, tendrían
Valer—valdría, valdrías, valdría, valdríamos, valdrían
Venir—vendría, vendrías, vendría, vendríamos, vendrían
Decir—diría, dirías, diría, diríamos, dirían
Hacer—haría, harías, haría, haríamos, harían
```

The conditional is sometimes used instead of the imperfect, and the conditional perfect instead of the pluperfect (past perfect) to express probability.

¿A qué hora llegó Vd.?	At what time did you arrive?
Serían las dos.	It was probably two o'clock.
Juan no vino a la escuela ayer; Estaría malo.	Juan did not come to school yesterday; he was probably sick.
¿Quién sería él?	I wonder who he was. Who could he have been?
La mujer habría estado mala.	The woman had probably been sick.

CONDITIONAL PERFECT TENSE

The conditional perfect is formed by placing the conditional tense of the verb "haber" before the past participle of the main verb.

IR

habría ido—I would have gone

habrías ido—You would have gone

habría ido—He would have gone

habríamos ido—We would have gone

habrían ido—They would have gone

VOCABULARY

el permiso—the permission, the permit
el oro—the gold
el anillo—the ring
el número—the number
la botella—the bottle
el vino—the wine
la semana que entra—next week
la próxima semana—next week

el juego—the game
al fin de . . .—at the end of
durante—during
a la caída del sol—at sunset
levantar—to pick up
hacer preguntas—to ask questions
llamar—to call
prometer—to promise
estar ocupado—to be busy

1. Did you say that you would give me permission to go to the city?
2. I told him that I would pick him up early.
3. He would buy the gold ring from the man, but he doesn't have any money.
4. If he asks you any questions, can you tell him the truth?
5. I would call him by (por) telephone, but I do not know his number.
6. Luis told me that he would have the money next week.
7. They told us that you would take us to town.
8. Did he know that he would be able to do it?
9. What would you do during that time?
10. I did not go to see him because he said he would not be there.
11. I would have given him the bottle of wine, but he was not there.
12. Did he promise that he would pay you at the end of the month?
13. He told us that he would not come to visit us because he was very busy.
14. I told them that I would do it, but they wouldn't listen to me.
15. Miguel told my friend that he would leave Brownsville at sunset.
16. I wonder who was with Manuel at the game.
17. It was probably his cousin from New York.
18. He probably took her to the game as soon as she arrived.
19. Mr. Lopez was probably going to the theater.
20. They probably saw the children arrive.

Lesson XVIII

REFLEXIVE VERBS

The verb is said to be reflexive when the subject and the object pronoun are the same person or thing; that is, the subject does something to, or acts upon itself. A verb is made reflexive by the use of the following reflexive pronouns:

me—myself	nos—ourselves
te—yourself (familiar)	
se—himself, herself	se—themselves
se—yourself	se—yourselves

The reflexive pronouns follow the same rule for their location as do the direct and indirect object pronouns (see Lesson IX). In the infinitive form for vocabulary and dictionary research, the reflexive verb is written with the third person reflexive pronoun attached.

The addition of reflexive pronouns does not alter the original form of the verb; therefore, all reflexive verbs will follow the model given here:

Levantarse—to get (oneself) up

Yo me levanto	I get (myself) up
Tú te levantas	You get (yourself) up
Él se levanta	He gets (himself) up
Ella se levanta	She gets (herself) up
Vd. se levanta	You get (yourself) up
Nosotros (as) nos levantamos	We get (ourselves) up
Ellos se levantan	They get (themselves) up
Ellas se levantan	They get (themselves) up
Vds. se levantan	You get (yourselves) up

Many verbs may be reflexive or not, according to whether the subject acts upon itself (reflexive) or upon something or someone else (not reflexive).

Me lavo las manos.	I wash my hands. (reflexive)
Yo lavo la ropa.	I wash the clothes. (not reflexive)
El se levantó temprano.	He got up early. (reflexive)
Su mamá lo levantó.	His mother got him up. (not reflexive)

Many verbs that are used reflexively in Spanish are not so used in English, consequently these do not "make sense" if attempt is made to parallel them to the English usage. The only manner of approaching them is to commit them to memory. Following is a list of some of the most common verbs which are reflexive in Spanish but not in English:

acordarse de (ue)—to remember
acostarse (ue)—to go to bed
bañarse—to take a bath
caerse—to fall
callarse—to be quiet
cansarse—to get tired
casarse (con)—to marry
dormirse (ue)—to fall asleep
escaparse—to escape
esconderse—to hide
bajarse—to alight, to get out
(of a car or other vehicle)
hacerse—to become (plus noun)

lavarse—to wash (oneself)
levantarse—to get up
llamarse—to be called, to be named
pararse—to stop, to stand up
ponerse—to put on (clothing) to become (plus adjective)
quedarse—to stay, to remain
quitarse—to take off (clothing)
sentarse (ie)—to sit down
subirse—to climb, to get in (a car or other vehicle)
vestirse—to get dressed

REFLEXIVE PRONOUNS AFTER PREPOSITIONS

In Spanish, the reflexive pronouns after prepositions have the following forms:

mí—myself
ti—yourself (familiar)
sí—himself, herself, yourself

nosotros, as—ourselves

sí—themselves, yourselves

Ella siempre piensa en sí.
Él no habla nunca de sí.
No estamos pensando en nosotros.

She always thinks of herself.
He never speaks of himself.
We are not thinking of ourselves.

The above may be intensified by the use of "mismo, a, os, as."

Ella siempre piensa en sí misma.
Él nunca habla de sí mismo.
No estamos pensando en nosotros mismos.

She always thinks of herself.
He never speaks of himself.
We are not thinking of ourselves.

RECIPROCAL VERBS

A reflexive pronoun may be used in a reciprocal sense, that is, the action is exchanged between various members of the subject. Such a use of a reflexive verb is translated by the expression "each other."

Se **odian con pasión.**	They hate each other passionately.
Nos queremos mucho.	We love each other very much.
Nos necesitamos.	We need each other.

REFLEXIVE SUBSTITUTE FOR PASSIVE VOICE

A reflexive construction is often used in place of the true passive when the doer of the action is not stated and the subject of the passive sentence is not a person. The receiver of the action of a passive sentence becomes the subject of a normal reflexive construction in Spanish (as if it had done the action to itself, or they, to themselves). If the subject under consideration is singular, the verb goes in the singular; if the subject is plural, the verb goes in the plural.

Se **vendió la casa ayer.**	The house was sold yesterday.
Se **han escrito muchas novelas sobre este tema.**	Many novels have been written about this theme.

Notice that the reflexive verb will normally precede the subject when it is used passively.

VOCABULARY

los pobres—the poor	**el lado**—the side
el policía—the policeman	**el chaparral**—the brush
la guerra—the war	**al mayoreo**—wholesale
la fecha—the date	**triste**—sad
la cara—the face	**el mes pasado**—last month
el pelo—the hair	**más temprano**—earlier
la cárcel—the jail	**estar acostumbrado a**—to be used to
el edificio—the building	**estar cansado**—to be tired
el apartamiento—the apartment	**telefonear**—to telephone
la orilla—the edge, the bank	**gatear**—to crawl
el arroyo—the creek	

EXERCISE

1. At what time did you get up this morning?
2. I got up at six this morning, but I am used to getting up earlier.
3. How long did John stay in Juarez before entering the United States?
4. I don't remember the date, but I think he arrived the fifth of last month.
5. When I entered the house last night, I took off my hat, I washed my face and hands, and I sat at the table to eat.

6. Maria told me that she didn't wash her hair because she didn't have time.
7. How many times did you stop when you were going to Las Vegas, and how long did you stay in each place?
8. Enrique was taking a bath when Maria telephoned him.
9. I was trying to escape when the officers arrested me.
10. How did you escape from jail the last time you were arrested?
11. Here, clothes are sold wholesale.
12. He put on his hat, got in the car, and went home where he was arrested by the policeman.
13. In this building, rooms and apartments are sold to the poor.
14. (At) what time did you go to bed last night?
15. At eleven, but it was about 2:30 when I fell asleep.
16. I put the newspaper on the table, but it is not there now.
17. He sat down and began to talk to me about the war.
18. The child's mother bathes him every morning at nine o'clock.
19. Her mother got her up very early yesterday.
20. Get in the car, but be careful not to fall.
21. The two men took off their shoes and crawled through the brush until they reached (llegar a) the bank of the creek.
22. Many cows are sold on this ranch.
23. She has to get dressed in thirty minutes.
24. Be quiet ! I am tired of hearing you.

Lesson XIX

EXPRESSIONS OF COMPARISON

There are two ways of comparing adjectives and adverbs in English:

Positive	Comparative	Superlative
slow	slower	slowest
beautiful	more beautiful	most beautiful

In Spanish the comparison of adjectives is formed similar to the second example above. The word "más" is placed before the positive for the comparative degree, and the definite article is placed before the comparative degree to obtain the superlative.

Positive	Comparative	Superlative
rico (rich)	más rico (richer)	el más rico (richest)
rica (rich)	más rica (richer)	la más rica (richest)
ricos (rich)	más ricos (richer)	los más ricos (richest)
ricas (rich)	más ricas (richer)	las más ricas (richest)

The comparison of adverbs is the same as for adjectives except that in the superlative degree the definite article is not used as it is in the comparison of adjectives.

Positive	Comparative	Superlative
rápido (fast)	más rápido (faster)	más rápido (fastest)
despacio (slow)	más despacio (slower)	más despacio (slowest)

When introducing a phrase or clause not containing a conjugated verb, "than" is expressed by "que"; however, if it precedes a number, "de" is used.

Soy más alto que María.	I am taller than Maria.
Ella es más rica que Juan.	She is richer than Juan.
La casa vale más de diez mil dólares.	The house is worth more than ten thousand dollars.
Este mes se pasó más despacio que el mes pasado.	This month went by slower than last month.
Yo corro más rápido que tú.	I run faster than you.

But when the "than" clause contains a conjugated verb, "than" is rendered in Spanish by the full forms: (a) **del que**, (b) **de la que**, (c) **de los que**, etc. **"De lo que"** is used when the antecedent is an adjective or adverb, the inflected forms are used when the antecedent is a noun.

La ofensa era más seria de lo que creíamos.
The offense was more serious than (what) we thought.

Juan corre más rápido de lo que me imaginaba.
Juan runs faster than I imagined.

Él tiene más dinero del que necesita.
He has more money than (what) he needs.

Ella vendió más canastas de las que esperaba vender.
She sold more baskets than (what) she expected to sell.

In the superlative degree, "of" or "in" is translated by "**de.**"

Este hombre es el más rico del pueblo.
This man is the richest in town.

María es la más linda de la clase.
Maria is the prettiest of the class.

La mujer más alta no vino.
The tallest woman didn't come.

La más alta mujer no vino.
The tallest woman didn't come.

As seen in the last two examples above, the word order of the superlative may take either form. The first is the most common.

The possessive adjective may take the place of the definite article.

Mi primo más alto está aquí.	My tallest cousin is here.
Su amigo más íntimo está malo.	His closest friend is sick.

The comparative of an adjective or adverb may be of a lesser degree rather than a greater degree. In this case the word "**menos**" is used instead of "**más**". In all the foregoing examples, "**menos,**" meaning "less," can replace "**más**" to render the opposite effect.

There are four adjectives that are compared irregularly in Spanish. Of the four "**grande**" and "**pequeño**" are also compared regularly, in which case they have their regular meaning of size. The irregular comparisons of "**grande**" and "**pequeño**" generally refer to age.

Positive	*Comparative*	*Superlative*
bueno (good)	mejor (better)	el mejor (the best)
malo (bad)	peor (worse)	el peor (the worst)
grande (large, old)	mayor (older)[1]	el mayor (the oldest)
pequeño (small, young)	menor (younger)	el menor (the youngest)

---

[1] Old (viejo) and young (joven) can also be compared regularly, but this is generally for animals and things.

Este hombre es mayor que mi hermano, pero es más pequeño.
This man is older than my brother, but he is smaller.

Juan es el más pequeño de mis hijos, pero no es el menor.
Juan is the smallest of my sons, but he is not the youngest.

Notice the following uses of **"mayor"** and **"menor"**.

Perdí la mayor parte de mi dinero.
I lost the greater part (most) of my money.

Esta tienda vende al por mayor.
This store sells at wholesale.

Aquella tienda vende al por menor.
That store sells at retail.

There are also four adverbs which are compared irregularly:

Positive	Comparative	Superlative
bien (well)	**mejor** (better)	**mejor** (best)
mal (badly)	**peor** (worse)	**peor** (worst)
mucho (much)	**más** (more)	**más** (most)
poco (little)	**menos** (less)	**menos** (least)

ABSOLUTE SUPERLATIVE

The absolute superlative is formed by adding **"ísimo, ísima, ísimos, or ísimas"** to the adjective or adverb. If the adjective ends in a vowel, remove the vowel before attaching the endings. Do the same for adverbs. The absolute superlative does not directly compare one thing to another, but merely states "a greater amount of," and can be translated into English by placing "very" before the adjective or adverb.

Adjective or Adverb	Absolute Superlative	English
linda	**lindísima**	very pretty
rico	**riquísimo**	very rich
mucho	**muchísimo**	very much
feo	**feísimo**	very ugly

The same idea can be expressed by using the adverb **"muy"** in front of the adjective; however, the absolute superlative is stronger. **"Muy"** cannot be properly used before **"mucho, a,"** or **"muchos, as."**

María es lindísima.	Maria is very pretty. (emphatic)
María es muy linda.	Maria is very pretty.
Muchísimas gracias.	Thank you very, very much.
Hay muchísimas casas.	There are very many houses.
Esta sopa es riquísima.	This soup is extremely rich.

COMPARISON OF EQUALITY

In making comparisons of equality in Spanish, the English words "as," "as much," and "as many" are replaced by the Spanish words **"tan," "tanto, a," "tantos, as"** respectively. The second word "as," translated into Spanish by **"como,"** is invariable.

tan	como	as		as
tanto, a	como	as much		as
tantos, as	como	as many		as

In the first case in the foregoing examples the comparison is of an adjective and the word **"tan"** is an adverb and is invariable. In the second and third cases above the comparisons are of amount and number of nouns, and the words stating the amount or number are adjectives and as such are variable as adjectives and agree in number and gender with the word modified.

María es tan alta como Juan.	Maria is as tall as Juan.
Este libro es tan grande como el suyo.	This book is as large as yours.
Juan tiene tanto dinero como Eduardo.	Juan has as much money as Eduardo.
Hay tanta tinta en este tintero como en aquél.	There is as much ink in this inkwell as in that one.
José tiene tantos libros como Ana.	Jose has as many books as Ana.
Él ha escrito tantas cartas como Vd.	He has written as many letters as you.

"SINO"—How Used

The connective **"sino"**, meaning "but", is used instead of **"pero"** in an affirmative statement in which the verb is omitted following a negative statement.

No voy al teatro sino a la iglesia.	I am not going to the theater but to church.
Él no es americano sino español.	He is not an American but a Spaniard.

but:

No tengo libros pero tengo plumas.	I do not have any books, but I have some pens.

"ONLY"—How Expressed

The English word "only" is expressed in several different ways in Spanish.

No leo sino libros ingleses.	I read only English books.
No tengo sino cuatro pesos.	I have only four dollars.

Tengo sólo cuatro pesos.	I have only four dollars.
Tengo cuatro pesos no más.	I have only four dollars.
	(I have four dollars, no more.)
No tengo más que cuatro pesos.	I have only four dollars (no more than four dollars).

but:

Tengo más de cuatro pesos.	I have more than four dollars.
Tengo menos de cuatro pesos.	I have less than four dollars.

VOCABULARY

la cicatriz—the scar	jugar—to play
el café—the coffee	ocupar—to hire
el recibo—the receipt	correr—to run
la taza—the cup	terminar—to finish
el fútbol—the football	sembrar—to plant (seed)
el béisbol—the baseball	nacer—to be born
nadie—no one, nobody, anybody	expedir—to issue
corto—short	prometer—to promise
rápido—fast	parecer—to seem
gastar—to spend	

EXERCISE

1. He has as many children as your friend, but his children are in Mexico.
2. His scar is larger than hers.
3. Your coffee is better than mine.
4. This receipt is older than that one, but that one is better.
5. He intends to come later than anyone.
6. The cups they have are prettier than the ones they sold.
7. Girls are wearing shorter skirts now.
8. Teofilo looks younger than his brother.
9. The card was issued sooner than the promised date.
10. My wife spends more money than I earn.
11. I didn't intend to buy it, but I bought it.
12. I do not want to buy it but borrow it.
13. He doesn't play football but baseball.
14. We have only four days to work.
15. They have more than five days to get their passports.
16. The children can run faster than you or I.
17. They will finish sooner than those men.
18. The farmers have planted more corn this year than last year.
19. They owe me more than fifty dollars.
20. Mr. Jones is the richest man in our town, but he is sick.

23. He lives in the tallest building on Tenth Avenue.
24. John does not earn more than five dollars a day, but he doesn't spend as much as his brother.
25. My youngest son was born in the United States in 1958.
26. His best friend is extremely tall.
27. Thanks a million!

LESSON XX

SUBJUNCTIVE MOOD

There are three moods in Spanish as well as in English; namely, the indicative, the subjunctive, and the imperative.

The indicative mood points out a thing as material or existing either affirmatively or negatively, and is based upon certainties or facts.

The imperative mood commands.

The subjunctive mood expresses an attitude, and is subservient to, or contingent upon some leading or governing idea expressed in an independent clause of causation, doubt, desire, emotion, or uncertainty. The subjunctive is a secondary or dependent thought or idea, and is found in the dependent clause. The subjunctive never makes a direct statement, nor asks a direct question.

PRESENT SUBJUNCTIVE

Like the polite commands, the present subjunctive is formed by attaching the following endings to the stem of the first person singular of the present indicative of regular and irregular verbs:

"AR" verbs: e, es, e, emos, en
"ER" verbs: a, as, a, amos, an
"IR" verbs: a, as, a, amos, an

Hablar	*Comer*	*Escribir*
hable	coma	escriba
hables	comas	escribas
hable	coma	escriba
hablemos	comamos	escribamos
hablen	coman	escriban

The same verbs that do not adhere to the above rules in the command form do not adhere in the present subjunctive.

dar	....	dé, des, dé, demos, den
estar	....	esté, estés, esté, estemos, estén
haber	....	haya, hayas, haya, hayamos, hayan
ir	....	vaya, vayas, vaya, vayamos, vayan
saber	....	sepa, sepas, sepa, sepamos, sepan
ser	....	sea, seas, sea, seamos, sean

PRESENT PROGRESSIVE SUBJUNCTIVE

The present progressive subjunctive is formed by placing the present subjunctive of the auxiliary verb "estar" in front of the present participle of the principal verb.

Tomar	*Vender*	*Escribir*
esté tomando	esté vendiendo	esté escribiendo
estés tomando	estés vendiendo	estés escribiendo
esté tomando	esté vendiendo	esté escribiendo
estemos tomando	estemos vendiendo	estemos escribiendo
estén tomando	estén vendiendo	estén escribiendo

PRESENT PERFECT SUBJUNCTIVE

The present perfect subjunctive is formed by placing the present subjunctive of the auxiliary verb "haber" in front of the past participle of the principal verb.

Tomar	*Vender*	*Escribir*
haya tomado	haya vendido	haya escrito
hayas tomado	hayas vendido	hayas escrito
haya tomado	haya vendido	haya escrito
hayamos tomado	hayamos vendido	hayamos escrito
hayan tomado	hayan vendido	hayan escrito

IMPERFECT SUBJUNCTIVE

There is only one simple past tense in the subjunctive mood, and this is formed by adding the following endings to the third person plural of the preterite indicative after dropping the final "on". These endings are the same for all three conjugations of regular and irregular verbs: **a, as, a, amos, an.** The first person plural bears a written accent over the last vowel before the last "r".

Tomaron	*Vendieron*	*Escribieron*
tomara	vendiera	escribiera
tomaras	vendieras	escribieras
tomara	vendiera	escribiera
tomáramos	vendiéramos	escribiéramos
tomaran	vendieran	escribieran

Anduvieron	*Hicieron*	*Dijeron*
anduviera	hiciera	dijera
anduvieras	hicieras	dijeras
anduviera	hiciera	dijera
anduviéramos	hiciéramos	dijéramos
anduvieran	hicieran	dijeran

PAST PROGRESSIVE SUBJUNCTIVE

The past progressive subjunctive is formed by placing the imperfect subjunctive of the auxiliary verb **"estar"** in front of the present participle of the principal verb.

Tomar	*Vender*	*Decir*
estuviera tomando	estuviera vendiendo	estuviera diciendo
estuvieras tomando	estuvieras vendiendo	estuvieras diciendo
estuviera tomando	estuviera vendiendo	estuviera diciendo
estuviéramos tomando	estuviéramos vendiendo	estuviéramos diciendo
estuvieran tomando	estuvieran vendiendo	estuvieran diciendo

PLUPERFECT SUBJUNCTIVE

The pluperfect subjunctive is formed by placing the imperfect subjunctive of the auxiliary verb **"haber"** in front of the past participle of the principal verb.

Tomar	*Hacer*	*Decir*
hubiera tomado	hubiera hecho	hubiera dicho
hubieras tomado	hubieras hecho	hubieras dicho
hubiera tomado	hubiera hecho	hubiera dicho
hubiéramos tomado	hubiéramos hecho	hubiéramos dicho
hubieran tomado	hubieran hecho	hubieran dicho

USES OF THE SUBJUNCTIVE
AFTER VERBS OF CAUSING

One of the principal uses of the subjunctive is after verbs expressing an action calculated to cause another person or thing to act or not to act. The force of the verb of causing varies from an authoritative command to a mild request or preference. What is true of the above is equally applicable to verbs of opposite effect, i.e., tending to prevent another from doing something. The following verbs in the independent clause require the verb of the dependent clause to be in the subjunctive provided that there is a change of subject in the clauses.

decir—to tell (order)	permitir—to permit
desear—to wish	preferir (ie)—to prefer
dejar—to let, allow	prohibir—to prohibit
mandar—to order, command	querer—to want
pedir (i)—to ask	rogar (ue)—to beg, pray

All verbs of causing, except "prefer", in English are followed by the infinitive, consequently there is no clue as to whether to use a present or past subjunctive in the dependent clause in Spanish. With these verbs, the translator must refer to the principal clause in order to determine what tense to use. If the verb in the main clause is in the present, present progressive, present perfect, command, or future, the verb in the dependent (subjunctive) clause is in the present tense. If the verb in the main clause is in the imperfect, preterite, past perfect, past progressive, or conditional, the verb in the dependent clause is in the imperfect subjunctive.

Le digo que vaya.	I tell him to go.
Le he dicho que vaya.	I have told him to go.
Quería que John fuera.	I wanted John to go.
Les mandarán que pasen.	They will order them to pass.

The verbs **"decir"**, **"mandar"**, **"pedir"**, and **"rogar"** generally use an indirect object pronoun even though there may be a noun in the English sentence. This noun serves both as the indirect object of one of the four verbs mentioned and as the subject of the subjunctive clause. With these four verbs, it is generally not necessary to use the subject in the subjunctive clause.

Le dije a Guillermo que fuera conmigo.	I told Guillermo to go with me.

The verbs **"dejar"**, **"permitir"**, and **"prohibir"** may be followed by an infinitive provided that indirect object pronouns are used.

Él deja que traigamos a nuestros padres.	He lets us bring our parents.
or	
Él nos deja traer a nuestros padres.	
Prohibo que Mario vaya.	I prohibit Mario from going.
or	
Le prohibo a Mario ir.	

VOCABULARY

aduaneros—customs officers	necesario—necessary
el aeropuerto—the airport	unos cuantos—a few
el gobierno—the government	unos pocos—a few
la elección—the election	reportar (slang)—to report
la autoridad—the authority	votar—to vote
otro—another	registrarse—to register

EXERCISE NO. 1

1. The consul told Mr. Lopez to return next week.
2. Mr. Guerra told him that he couldn't obtain the necessary papers.
3. Tell them to stay on that side for a few days.
4. The customs agents ordered us to show them our suitcases.
5. They asked us to open them and[1] to take out our clothes.
6. Does Eloisa want us to take her to the airport?
7. We begged her to stay for a few more weeks.
8. I prohibit you from telling your friend about us.
9. We wanted to come to this side with our parents.
10. Tell your mother to write the consul for a visa.

EXPRESSIONS OF FEELING OR EMOTION

If the verb of the main clause expresses emotion or feeling, the verb of the dependent clause will be in the subjunctive. When there is no change of subject with these verbs or expressions, the infinitive is more common. Some verbs of feeling or emotion are:

alegrarse de—to be glad
esperar—to hope, to expect
extrañarse—to be surprised
sentir (ie)—to be sorry
sorprenderse—to be surprised
temer—to fear
tener miedo—to be afraid

Espero que Carlos llegue a tiempo.	I hope that Carlos arrives on time.
Nos alegramos de que Vds. no estuvieran malos.	We are glad that you were not ill.
Se sorprendió que yo no hubiera trabajado más.	He was surprised that I had not worked more.
Siento que él estuviera enfermo.	I am sorry that he was sick.
Espero ir.	I hope to go. (No change of subject; therefore, no subjunctive.)

---

[1] When the independent verb governs two or more subjunctive verbs, it is generally better Spanish to repeat the conjunction "que".

The subjunctive is used after "ojalá" (that God grant) which has the force of a verb of wishing. "Ojalá" means "I wish" or "I hope" and is used with the first person singular only.

Ojalá que recibamos la carta hoy.	I hope that (O that) we receive the letter today.
Ojalá que él venga mañana.	I hope he comes tomorrow.
Ella desea que su prima estuviera aquí.	She wishes that her cousin were here.
Ojalá que yo hubiera ahorrado más dinero.	I wish I had saved more money.
Ojalá que ella vaya.	I hope she goes.

EXPRESSIONS OF DOUBT OR DENIAL

When the verb of the main clause expresses doubt or denial, or is used negatively or interrogatively expressing belief or understanding, the verb of the dependent clause will be in the subjunctive. Some of the most common verbs of doubt or denial are:

dudar—to doubt
negar (ie)—to deny
no creer—not to believe

Yo dudo que él tenga tanto dinero.	I doubt that he has so much money.
María no creía que Juan estuviera en ese lugar.	Maria didn't believe that Juan was in that place.
Él niega que él le haya dado el dinero a ella.	He denies that he has given her the money.
No dudo que él está loco.	I do not doubt that he is crazy. (There is no doubt.)
Enrique no niega que ella lo hizo.	Enrique does not deny that she did it.

Verbs of doubt or denial are usually followed by the infinitive when there is no change of subject.

IMPERSONAL EXPRESSIONS

Provided there is a change of subject, the subjunctive is used after impersonal expressions unless certainties are expressed. A few impersonal expressions are:

Ser dudoso—to be doubtful
Ser importante—to be important
Ser imposible—to be impossible
Ser lástima—to be a pity
Ser necesario—to be necessary
Ser posible—to be possible

Es lástima que ella no esté aquí.	It is a pity that she isn't here.
Era imposible cruzar de día.	It was impossible to cross by day.
No es necesario que Vd. lo firme.	It isn't necessary for you to sign it.
Es dudoso que él lo haya hecho.	It is doubtful that he has done it.
Será importante llegar a tiempo.	It will be important to arrive on time.

VOCABULARY

el equipaje—the luggage, baggage
el sueldo—the wages
la propiedad—the property
el banquero—the banker
el corralón—the large yard

perdido—lost
pronto—soon
continuar—to continue
vadear—to wade
ser dueño de—to own

EXERCISE NO. 2

1. Are you surprised that Eliseo is still living here?
2. Their relatives were glad that they were not arrested.
3. Why are you glad that Minerva has not arrived?
4. His mother hopes that he will marry soon.
5. Aren't you afraid to continue without washing your hands?
6. I am sorry that you have lost your baggage.
7. We cannot deny that we waded the river.
8. Marcos knows that he will be released by tomorrow.
9. It was necessary that we send him his wages.
10. It is a pity that you are not going with us.
11. Is it true that you knew the banker?
12. They hoped that it would be important.

AFTER RELATIVE PRONOUNS

The subjunctive is used in the dependent clause after a relative pronoun referring to a person or thing that is indefinite or unknown.

Busco una criada que sepa cocinar.	I am looking for a servant (unknown to speaker) who knows how to cook.
Le daré dos pesos al muchacho que me enseñe la casa del contrabandista.	I will give two pesos to the boy (unknown) who shows me the smuggler's house.
Le dí dos pesos al muchacho que me enseñó la casa del contrabandista.	I gave two pesos to the boy (now known) who showed me the smuggler's house.

AFTER CONJUNCTIVE EXPRESSIONS

The subjunctive is used after these conjunctive expressions expressing supposition, purpose, result, concession, or provision.

antes (de) que—before

a menos que—unless
con tal (de) que—provided that

Iré antes de que él vuelva.
Aquí la traigo a menos que la haya perdido.
Con tal que Vd. nos diga la verdad, le soltaremos mañana.

para que—in order that (for), so that
siempre que—provided that
suponiendo que—supposing that

I will go before he returns.
I have it here unless I have lost it.
Provided (that) you tell us the truth, we will let you go tomorrow.

When there is future time expressed or implied, the subjunctive is used with the following expressions.

cuando—when
después (de) que—after
hasta que—until
luego que—as soon as

para cuando—by the time
quizá(s)—perhaps, maybe
tal vez—perhaps, maybe
tan pronto como—as soon as

Estaré aquí cuando él venga.
Él esperará hasta que Vd. diga.
Estará lista para cuando él llegue.
Él dijo que me pagaría luego que ganara el dinero.
Hablamos hasta que se fué.

I shall be here when he comes.
He will wait until you say.
It will be ready by the time he arrives.
He said he would pay me as soon as he earned the money.
We talked until he left. (Both definitely completed past actions; therefore no subjunctive.)

VOCABULARY

la recámara—the bedroom
la casa de remolque—the house trailer
la secretaria—the secretary
la sala de espera—the waiting room
el correo—the mail; the post office
el paquete—the package
guapo—handsome

inteligente—intelligent
permanente—permanent
plantar—to plant
sembrar (ie)—to sow, to plant (seed)
llover (ue)—to rain
regar (ie)—to irrigate
volverse (ue) loco—to go crazy
tener listo—to have ready

EXERCISE NO 3

1. We need a house that has three bedrooms.
2. They have a house trailer that is too small.
3. She is looking for a man who is handsome, intelligent, and rich.
4. Mr. Billings wants a secretary who can speak Spanish.
5. He has a sister who went crazy many years ago.

6. The farmer is looking for a man who will work for him.
7. The laborers have to plant the cotton before it rains.
8. We plan to leave unless he pays us more money.
9. Bring your documents here as soon as you find them.
10. I will have them ready so that you may sell them tomorrow.
11. Supposing you bring her, what will she say?
12. Tell him to wait in the waiting room until we come.
13. Enrique waited until the mail left.
14. As soon as Alfonso became rich, he forgot his old friends.
15. When you obtain the necessary papers you can begin to live here.
16. I want you to have it ready by the time they come.
17. Marta and Gloria were here by the time the packages arrived.
18. He said he would leave whenever you told him.

IN CONDITIONS CONTRARY TO FACT

A condition contrary to fact is a most obvious case of unreality. Exactly as in English, when a clause introduced by "if" makes a supposition that is contrary to fact (If I were you, but I am not, etc.), a past subjunctive must be employed in the "if" clause.

CONDITIONS CONTRARY TO FACT IN PRESENT TIME

The verb in the "result" clause may be in the conditional indicative or the imperfect subjunctive, and the verb in the "if" clause must be in the imperfect subjunctive. The order of these two clauses does not matter; either may come first. In the following examples, the "result" clause is underlined in both English and Spanish.

> I would buy the house if I had the money.
> Yo compraría la casa si tuviera el dinero.
> Yo comprara la casa si tuviera el dinero.

> If he were here, would you tell him the truth?
> Si él estuviera aquí, ¿le diría Vd. la verdad?
> Si él estuviera aquí, ¿le dijera Vd. la verdad?

If the "result" clause in English is in any tense other than the conditional, the indicative is used in the "if" clause.

> I will buy the house if I have the money.
> Yo compraré la casa si tengo el dinero.

> If he is here, will you tell him the truth?
> Si él está aquí, ¿le dirá Vd. la verdad?

CONDITIONS CONTRARY TO FACT IN PAST TIME

The verb in the "result" clause may be in the conditional perfect or the pluperfect subjunctive, and the verb in the "if" clause must be in the pluperfect subjunctive. It does not matter which of these two clauses precedes. The "result" clause is underlined in both Spanish and English.

I would have bought the house if I had had the money.
Yo habría comprado la casa si yo hubiera tenido el dinero.
Yo hubiera comprado la casa si yo hubiera tenido el dinero.

If he had been here, would you have told him the truth?
Si él hubiera estado aquí, ¿le habría dicho Vd. la verdad?
Si él hubiera estado aquí, ¿le hubiera dicho Vd. la verdad?

VOCABULARY

el empleo—the job	bastante—enough, plenty
la oportunidad—the opportunity	suficiente—enough, plenty
la novia—the girl friend	escuchar—to listen
el edificio—the building	hacer calor—to be warm
la fiesta—the party, the celebration	advertir (ie)—to warn

EXERCISE NO. 4

1. If there were plenty of work in the fields, would you work there?
2. If Manuel has enough money, will he buy it?
3. You would not be in jail now if you had listened to me.
4. Would they have escaped if you had not told them?
5. If you did not have employment, I would help you.
6. I would go to town if it were not so warm.
7. Would you return to that country if you had the opportunity?
8. If there had been an officer there, would your girl friend have warned you?
9. If you had known that you were going to be arrested, would you have entered the building?
10. I would have remained at the party if I had seen you.

LESSON XXI

WORD STUDY

The following suggestions should be of help to a beginner in the study of the Spanish language. They are not at all complete so should be remembered only as general suggestions.

The principal method of combining nouns is by placing the secondary or modifying noun last and connecting the two by "de".

> traje de baile—ball dress
> jugo de limón—lemon juice
> anillo de oro—gold ring
> labor de betabel—beet field
> caballo de silla—saddle horse
> molino de viento—windmill
> traje de lana—woolen suit
> tarjeta de bracero—bracero card

If the secondary noun expresses purpose or use for which the first is intended, use "para" instead of "de".

> estante para libros—book case
> vaso para cerveza—beer glass
> percha para sombreros—hat rack
> vestidos para niñas—children's dresses

An infinitive is often used as a verbal noun expressed in English by the gerund.

> máquina de coser—sewing machine
> pluma de dibujar—drawing pen
> papel de escribir—writing paper
> máquina de escribir—typewriter

"Ero" added to words of commerce forms the noun denoting the dealer in those articles, while "ería" added to those words usually denotes the shop or place of business.

zapato	zapatero	zapatería	reloj	relojero	relojería
shoe	shoemaker	shoe shop	watch	watchmaker	watch shop

leche	lechero	lechería	joya	joyero	joyería
milk	milkman	dairy	jewel	jeweler	jewelry store, shop

The names of many fruit trees ending in "o" change the "o" to "a" for the fruit.

cerezo	**cereza**	**naranjo**	**naranja**
cherry tree	cherry	orange tree	orange
manzano	**manzana**	**ciruelo**	**ciruela**
apple tree	apple	plum tree	plum

The feminine form of a past participle often expresses the completed action of the verb from which it came.

llegar—to arrive   llegada—arrival
entrar—to enter   entrada—entrance
venir—to come   venida—arrival, coming
salir—to leave   salida—departure, leaving

The following words, opposite in meaning, should be noted:

caballero—gentleman   dama—lady
caballo—horse   yegua—mare
yerno—son-in-law   nuera—daughter-in-law
toro—bull   vaca—cow

"Ito, a"; "cito, a"; "ecito, a", when added to a noun convey the additional idea of sweet, nice, or little.

madrecita	dear mother	**hermanito**	little brother
pobrecito	poor little one	**cabrito**	kid (little goat)
chiquito	very small	**perrito**	pup (little dog)

Proper names often add **"ito"**, and **"ita"**, as follows:

Juan	**Juanito**	Johnny
Carlos	**Carlitos**	Charlie
Ana	**Anita**	Annie
Ricardo	**Ricardito**	Dickie

"Illo", **"cillo"**, and **"ecillo"** are added to words to form diminutives:

campana	bell	**campanilla**	hand bell
muestra	sample	**muestrecilla**	little sample
chico	little	**chiquillo**	very little

Note the diminutive form of the following adjectives and adverbs:

ahora	**ahorita**	**pronto**	**prontito**
now	right now	soon	very soon
cerca	**cerquita**	**poco**	**poquito**
near	very near	little	very little

Some nouns form the augmentatives by adding "**ón**" for the masculine and "**ona**" for the feminine.

hombre—man	hombrón—large man
mujer—woman	mujerona—large woman
soltera—woman (single)	solterona—woman (old maid)
zapatos—shoes	zapatones—very large shoes

Certain Spanish verbs include the English preposition.

escuchar—to listen to	mirar—to look at
esperar—to wait for	buscar—to look for
pedir—to ask for	ponerse—to put on
quitarse—to take off	sacar—to take out

Verbs of motion, teaching, learning, and beginning require "a" before a following infinitive.

venir—to come	Vengo a trabajar	I come to work.
enseñar—to teach	Les enseñó a pizcar.	He taught them to pick (cotton, etc.).
aprender—to learn	Aprendemos a escribir.	We are learning to write.
empezar—to start	Empezarán a lavar.	They will start to wash.

Some verbs require "**de**" before a following infinitive, noun, or pronoun.

acordarse de—to remember
tratar de—to try to
acabar de—to have just
dejar de—to cease, to stop

No me acuerdo de él.	I don't remember him.
Acabo de estudiar mi lección.	I have just studied my lesson.
Él trató de hacerlo.	He tried to do it.
El niño dejó de llorar.	The child stopped crying.

Some verbs require "**en**" before a following infinitive, noun, or pronoun.

insistir en—to insist
convenir en—to agree
tardar en—to be late
fijarse en—to notice

Insiste en hablar contigo.	He insists on talking to you.
Convinieron en pagar por el cuarto.	They agreed to pay for the room.
No tardaré en llegar.	I will not be late in arriving.
Fíjese en esa muchacha.	Notice that girl.

WORDS SIMILAR IN ENGLISH AND SPANISH

Following is a list of Spanish words alike or almost alike in spelling, and alike in meaning in at least one acceptation to their English equivalents. However, the following orthographic peculiarities are to be observed:

Spanish admits of no doubled consonants except "cc" and, in very few cases, the "nn". The "ll" is not regarded as a double consonant, but as the sign for a particular sound; hence "college" is **"colegio"**. And "cc" occurs only before "e" and "i"; hence "accumulative" is **"acumulativo"**.

The "n" of the prefixes **"in"** and **"con"** does not change to "m" before a word beginning with "m", as is the case in English; therefore "immersion" is **"inmersión"**; "immortal" is **"inmortal"**; "commotion" is **"conmoción"**.

"Qu" becomes "cu": "frequent" is **"frecuente"**; "consequence" is **"consecuencia"**; "adequate" is **"adecuado"**.

Initial "s", followed by a consonant, takes an "e" before it: "squadron" is **"escuadrón"**; "spiral" is **"espiral"**; "strict" is **"estricto"**.

In this list of words a slight change is made in the ending of the English word to obtain the Spanish.

abrupto	agente	arrogante	bote (boat)
absceso	agresivo	asalto	bravo
absoluto	agresor	asfalto	burlesco
absorbente	aire	astuto	busto
abstinente	alarma	Atlántico	
abstracto	alarmista	átomo	cablegrama
absurdo	amazona	atractivo	calendario
abundante	alfabeto	autócrata	calma
abusivo	altitud	automático	candidato
acceso	antecedente		canino
accidente	antídoto	bálsamo	canoa
acento	aparte	banco	carácter
ácido	apetito	banquete	caravana
acróbata	aplauso	barbarismo	carbonato
activo	apóstol	barbero	carpintero
acto	apto	barómetro	caso
adjetivo	archivo	baronesa	católico
adulterante	argumento	bastardo	causa
adulto	árido	bautismo	caverna
adverbio	aristócrata	bayoneta	cemento
aeroplano	arma	Biblia	centínela
ágata	artico	biplano	centro

cigarro	diadema	femenino	inteligente
cisterna	diferente	festivo	intento
clase	diminutivo	figura	intolerante
cliente	dinamita	final	
coexistente	directo	firme	justicia
columna	discordia	forma	
comandante	discreto	fortuna	kilogramo
comando	disputa	fractura	kilómetro
combate	distancia	fragante	
cometa	distante	frágil	límite
cómico	distinto	fragmento	línea
compatriota	distrito	franco	lista
complemento	divino	frecuente	lógica
completo	do(u)ble	frontera	lotería
complexo	doctrina	fruta	
componente	documento	futuro	madama
compromiso	domicilio		magnitud
común	dramático	galante	mapa
concepto		galore	marcha
conciso	edicto	garantía	margen
concreto	edificio	gasolina	marinero
concubina	efectivo	globo	masculino
conducta	efecto	grupo	matrona
conductivo	egoísta	guarda	mayo
confidencia	elástico		mérito
conflicto	electivo	humano	modelo
congreso	electo		moderno
consonante	eléctrico	idea	monoplano
constante	elegancia	idealista	monte
constructivo	elegante	idiota	moralista
contacto	emigrante	ídolo	motor
contento	eminente	ignorante	música
continente	época	ilegal	
contrabando	etiqueta	imbécil	narcótico
contraste	evidencia	importante	negligente
conveniente	excesivo	incidente	noticia
convento	exceso	indiferente	novela
convicto	existencia	indirecto	novelista
cooperativo	expansivo	individual	novicio
correcto	experiencia	indulgente	
costa	experimento	infante	obscuro
credencial	experto	infinitivo	occidente
crédito	expresivo	infrecuente	océano
cresta	exquisito	inherente	ofensivo
criatura	extensivo	inmenso	orgánico
	extinto	inmigrante	organismo
defecto	extracto	inminente	órgano
demanda		insolente	oriental
democrático	falso	instante	oriente
demonio	famoso	instrumento	original
depósito	fanático	insuficiente	
despotismo	favorito	insulto	pacto

paganismo	público	secta	transparente
palacio	pútrido	sereno	triunfo
palma		severo	trópico
pánico		sexo	trote
parte	radiante	sincero	tubo
patriota	rancho	símbolo	tumulto
patriotismo	rápido	socialista	turbulento
penitente	rata	solemne	turno
período	realista	suma	
persona	reforma	sólido	
piloto	relativo	suficiente	uniforme
pistola	renta	supremo	union
planeta	república		
planta	reserva		válido
poema	residente	tacto	valiente
poeta	respeto	talento	verbo
portero	restaurante	teléfono	verso
presidente	resto	telegrama	víctima
pretexto	resulta	temperatura	violencia
prcblema	rollo	texto	violeta
producto	romántico	tímido	violinista
programa		tolerante	vista
prostituta		tomate	volcán
proverbio	sacramento	tormento	
prudente	sarcasmo	tráfico	
	secreto	tranquilo	zona

The following list of words ending in **"tad"** or **"dad"** in Spanish are feminine and end in "ty" in English. They are of the neuter gender in English.

absurdidad	autoridad	cristiandad	falsedad
aceptabilidad		crueldad	familiaridad
actividad	barbaridad	curiosidad	fatalidad
actualidad	brevedad		fecundidad
adaptabilidad	brutalidad	debilidad	felicidad
adversidad		densidad	ferocidad
afabilidad	calamidad	dificultad	fertilidad
afinidad	calidad	dignidad	fidelidad
agilidad	cantidad	divinidad	flexibilidad
alterabilidad	capacidad	durabilidad	formalidad
ambigüedad	caridad		fragilidad
amabilidad	casualidad	elasticidad	
amenidad	cavidad	electricidad	generalidad
anabilidad	civilidad	entidad	generosidad
animosidad	claridad	especialidad	gravedad
ansiedad	comodidad	esterilidad	
anterioridad	compatibilidad	eternidad	habilidad
antigüedad	complicidad	eventualidad	honestidad
atrocidad	comunidad	extremidad	humanidad
austeridad	conformidad		
autenticidad	continuidad	facilidad	identidad
		facultad	igualdad

imposibilidad	moralidad	posteridad	severidad
incredulidad	multiplicidad	prioridad	simplicidad
individualidad		probidad	sinceridad
infinidad	nacionalidad	probabilidad	singularidad
informalidad	natividad	profundidad	sociedad
ingenuidad	necesidad	prosperidad	solemnidad
iniquidad	neutralidad	proximidad	solidaridad
inmensidad		puntualidad	suavidad
inmoralidad	obscuridad		superioridad
inmunidad	oportunidad	raridad	
integridad		realidad	temeridad
intensidad	paternidad	receptabilidad	totalidad
irregularidad	peculiaridad	regularidad	tranquilidad
	personalidad	removibilidad	
liberalidad	perversidad	responsabilidad	universidad
libertad	piedad		utilidad
localidad	pluralidad	sagacidad	
	popularidad	seguridad	
maternidad	porosidad	sensibilidad	variedad
majestad	posibilidad	serenidad	velocidad

The following list of words ending in **"ción"** in Spanish end in "tion" in English and mean the same thing in at least one definition:

abducción	aserción	comunicación	convención
absolución	asimilación	concentración	conversación
abstracción	asociación	concepción	convicción
aceptación	aspiración	conciliación	convocación
acción	atención	condenación	cooperación
acumulación	atracción	condición	coordinación
acusación	aumentación	confección	corporación
administración	autorización	confederación	corrección
admiración	aviación	confirmación	corrupción
adoración		conflagración	creación
adulteración	calificación	congratulación	cristalización
adquisición	capitalización	congregación	cultivación
adulación	capitulación	conjugación	
afección	celebración	conjunción	declamación
agitación	certificación	conmoción	declaración
agregación	circulación	conservación	decoración
alternación	civilización	consideración	**dedicación**
ambición	clasificación	constelación	definición
amputación	colaboración	constitución	degeneración
animación	colección	construcción	deliberación
anticipación	colonización	contaminación	demostración
aplicación	combinación	contemplación	denominación
aposición	comparación	contención	deportación
apropiación	compensación	continuación	deposición
arbitración	competición	contracción	depreciación
argumentación	complicación	contradicción	derivación
articulación	composición	contribución	descripción

deserción
designación
destitución
destrucción
detención
determinación
detonación
devastación
devoción
dirección
discreción
disipación
disolución
disposición
distinción
distracción
distribución
dominación
duración

edición
educación
ejecución
elección
elevación
elocución
emancipación
emigración
emoción
enumeración
equivocación
erudición
erupción
estación
estimación
estrangulación
evacuación
evaporación
evicción
evolución
exageración
exaltación
excavación
excepción
exclamación
exhibición
expedición
expiración
exploración
explotación
exportación
exposición
extracción

extradición

fabricación
facción
fascinación
federación
ficción
formación
fortificación
fricción
fumigación
función

generación
generalización
glorificación
graduación

habitación

identificación
iluminación
ilustración
imaginación
imitación
imperfección
imploración
importación
imposición
inauguración
inclinación
indicación
indignación
infección
información
infracción
iniciación
inmigración
inscripción
insinuación
inspección
inspiración
instigación
institución
instrucción
insurrección
intención
interjección
interpretación
interrogación
intervención
introducción
invención

investigación
invitación

jurisdicción

lamentación
legación
legalización
legislación
liberación
limitación
lubricación

mancipación
manifestación
manipulación
mediación
meditación
mención
mitigación
moción
moderación
modificación
mortificación
multiplicación
munición

nación
narración
natación
naturalización
navegación
negación
negociación
noción
nominación
notación
notificación
numeración
nutrición

objeción
obligación
observación
obstrucción
ocupación
operación
oposición
oración
orientación
organización
oscilación
osificación

ostentación
ovación
oxidación

palpitación
participación
penetración
percepción
perfección
perforación
persecución
petición
porción
posición
precaución
precipitación
predicción
predilección
predisposición
premeditación
preocupación
preparación
preposición
presentación
preservación
presunción
prevaricación
prevención
privación
probación
proclamación
producción
prohibición
prolongación
promoción
promulgación
pronunciación
proporción
proposición
prosecución
prostitución
protección
provocación
publicación
pulverización
puntuación
purificación

ración
radiación
ratificación
reacción
realización

recapitulación · reparación · salvación · tracción
recepción · repetición · sanción · tradición
reciprocación · representación · satisfacción · transacción
recitación · reproducción · saturación · transición
reclamación · repudiación · sección · translación
recomendación · reputación · selección · transmigración
reconciliación · requisición · sensación · transportación
recreación · reservación · separación · transposición
rectificación · resignación · significación
reducción · resolución · simplificación
reelección · respiración · simulación · vacilación
refracción · restauración · situación · vaporación
refrigeración · resurrección · solidificación · variación
rehabilitación · retención · solución · vegetación
relación · revelación · subscripción · ventilación
relegación · reverberación · suposición · vibración
remuneración · revolución · substitución · vindicación
rendición · rotación · · visitación
renovación · · · violación
renunciación · · terminación · vocación
reorganización · salutación · testificación · vociferación

In the following list of words the Spanish "io" and "ia" end in "y" in English. In a few of the words listed below there is a slight change in spelling. In some instances, shown with parentheses, the English letter is omitted in the Spanish word:

academia · ceremonia · extraordinario · matrimonio
accesorio · colonia · · melodía
adulterio · comedia · farmacia · memoria
adversario · comentario · familia · mercurio
agencia · comisario · fantasía · ministerio
agonía · compañía · frecuencia · miseria
analogía · constancia · func(t)ionario · modestia
aniversario · contrario · furia · monasterio
antropología · copia · · monopolio
arbitrario · coquetería · galantería
armonía · cortesía · galería · observatorio
arteria · · geografía · oratorio
artillería · depositario · gloria · ordinario
auditorio · dinastía · · orgía
· diplomacia · idolatría
batería · directorio · industria · patrimonio
blasfemia · disentería · infamia · pedagogía
· dormitorio · infancia · perfidia
calvario · · injuria · perfumería
canario · economía · · plenipotenciario
categoría · energía · · prodigio
centenario · estudio · laboratorio

promontorio	salario	sociología	tiranía
purgatorio	san(c)tuario	sumario	tragedia
	satisfactoria		
remedio	secretario	territorio	victoria
rosario	seminario	testimonio	voluntario

Drop the infinitive ending in Spanish for the English verb:

abandonar	confesar	estampar	ocasionar
absorber	confirmar	exaltar	ocurrir
abundar	conformar	exclamar	ofender
aceptar	confrontar	exhortar	omitir
aclamar	consentir	existir	
acordar	considerar	expeler	partir
acreditar	consignar	experimentar	pasar
adaptar	consistir	exportar	perdonar
administrar	consultar	expresar	permitir
adoptar	contar	extender	persistir
adornar	contender		perturbar
aducir	contentar	filtrar	ponderar
afectar	contrastar	fomentar	preferir
afirmar	convertir	frecuentar	presentar
alarmar	corresponder	func(t)ionar	preservar
alterar	costar	fundar	pretender
anexar			proclamar
anular		guardar	profesar
apelar	debutar		prolongar
aplaudir	defender		proporcionar
aprehender	deferir	honrar	prosperar
aprisionar	defraudar		protestar
armar	demandar	importar	proyectar
arrestar	departir	incurrir	
asaltar	depender	inferir	razonar
ascender	deportar	informar	reclamar
asentir	depositar	insertar	recordar
asignar	desarmar	insistir	referir
atacar	descender	inspeccionar	reformar
atender	descontar	instalar	refrenar
	desembarcar	insultar	registrar
balancear	desistir	interesar	remitir
batallar	despachar	internar	repetir
	destilar		rescindir
calmar	detallar	laborar	responder
cancelar	detestar	lamentar	representar
combatir	divorciar	limitar	resignar
comentar			resistir
comisionar	embarcar	manifestar	respetar
concernir	emitir	marcar	retardar
concurrir	enamorar	marchar	robar
conducir	engendrar	molestar	
conferir	entrar	murmurar	salvar

sanc(t)ionar	sufrir	tostar	usurpar
solicitar	sumar	transformar	
soportar	suspender	transmitir	vender
subsistir		transportar	visitar
sucumbir	telefonear	triunfar	vomitar

In this list of words the Spanish infinitive is replaced by a silent "e" in English. Some of these words have slight changes in spelling. English double letters are single in Spanish. Soft "c" before "a" or "o" is changed to "z". The "dv" combination in many English words changes to "v" in Spanish.

abjurar	computar	eludir	mover
absolver	conceder	equipar	
abusar	condensar	escalar	notar
acceder	confinar	escandalizar	
acreditar	conjurar	escapar(se)	obligar
acusar	consolar	evadir	observar
admirar	conspirar	evocar	opinar
adorar	consumir	examinar	organizar
adherir	continuar	exceder	
adquirir	convencer	excitar	paralizar
aludir	conversar	excusar	perfumar
analizar	curar	exhalar	persuadir
aprobar		expirar	practicar
argüir	danzar	explorar	preparar
aspirar	datar	expulsar	preseverar
asumir	decidir		presidir
autorizar	declarar	fatigar	presumir
avanzar	declinar	figurar	procurar
a(d)vanzar	deducir	fingir	producir
aventurar	definir	forzar	profanar
a(d)venturar	defraudar	fracturar	prolongar
a(d)visar	denotar		pronunciar
	denunciar		proscribir
basar	deplorar	ignorar	provocar
	depravar	imaginar	pulverizar
capitalizar	describir	impedir	
capturar	desfigurar	implorar	realizar
caracterizar	desolver	improvisar	recibir
carbonizar	destinar	incitar	reclinar
causar	determinar	inclinar	recompensar
censurar	dilatar	inducir	redo(u)blar
citar	dispensar	inflamar	reducir
civilizar	dispersar	inquirir	refinar
coincidir	dividir	inspirar	relatar
combinar	divulgar	intervenir	remover
comenzar	do(u)blar	introducir	renunciar
comparar		invadir	reparar
competir	economizar	invitar	repasar
completar	eclipsar	invocar	reposar

reproducir	retirar	sentenciar	tributar
reservar	revocar	separar	
residir	revolver	servir	usar
resolver		subscribir	utilizar
respirar	saludar		
resumir	seducir	tranquilizar	votar

The following verbs end in "ar" in Spanish and in "ate" in English:

abdicar	contemplar	facilitar	navegar
abreviar	cooperar	fascinar	necesitar
abrogar	coordinar	felicitar	negociar
acelerar	crear	formular	nominar
acentuar	cultivar	fluctuar	
acomodar			
actuar		graduar	obligar
acumular	debilitar	granular	oficiar
adulterar	decorar		operar
agitar	dedicar		orientar
aglomerar	degenerar	habilitar	originar
agravar	delegar	habitar	oscilar
agregar	deliberar	habituar	
aliviar	demo(n)strar		
alternar	denominar	iluminar	palpitar
amputar	depredar	ilustrar	participar
animar	designar	implicar	penetrar
anotar	desolar	inaugurar	perpetuar
anticipar	devastar	incorporar	precipitar
apreciar	dictar	indicar	predominar
aprop(r)iar	diferenciar	iniciar	premeditar
arbitrar	dilatar	inocular	promulgar
articular	disimular	insinuar	propagar
asesinar	disipar	instigar	pun(c)tuar
	dislocar	interrogar	
	dominar	intimar	radiar
calcular	donar	invalidar	reanimar
calumniar	duplicar	investigar	recapitular
castigar		irritar	reciprocar
celebrar			recrear
circular	educar	libertar	refrigerar
complicar	elevar	lubricar	regenerar
comunicar	emanar		remunerar
concentrar	emancipar	manipular	renovar
conciliar	emigrar	mediar	renunciar
confiscar	enumerar	meditar	resucitar
congratular	enunciar	mitigar	
congregar	especificar	moderar	
conjugar	estimar	modular	saturar
conmemorar	evacuar	motivar	separar
consolidar	exagerar	mutilar	simular
consumar	excavar		situar
contaminar	exterminar	narrar	sofocar

subyugar	tolerar	vacilar	vibrar
suplicar	transmigrar	vegetar	vindicar
		venerar	violar
terminar	ulcerar	ventilar	vociferar

Below is given a list of words that are spelled alike, or almost alike, in Spanish and English and mean the same thing in at least one acceptation:

abdomen	bonanza	consular	eczema
abominable	brutal	continental	editorial
abrasión	billón	convoy	elector
accesible		corral	electorial
accidental	cable	cordial	elemental
acre	calibre	corporal	era
actor	calicó	coyote	error
actual	calomel	cráter	especial
admirable	canal	criminal	estimable
adobe	cáncer	crisis	etcétera
adorable	candor	cristal	evasión
adverbial	caníbal	cruel	excursión
agresión	cañón	cuestión	experimental
álbum	canon	culpable	explosión
álcali	capital	curable	expresión
alcohol	cardinal	champaña	expulsión
alfalfa	carnal	charlatán	extensión
altar	cartel	chasis	exterior
alusión	casual		
aluvial	celestial	deán	facial
amén	censor	debate	factor
ángel	central	decimal	familiar
angular	cereal	decisión	fatal
animal	chocolate	déficit	favor
antena	circular	depresión	favorable
anterior	civil	derivable	federal
anual	clamor	detestable	felón
apendicitis	clerical	detector	fértil
aplicable	clímax	diagnosis	fervor
área	colisión	difusión	fiasco
arena	colonial	digestible	filial
armada	color	digestión	final
artificial	comercial	dimensión	flexible
ascensión	comisión	director	formal
atlas	comparable	dirigible	formidable
audible	compulsión	diván	fórmula
auto	concesión	diversión	fraternal
automóvil	conclusión	división	fundamental
aversión	cóndor	doctor	funeral
axioma	confesión	dogma	
	confusión	dorsal	galón
balance	considerable	dragón	gas
bulevar	cónsul	drama	general

genial	integral	mortal	perpendicular
glacial	intelectual	mosquito	personal
gonorrea	inteligible	motor	piano
gorila	interior	mulato	pistón
gradual	interminable	múltiple	placer
gratis	intolerable	municipal	plan
guardián	intrusión	mural	plural
	invariable	musical	polar
habitual	invasión		popular
hangar	inventor		portal
honor	invisible	natal	posible
horrible	irregular	natural	postal
horizontal	irremediable	naval	posterior
horror	irresistible	negociable	practicable
hospital		negro	preceptor
hotel		neuralgia	precisión
humor	jovial	neutral	prior
	judicial	no	probable
idea		noble	profesional
ideal		nominal	promotor
ilusión	kodak	normal	propaganda
imaginable		notable	provincial
imitable	labor	numeral	provisional
imperceptible	lamentable		provisión
imperial	lateral		pulmotor
impersonal	latín	oasis	pus
implacable	laudable	ocasión	
imposible	laurel	occidental	
impresión	legal	omisión	radial
incomparable	legion	oficial	radiar
incompatible	liberal	ómnibus	radical
incomprehensible	local	ópera	radio
incurable	lustre	opinión	rebelión
indigestion		ordinal	región
indispensable		oriental	regular
indisputable	magnate	oral	religión
individual	magneto	origen	remediable
indivisible	maíz	original	reparable
industrial	mamá	ornamental	repulsión
inestimable	mansión		resistible
inevitable	manual	panorama	reversible
infalible	marginal	par	revisión
inferior	marital	particular	revocable
infernal	maternal	pasión	revólver
inflamable	melón	pastoral	rifle
informal	memorable	paternal	rigor
inimitable	memorial	peculiar	ritual
innumerable	mental	pedestal	romance
insensible	metal	penal	rufián
inseparable	mineral	península	rumor
inspector	miserable	peninsular	rural
instructor	misión	pensión	
instrumental	moral	peón	salón
	mormón	perfume	secular

sensible	superficial	transferible	variable
sentimental	superior	tribunal	venerable
separable	suspensión	trío	verbal
sexual		triple	versión
similar	tango	trivial	viceversa
simple	temporal	tropical	vigor
singular	tenis	tumor	violín
sentimental	tenor	tutor	virginal
social	tensión		virtual
sofá	terrible	unión	visible
soluble	terror	universal	visión
suave	tolerable	usual	visual
sublime	total		vital
sultán	tractor	vapor	vocal

The following list of words ending in "ista" in Spanish refers to one who is of that occupation or a member of the group.

The word is masculine or feminine according to the gender of the person.

absolutista	bautista	economista	naturalista
adornista	biciclista	electricista	novelista
agrarista	bimetalista		
alarmista	bolchevista	fatalista	oculista
alienista			
alquimista	capitalista		pianista
analista	comunista	huelguista	protagonista
anarquista	comisionista		
antagonista	conformista	idealista	realista
archivista	contrabandista		
artista			
automovilista		maquinista	socialista
	dentista	moralista	
bañista	duelista	motorista	violinista

STATES OF MEXICO AND THEIR ABBREVIATIONS

Aguascalientes—Ags.
Baja California—B. C.
Campeche—Camp.
Chiapas—Chis.
Chihuahua—Chih.
Coahuila—Coah.
Colima—Col.
Distrito Federal—D. F.
Durango—Dgo.
Guanajuato—Gto.
Guerrero—Gro.
Hidalgo—Hgo.
Jalisco—Jal.
México—Mex.
Michoacán—Mich.
Morelos—Mor.

Nayarit—Nay.
Nuevo León—N. L.
Oaxaca—Oax.
Puebla—Pueb.
Querétaro—Qto.
Quintana Roo (no abbreviation)
San Luis Potosí—S. L. P.
Sinaloa—Sin.
Sonora—Son.
Tabasco—Tab.
Tamaulipas—Tamps.
Tlaxcala—Tlax.
Veracruz—Ver.
Yucatán—Yuc.
Zacatecas—Zac.

OCCUPATIONS

agent—agente
artist—artista
aviator—aviador
ballplayer—pelotero
barber—peluquero
   barbero
blacksmith—herrero
bookkeeper—tenedor de libros
book seller—librero
bootblack—limpiabotas, bolero
butcher—carnicero
carpenter—carpintero
cattleman—ganadero
chauffeur—chofer, chófer
chicken raiser—gallinero
clerk—dependiente
conductor—conductor
constable—alguacil
cook—cocinero
cotton grower—algodonero
cowboy—vaquero
customs agent—agente de aduana
   aduanero
dairyman—lechero
dancer—bailador
   bailarina
dentist—dentista
director—director
doctor—doctor
   médico
driver—muletero (horses)
   cochero (coach)
druggist—boticario
   droguista
   droguero
engineer—ingeniero
farmer—hacendado
   agricultor
fisherman—pescador
gardener—jardinero
goatherd—chivero
   cabrero
guide—guía
harvester—cosechero
hatmaker—sombrerero
inventor—inventor
irrigator—regador
jeweler—joyero
laborer—jornalero, bracero
   trabajador
   labrador

lawyer—abogado
   licenciado
machinist—maquinista
mailcarrier—cartero
manufacturer—fabricante
mason—albañil
merchant—comerciante
mechanic—mecánico
midwife—partera
miller—molinero
miner—minero
musician—músico
nurse—enfermera
obstetrician—partero
official—oficial
painter—pintor
peddler—comerciante ambulante
   buhonero
picker (cotton)—pizcador
pilot—piloto
pimp—palo blanco
   alcahuete
plasterer—emplastador
plumber—plomero
planter—plantador
   sembrador
porter—portero
   cargador
priest—cura, padre
promoter—promotor
rancher—ranchero
sailor—marinero
seller—vendedor
servant—mozo
   sirviente
   criado
seamstress—costurera
sharecropper—mediero
shepherd—pastor
   borreguero
sheriff—alguacil
   policía
shoemaker—zapatero
shoplifter—ratero de tienda
smuggler—contrabandista
soldier—soldado
stenographer—taquígrafo
surgeon—cirujano
swineherd—porquero
tailor—sastre

teacher—profesor
    maestro
tinsmith—hojalatero
usher—conserje, acomodador
valet—camarero
waiter—mozo, mesero

washerwoman—lavandera
watchmaker—relojero
wet nurse—nodriza
woodchopper—leñero
worker—trabajador
    obrero

Appendix

ACCEPTABLE TRANSLATIONS FOR EXERCISES CONTAINED IN THE TEXT

LESSON V

1. El muchacho compra un lápiz.
2. ¿Vive ella en El Paso?
3. Nosotros estudiamos mucho.
4. ¿Escribimos nosotros las lecciones cada día?
5. ¿Trabaja él hoy?
6. ¿Toma él el autobús mañana?
7. Alberto lleva el libro a su cuarto.
8. Yo siempre tomo un taxi.
9. Él y Pepe ganan bastante dinero.
10. Luis y María no ganan mucho dinero.
11. Nosotros no hablamos español.
12. Él saca su visa hoy.
13. Simón llega temprano cada día.
14. ¿Maneja Vd. el carro de su patrón?
15. Ellos esperan el tren.
16. Él no toma mucha agua.
17. Ellas trabajan mucho.
18. ¿Debe esta señora mucho dinero?
19. La mádre del muchacho pasa por esta ciudad cada mes.
20. La enfermera de ese doctor vive en aquella casa azul.
21. ¿Compran esos abogados estos dos carros?

LESSON VI

1. ¿Cuántos parientes tiene Vd.?
2. ¿Qué trae Vd.?
3. ¿Tiene Vd. cortadas o lunares?
4. Sí señor, yo tengo una cortada en la mano derecha.
5. Una semana tiene siete días.
6. ¿Va ella con nosotros la semana que viene?
7. Yo no tengo los documentos de mi hermano.
8. Este hombre tiene mis cosas.
9. Esta muchacha viene y va cada día.
10. ¿Tiene ella esposo?
11. ¿Por qué quiere Vd. una visa?
12. El mayordomo pide ayuda.
13. Estos hombres no saben nada.
14. Manuel no sabe el nombre del oficial.
15. ¿Por qué miente Vd. siempre?
16. Ellos no entienden el problema.
17. La señora Silva sabe las lecciones de español muy bien.

LESSON VII

1. ¿Es Vd. ciudadano mexicano?
2. Esta casa es muy grande.
3. ¿Quién es el presidente de México?
4. ¿En dónde trabaja Rogelio ahora?
5. Ellos siempre están enfermos.
6. La señorita García no es bonita, porque ella es muy vieja.
7. El sobrino de Vd. es de México, pero ¿qué hace él aquí?
8. Sí señor, ellos son de Puebla.
9. Estos son los pantalones de Pedro.
10. La señorita Cabaza no es muy alta.
11. Nuestros papeles están mojados.
12. Este muchacho es el hijo de esa mujer.
13. Mi padre y mi hermano están en California, pero ellos son de México.

14. Vd. está mintiendo ahorita.
15. El cuñado del hombre no está aquí.
16. ¿Qué tan lejos está la tienda de la casa de Vd.?
17. Vd. no está diciendo la verdad.
18. ¿Cuánto gana Vd. por mes?
19. ¿Qué hora es?
20. ¿Cuánto vale la camioneta de Vd.?
21. Mi primo es de México, y él está trabajando en una fábrica
22.   allá.
    Hoy es sábado, y nosotros vamos al pueblo esta noche.
23. El señor Moreno es un buen trabajador, pero siempre está
24.   enfermo.
    ¿De qué color es el saco nuevo de Vd.?

LESSON VIII

1. Hay un libro en la mesa.
2. ¿Tiene Vd. mucho sueño?
3. ¿Por qué ha mentido Vd.?
4. Hay doce sillas en el cuarto.
5. ¿Cómo está su esposa?
6. Yo no he visto a ese hombre antes.
7. ¿En dónde está la carta? ¡Allí está!
8. Nosotros hemos traído nuestros documentos hoy.
9. Nosotros no hemos abierto la puerta.
10. El amigo de él no tiene dinero.
11. ¿Ha cruzado el padre de Vd. la línea antes?
12. Yo he llevado el carro al pueblo.
13. ¿Qué ha hecho Vd. hoy?
14. Ellos han ido al pueblo varias veces.
15. ¿Hay hombres en ese rancho?
16. Él no ha dicho la verdad.
17. Alguien ha puesto la tinta en la mesa.
18. ¿Ha estado Vd. en Chicago alguna vez?
19. ¿Cuántas veces ha vuelto Vd. a este país?
20. ¿Tiene el patrón de Vd. un avión verde?
21. Él tiene mucho cuidado cuando cruza la calle.
22. Yo tengo mucha hambre y mucha sed, porque no he comido
    nada por mucho tiempo.

LESSON IX
Exercise No. 1

1. Josefa tiene mis papeles legales. Ella los trae en su bolsillo.

2. Él no ha visto la pistola de Vd. ¿La trae Vd.?
3. Nosotros compramos nuestra comida en esa tienda. No es muy cara allí.
4. Miguel vende su casa. La vende barata.
5. ¿Entiende Vd. las reglas? Sí, ya las he aprendido.
6. Yo tengo las armas en casa. Mi esposa ya las ha visto.
7. Él ha cruzado el río antes. Lo cruza cada semana.
8. ¿Ha visto Vd. a Felipe? No, no lo he visto todavía.
9. ¿Han visto Vds. a mi esposa? Sí, la vemos en la tienda de vez en cuando.
10. Vemos a Gabriel y a su hermana cada semana. Los vemos en la iglesia cada domingo.
11. **Timoteo visita a sus abuelos a menudo. Los visita una vez por semana.**
12. ¿Lo conoce él a Vd. muy bien? No, él no me conoce muy bien.
13. ¿Ha pagado Vd. la cuenta? Sí, ya la he pagado.

LESSON IX
Exercise No. 2

1. Él me está dando su nombre correcto.
2. Ella nos lee el periódico.
3. ¿Le ha escrito Vd. a Mary esta semana?
4. Nosotros le estamos comprando los cintos al señor Jones.
5. Osvaldo le vende su bicicleta a Pepe.
6. ¿Le ha pedido Vd. dinero?
7. ¿No le han pedido Vds. al cónsul un permiso?
8. ¿Por qué no le pide prestado el radio a Martín?
9. Él le está pidiendo prestados cinco dólares a su cuñada.
10. Él le ha robado muchas cosas a ese comerciante.
11. ¿Le ha robado algo él a Vd.?
12. Él le está diciendo la verdad al oficial.
13. Les estoy pidiendo más información tocante a sus compañeros.
14. Él le está comprando el ganado al señor Aguilar.
15. Ellos le han dado al oficial mucha información.
16. Él nunca nos ha ayudado antes.
17. ¿Le ha pagado Vd. al zapatero la cuenta?

LESSON IX

Exercise No. 3

1. ¿Por qué nos lo está enseñando?
2. Nosotros se los estamos mandando.
3. Andrés nos la ha pedido.
4. Guillermo me las está pagando ahora.
5. Nosotros lo hemos cruzado con él muchas veces.
6. Él se lo está comprando por diez dólares.
7. ¿Quién nos la está vendiendo?
8. ¿Por qué no se las pide?
9. Él se lo ha robado al comerciante.
10. Ellos ya se lo han dado.
11. ¿Se la ha mandado Vd. a Susana?
12. ¿Se lo ha pedido prestado él a la señorita Peña?
13. Jaime me lo ha dicho muchas veces.
14. Yo ya se lo he comprado al señor Garza.
15. ¿Quién se las manda?

LESSON X

1. ¿Sabe Vd. manejar un tractor?
2. ¿Va él a trabajar mañana por la mañana?
3. Nosotros no podemos ir esta tarde.
4. Tenemos que firmar este papel lo más pronto posible.
5. ¿Saben Vds. leer y escribir?
6. Ella quiere estar con su esposo lo más pronto posible.
7. Ellos piensan regresar mañana por la noche.
8. ¿Acaba de regresar Vd. de México?
9. Yo debo pagarle hoy.
10. Vd. debe comprárselo.
11. Vd. tiene que salir de este lugar ahorita.
12. ¿Cómo ha podido Antonio hallar trabajo en los Estados Unidos?
.13. ¿Qué va a hacer él esta noche?
14. Yo he tratado de hacerlo antes.
15. Ellos acaban de entrar, pero no han podido hallar trabajo.
16. ¿A quién piensa dárselo él?
17. Nosotros acabamos de llegar a esta ciudad.
18. ¿No sabe Vd. que no puede llevarlo con Vd.?

19. ¿Le permiten ver al cónsul sin una cita?
20. ¿Comienza Jorge a trabajar muy temprano?
21. ¿Por qué ha dejado de trabajar como enfermera?

LESSON XI

1. Enséñeme el camino.
2. Espere hasta mañana.
3. Ayúdenos a hacer la asignatura.
4. No corra tan rápido.
5. No cierre la puerta.
6. Díganos la verdad.
7. Déselo a ellos.
8. Llévenos temprano en su carro.
9. Páguenos con un cheque.
10. Déjeme ver su cartera.
11. Súbase al carro.
12. No crucen juntos.
13. Haga esto primero y luego abra la caja.
14. Dígale que su esposo está mintiendo.
15. No le pague todavía.
16. Vaya a casa y tráiganos esos documentos.
17. Venga a la oficina mañana y ayúdeme.
18. Tráigame la pluma amarilla de él, por favor.
18. Esté aquí temprano mañana.
20. Obtenga una visa lo más pronto posible.

LESSON XII

1. Anita no vino de México con su padrastro.
2. Simón no me trajo mi maleta.
3. Ella dijo que no le dijo la verdad al oficial.
4. ¿Cuántos años vivieron sus padres en Sonora?
5. Yo no pude hacer el trabajo ayer por la mañana.
6. Nosotros no vimos al criminal.
7. ¿Dejó él su pasaporte con Vd.?
8. La mujer le mandó siete dólares a su hija el mes pasado.
9. Los papeles legales no le costaron mucho a ella.
10. Él me dejó ir porque yo le dije la verdad.
11. Ellos salieron de aquí con mi tío hace cinco días.

12. ¿Por qué dejó Vd. a su esposa en ese lugar?
13. Yo no creí lo que él dijo.
14. ¿Le pidió Vd. dinero?
15. Él no quiso darme la navaja cuando se la pedí.
16. ¿A qué hora supo él?
17. ¿Cuándo fué la última vez que Vd. vió a este hombre?
18. Yo trabajé en esa fábrica por mucho tiempo.
19. ¿Cuántas botellas de tequila trajo Vd. de México?
20. ¿Cuántas millas anduvo Vd. por el desierto?
21. ¿Qué hizo Vd. cuando llegó a Chicago?
22. Él me dijo que vió al señor Moreno ayer.

LESSON XIII

1. ¿Por qué lo arrestaron los oficiales?
2. Ellos me arrestaron por una ofensa muy pequeña.
3. Eliseo tiene una cita para el lunes por la mañana.
4. Yo necesito un vaso para leche.
5. Él corrió hacia el oeste cuando yo lo ví.
6. Ella quiere ir a casa para los días de fiesta.
7. Yo le pagué al ranchero cien dólares por la vaca.
8. Los mineros fueron a las montañas para buscar plata.
9. Él vendió cada uno por cinco centavos.
10. Haga estos ejercicios para mañana.
11. Él gana muy poco dinero haciendo esta clase de trabajo.
12. Después de que salió él del hospital, comenzó a trabajar.
13. Ese abogado puede hacer mucho por Vd.
14. ¿Para qué es esta máquina? Es para escribir cartas.
15. Al llegar a la oficina, le llamé por teléfono.
16. Marta no puede ir a la tienda sin decirme.
17. Vd. no puede andar por el parque solo.
18. En vez de decirnos la verdad, ella mintió.
19. El oficial lo paró porque él empezó a correr.
20. Después de cambiar su mercancía por dinero, él fué al pueblo.
21. Él y sus dos amigos siempre viajan juntos.
22. Voltee a la derecha donde ve la iglesia.
23. Él quebró la botella sin saberlo.

LESSON XIV

1. Yo ya había comprado la casa cuando ellos llegaron.
2. Había mucho algodón en los campos.
3. ¿Había ido él a la oficina cuando Vd. fué a verlo?

4. Ella no vino por el dinero porque ella había recibido un cheque.
5. Vd. me dijo que había trabajado con él antes.
6. ¿Sabía Vd. que el hombre era contrabandista?
7. ¿Había braceros pizcando algodón?
8. Yo trabajaba con el señor Kent, pero ahora estoy trabajando en un rancho grande.
9. ¿Qué clase de trabajo hacía Vd. antes de venir a los Estados Unidos?
10. Él dijo que quería venir a San Antonio a trabajar.
11. Cuando yo trabajaba en ese rancho, Enrique estaba allí también.
12. El esposo de ella había estado trabajando en Cotulla por muchos años.
13. Ellos caminaban por el camino cuando yo los arresté.
14. ¿Quién manejaba el troque cuando Vds. iban a California?
15. Ellos pensaban venir a los Estados Unidos, pero no pudieron porque no tenían dinero.
16. ¿Había visto Vd. a este hombre antes?
17. Yo estuve muy enfermo ayer.
18. Había mucha gente sin trabajo cuando yo salí de México.
19. El alumno hacía la lección cuando yo entré en la sala de clase.
20. El tío de él necesitaba otros papeles para sacar un pasaporte.
21. ¿Sabía Vd. localizar la casa de este hombre?
22. ¿Conocía Vd. a Elías cuando Vd. trabajaba allí?

LESSON XV

1. ¿En dónde enterró el cuerpo?
2. Micaela nació el trece de febrero de mil novecientos treinta.
3. Ayer fué sábado; hoy es domingo.
4. Nosotros vendimos la última sandía a las diez veinte de la noche.
5. Yo voy de compras cada viernes.
6. Nuestros padres llegaron a las cuatro cuarenta de la tarde el viernes.
7. Ella decidió tomar el tren el martes a las ocho cincuenta y cinco de la mañana.
8. El mayordomo nos pagó a las seis y media de la mañana ayer.
9. Durante el verano salimos para Michigan.
10. ¿Vió Vd. a alguien anoche a las once y media?
11. ¿Qué hace Vd. los domingos?
12. Nosotros no tenemos que estar aquí hasta las doce y media de la tarde.

13. Lo conocí anteayer a mediodía.
14. La última vez que fuí allá fué el lunes, el veinte y siete de mayo de mil novecientos cuarenta y tres.
15. Vámonos, porque ya es muy tarde.
16. Los inspectores van a deportarlo mañana por la mañana.
17. Concha tiene treinta y un años, pero todavía vive con sus padres.
18. Felipe dice que ellos le pagan cada quincena.
19. Él me debe como trescientos cincuenta y un dólares por siete meses de trabajo.
20. Hoy es día de fiesta, y no tenemos que trabajar.
21. Él quiere vernos en el puente esta noche a las diez cuarenta y cinco.
22. ¿A qué hora llega el primo de Vd. aquí?
23. Perdí el primer pasaporte que saqué.
24. Son las doce del día, el treinta de noviembre de mil novecientos sesenta y seis.
25. Cien niños estuvieron enfermos ayer.

LESSON XVI
Exercise No. 1

1. Él fué arrestado por la policía en mil novecientos cuarenta y siete.
2. Nosotros hemos estado viviendo en ese lugar por mucho tiempo.
3. Esta casa fué vendida la semana pasada.
4. Fué enviado de aquí el quince de mayo.
5. La estación de tren estaba abierta cuando yo salí.
6. Todas las puertas fueron cerradas por los vientos fuertes.
7. Los muebles nuevos de ellos habían sido sacados del cuarto.
8. ¿A qué hora cierra el banco?
9. Cuando ellos llegaron, las puertas y las ventanas estaban cerradas.
10. Él estaba cansado porque había trabajado toda la noche.
11. Horacio fué mandado al mercado por pan.
12. Estos edificios fueron acabados el año pasado.

LESSON XVI
Exercise No. 2

1. Hacía mucho viento cuando el barco entró en el puerto.

2. Nos gusta ir a la pesca cuando hace sol.
3. El pasaporte de él fué cancelado hace tres semanas.
4. Ella fué encontrada en una casa abandonada hace como cinco horas.
5. Hace cinco años que yo no lo veo (a él).
6. Mario había trabajado en ese taller por ocho o nueve meses.
7. Hace siete días desde mi último día de pago.
8. La cueva estaba muy fría y muy mojada.
9. Le hicimos darnos las drogas que él pasaba de contrabando.
10. Ellos pueden hacernos rendir nuestras tarjetas locales.
11. ¿Vieron Vds. al contrabandista hablar con ellos?
12. Lo vimos tomar cerveza con esa mujer.
13. La fichera no pudo oír venir a su patrón.
14. A esos refugiados no les gusta trabajar en las labores.
15. A ella no le gustó los Estados Unidos, así que ella regresó a su país.
16. A mi nunca me ha gustado su compañía (amistad).
17. ¿Cómo le gustó la película?
18. A Eloísa le gusta comer en ese restaurante.
19. A ella siempre le gusta pedir la misma cosa.
20. A él le faltan nueve días para terminar este curso.

LESSON XVII

Exercise No. 1

1. Mañana por la mañana iré al correo.
2. ¿Cuándo irá Vd. al pueblo?
3. Voy a ver a Luís mañana por la mañana.
4. Mañana es día de fiesta, y todas las tiendas estarán cerradas.
5. Ricardo saldrá de aquí pasado mañana.
6. Vd. tendrá que volver lo más pronto posible.
7. ¿A qué hora abrirán la ventana?
8. Él estará aquí como a las nueve.
9. ¿Estará Vd. en casa esta noche a las seis?
10. No, tengo que ir a la iglesia a esa hora, pero estaré allí a las ocho.
11. Si Vd. ve al inspector, dígale que iré a su casa esta noche.
12. ¿Habrá mucho algodón en las labores este año?
13. Él tendrá que vender el maíz lo más pronto posible.
14. Ellos piensan ver al mayordomo mañana por la tarde.
15. ¿Por qué brincarán en ese lugar?
16. Los amigos de él tratarán de entrar por la madrugada.

LESSON XVII

Exercise No. 2

1. ¿Dijo Vd. que me daría permiso para ir a la ciudad?
2. Le dije que yo lo levantaría temprano.
3. Él le compraría al hombre el anillo de oro, pero él no tiene dinero.
4. Si él le hace preguntas, ¿le puede decir Vd. la verdad?
5. Yo le llamaría por teléfono, pero no sé su número.
6. Luis me dijo que él tendría el dinero la semana que viene.
7. Ellos nos dijeron que Vd. nos llevaría al pueblo.
8. ¿Sabía él que podría hacerlo?
9. ¿Qué haría Vd. durante ese tiempo?
10. No fuí a verlo porque él dijo que no estaría allí.
11. Yo le habría dado la botella de vino, pero él no estaba allí.
12. ¿Prometió él que le pagaría a Vd. al fin del mes?
13. Él nos dijo que no vendría a visitarnos porque estaba muy ocupado.
14. Les dije que lo haría, pero ellos no quisieron escucharme.
15. Miguel le dijo a mi amigo que él saldría de Brownsville a la caída del sol.
16. ¿Quién estaría con Manuel en el juego?
17. Sería su primo de Nueva York.
18. Él la llevaría al juego tan pronto como ella llegó.
19. El señor López iría al teatro.
20. Ellos verían a los niños llegar.

LESSON XVIII

1. ¿A qué hora se levantó Vd. esta mañana?
2. Me levanté a las seis esta mañana, pero estoy acostumbrado a levantarme más temprano.
3. ¿Cuánto tiempo se quedó John en Juárez antes de entrar en los Estados Unidos?
4. No me acuerdo de la fecha, pero creo que él llegó el (día) cinco del mes pasado.
5. Cuando entré en la casa anoche, me quité el sombrero, me lavé la cara y las manos, y me senté a la mesa para comer.
6. María me dijo que ella no se lavó el pelo porque no tuvo tiempo.
7. ¿Cuántas veces se paró Vd. cuando iba para Las Vegas, y cuánto tiempo se quedó en cada lugar?

8. Enrique se estaba bañando cuando María le telefoneó.
9. Yo estaba tratando de escaparme cuando los oficiales me arrestaron.
10. ¿Cómo se escapó Vd. de la cárcel la última vez que Vd. fué arrestado?
11. Aquí se vende ropa al por mayor.
12. Él se puso el sombrero, se subió al carro, y fué a casa donde fué arrestado por el policía.
13. En este edificio, se les venden cuartos y apartamientos a los pobres.
14. ¿A qué hora se acostó Vd. anoche?
15. A las once, pero eran como las dos y media cuando me dormí.
16. Puse el periódico en la mesa, pero no está allí ahora.
17. Él se sentó y empezó a hablarme acerca de la guerra.
18. La madre del niño lo baña cada mañana a las nueve.
19. Su mamá la levantó muy temprano ayer.
20. Súbase al carro, pero tenga cuidado de no caerse.
21. Los dos hombres se quitaron los zapatos y gatearon por el chaparral hasta que llegaron a la orilla del arroyo.
22. Se venden muchas vacas en este rancho.
23. Ella tiene que vestirse en treinta minutos.
24. ¡Cállese! Estoy cansado de oírlo.

LESSON XIX

1. Él tiene tantos niños como el amigo de Vd., pero los niños de él están en México.
2. La cicatriz de él es más grande que la de ella.
3. Su café es mejor que el mío.
4. Este recibo es más viejo que aquél, pero aquél es mejor.
5. Él piensa venir más tarde que nadie.
6. Las tazas que ellos tienen son más bonitas que las que vendieron.
7. Las muchachas usan faldas más cortas ahora.
8. Teófilo parece menor que su hermano.
9. La tarjeta se expidió más pronto que la fecha prometida.
10. Mi esposa gasta más dinero de lo que yo gano.
11. No pensaba comprarlo, pero lo compré.
12. No lo quiero comprar sino pedirlo prestado.
13. Él no juega fútbol sino béisbol.
14. Tenemos solo cuatro días para trabajar.

15. Ellos tienen más de cinco días para conseguir sus pasaportes.
16. Los niños pueden correr más rápido que Vd. o yo.
17. Ellos acabarán más pronto que aquellos hombres.
18. Los hacendados han sembrado más maíz este año que el año pasado.
19. Ellos me deben más de cincuenta dólares.
20. El señor Jones es el hombre más rico de nuestro pueblo, pero está malo.
21. Él vive en el edificio más alto de la avenida número diez.
22. John no gana más de cinco dólares por día, pero él no gasta tanto como su hermano.
23. Mi hijo menor nació en los Estados Unidos en mil novecientos cincuenta y ocho.
24. El mejor amigo de él es altísimo.
25. ¡Muchísimas gracias!

LESSON XX

Exercise No. 1

1. El cónsul le dijo al señor López que regresara la semana que viene.
2. El señor Guerra le dijo que él no podía conseguir los papeles necesarios.
3. Dígales que se queden en ese lado por unos cuantos días.
4. Los aduaneros nos mandaron que les enseñáramos nuestras maletas.
5. Nos pidieron que las abriéramos y que sacáramos nuestra ropa.
6. ¿Quiere Eloísa que la llevemos al aeropuerto?
7. Le rogamos que se quedara por unas cuantas semanas más.
8. Le prohibo que Vd. le diga a su amigo acerca de nosotros.
9. Queríamos venir a este lado con nuestros padres.
10. Dígale a su madre que le escriba al cónsul por una visa.

LESSON XX

Exercise No. 2

1. ¿Se sorprende que Eliseo todavía esté viviendo aquí?
2. Los parientes de ellos se alegraron de que ellos no fueran arrestados.

3. ¿Por qué se alegra Vd. de que Minerva no haya llegado?
4. La mamá de él espera que él se case pronto.
5. ¿No tiene miedo de continuar sin lavarse las manos?
6. Siento que Vd. haya perdido su equipaje.
7. No podemos negar que nosotros vadeamos el río.
8. Marcos sabe que lo soltarán para mañana.
9. Era necesario que nosotros le mandáramos el sueldo de él.
10. Es lástima que Vd. no vaya con nosotros.
11. ¿Es verdad que Vd. conocía al banquero?
12. Esperaban que fuera importante.

LESSON XX
Exercise No. 3

1. Necesitamos una casa que tenga tres recámaras.
2. Ellos tienen una casa de remolque que es muy pequeña.
3. Ella busca un hombre que sea guapo, inteligente, y rico.
4. El señor Billings quiere una secretaria que pueda hablar español.
5. Él tiene una hermana que se volvió loca hace muchos años.
6. El hacendado anda buscando un hombre que trabaje con él.
7. Los labradores tienen que sembrar el algodón antes de que llueva.
8. Pensamos salir a menos que él nos pague más dinero.
9. Traiga sus documentos aquí tan pronto como los halle.
10. Los tendré listos para que Vd. los venda mañana.
11. Suponiendo que Vd. la traiga, ¿qué dirá ella?
12. Dígale a él que espere en la sala de espera hasta que vengamos.
13. Enrique esperó hasta que salió el correo.
14. Tan pronto como Alfonso se hizo rico, él olvidó a sus viejos amigos.
15. Quiero que Vd. lo tenga listo para cuando ellos vengan.
16. Marta y Gloria estaban aquí para cuando llegaron los paquetes.
17. Él dijo que saldría cuando Vd. le dijera.

LESSON XX
Exercise No. 4

1. Si hubiera bastante trabajo en las labores, ¿trabajaría Vd. allí?
2. Si Manuel tiene suficiente dinero, ¿lo comprará?
3. Vd. no estaría en la cárcel ahora, si Vd. me hubiera escuchado.
4. ¿Se habrían escapado ellos, si Vd. no les hubiera dicho?
5. Si Vd. no tuviera empleo, yo le ayudaría.
6. Yo iría al pueblo si no hiciera tanto calor.
7. ¿Regresaría Vd. a ese país si Vd. tuviera la oportunidad?
8. Si hubiera habido un oficial allí, ¿le habría advertido su novia?
9. Si Vd. hubiera sabido que iba a ser arrestado, ¿habría entrado Vd. en el edificio?
10. Yo me habría quedado en la fiesta si lo hubiera visto a Vd.

USEFUL EXPRESSIONS

a cosa (eso) de las dos—at about
two

¿A cuánto estamos?—what is the
date?

a cuestas—on one's back; piggyback

a fines de—late in, towards the end
of (week, month, year, etc.)

a gatas—crawling

a lado de—beside

a mediados de—about the middle of
(week, month, year, etc.)

a menudo—often

a o(b)scuras—in the dark

a pie—on foot

a principios de—early in, about the
first of (week, month, year, etc.)

a propósito—incidently; by the way

¿a qué hora?—at what time?

a ratos—at times

a toda velocidad—at full speed

a todo correr—at full speed

a últimos del mes—at the end of the
month

a veces—sometimes; at times

a ver—let's see

ahora—now

a la buena (mala)—willingly (by
force; unwillingly)

a la caída de la tarde—at sunset

a la caída del sol—at sunset

a la derecha—to the right

a la izquierda—to the left

a la larga—in the long run

a la madrugada—in the wee hours
of the morning

a lo largo de—along

al amanecer—at dawn (daybreak)

al anochecer—at dusk (nightfall)

al contado—cash

al fiado—on credit

al fin—finally

al fin del año—at the end of the year

al fin y al cabo—in the end

al otro lado—to the (at the) other
side

al principio—at first

al último—at the end (last)

algo que comer—something to eat

alto—stop

ándele—hurry

¡basta!—enough!

caer bien (mal)—to fit well (badly);
to please (displease)

calle arriba (abajo)—up (down) the
street

camino de—on the road to; on the
way to

como a—at about

como de costumbre—as usual

como en—in about

con permiso—excuse me; with your
permission

¡con razón!—no wonder!

contar con—to rely on; to count on

creer que no—to believe (think) not

creer que sí—to believe (think) so

costar mucho trabajo—to be very
difficult; requiring much effort

¡Cuidado!—Be careful!

cueste lo que cueste—regardless of
cost; cost what it may

cumplir (con) su palabra—to keep
one's word

dar a—to face

dar atención—to pay attention

dar con—to chance upon

dar de comer—to feed

dar en—to hit upon

dar fianza por—to post bond for

dar la hora—to strike the hour

dar la mano—to help; to handshake

dar la vuelta—to take or go for
a ride

dar las gracias—to thank

dar un paseo—to take or go for a
ride or walk

dar una vuelta—(same as above)

darse cuenta de (que)—to notice;
to realize

darse por ofendido—to take offense;
to become offended

darse por vencido—to surrender; to
acknowledge defeat; to give up

darse prisa—to hurry

de ahí en adelante—from then on

de aquí en adelante—from now on

de aquel tiempo en adelante—from
that time on

de buena gana—gladly

de este modo—like this; in this
manner

de hoy en adelante—from now on

de mala gana—unwillingly

de moda—in vogue; stylish

de nada—you are welcome

¡De ninguna manera!—I should say
not! Under no circumstances!

de nuevo—again; anew

de oquis (dioquis)—idle; free (coll.)

de pie—standing

de pronto—suddenly

de punto—just right

¿De qué tamaño es?—What size is
it?

de todos modos—at any rate;
anyhow

¿de veras?—really?

de vez en cuando—from time to time

de vuelta—again

decir para sí—to say to oneself

dejar caer—to drop

dejar de (plus infinitive)—to stop
or cease

dentro de poco—within a short while

desde entonces—since then

dicho y hecho—sure enough; no
sooner said than done

Dispénseme.—Excuse me.

echar al correo—to mail

echar a perder—to ruin; to spoil

echar de menos—to miss; to feel the
absence of

en abonos—on installments

en casa—at home

en cuanto a—concerning; as far as

en otras palabras—in other words

en otros términos—in other words

en pleno día —in broad daylight

en punto—on the dot; sharp

¿En qué puedo servirle?—What can
I do for you?

en vez de—instead of

en voz alta—aloud

en voz baja—whisper

es decir—that is to say

¡Eso es!—That's it. That's right.

Está bien (bueno).—All right.;
Okay.

estación de gasolina—gas station

estar airoso—to be windy

estar bien de salud—to be in good
health

estar crudo—to have a hangover

estar de acuerdo—to agree; to be
in accordance

estar de prisa—to be in a hurry

estar de vacaciones—to be on
vacation

estar de vuelta—to be back

estar dispuesto—to be willing

estar listo (__para__ plus infinitive)—to
be ready

estar para (plus infinitive)—to be
about

estar por—to be in favor of

estar seguro—to be sure

expendio de gasolina—gas station

faltar a su palabra—to break one's
word; to break a promise

haber—there to be

haber lodo—to be muddy

haber luna—for the moon to be out

haber polvo—to be dusty

haber de—to be (supposed) to (plus
infinitive)

haber quienes—there to be those
who

haber sol—to be sunny

hacer (plus a period of time)—ago

hacer arreglos—to make arrange-
ments

hacer buen (mal) tiempo—to fare
well; to be good or bad weather

hacer calor—to be hot (weather)

hacer caso de—to mind; to pay
attention, heed

hacer falta—to lack; to be in need of

hacer frío—to he cold (weather)

hacer fresco—to be cool (weather)

hacer (un) juramento—to swear;
to make a statement under oath

hacer luna (sol)—to shine—moon
(sun)

hacer pedazos—to destroy; to tear
to pieces

hacer una pregunta—to ask a
question

hacer una visita—to make a visit

hacer un papel—to play a role

hacer un viaje—to make (take)
a trip

hacer viento(aire)—to be windy

hacerle la primera cura a—to render
first aid to

hacerse—to become

hacerse cargo—to be responsible for;
to take charge

hacerse el sordo—to pretend to be deaf

hacerse noche—to grow late; to get late (in the evening)

hacerse tarde—to get late

haga el favor de—please

hasta la vista—goodbye; so long

hasta luego—goodbye; until we meet again

hoy día—nowadays

ir al centro—to go downtown

ir a medias—to go 50-50

ir de compras—to go shopping

levantar la mesa—to clear the table

lo más pronto posible—as soon as possible

llegar a ser—to become (rich, doctor, etc.)

llevar puesto—to wear; to have on

llevarse bien (mal)—to get along well (badly)

mañana por la mañana—tomorrow morning

¿Mande?—I beg your pardon?; Yes?; What?; What can I do for you?

más acá de—on this side of; before you get to

más allá de—on the other side of; beyond

más que nunca—more than ever

montar a caballo—to ride horseback

no cabe duda—there's no question or doubt about it

no caer bien—to displease

No hay de (por) que.—You are welcome.; Don't mention it.

No le hace.—It doesn't matter.; It doesn't make any difference.

no poder con—not to be able to manage or handle; to be too much for one

no poder más—to be exhausted; to be all in

No vale la pena.—It is not worth while.

otra vez—again

¿Para qué lo usan?—What is it used for?

¿Para qué se usa?—What is it used for?

¿Para qué sirve?—What is it good for?

pasar las vacaciones—to spend one's vacation

¡Pase!—Come in!

pedir prestado—to borrow

perder cuidado—to be at ease; not to worry

perder de vista—to lose sight of

perder el tiempo—to lose time

perder el tren—to miss the train

poco a poco—little by little

poner la mesa—to set the table

poner una queja—to file a complaint

ponerse—to put on; (plus an adjective) to become

ponerse a—to begin; to start

ponerse en pie—to stand up

por aquí—this way

por eso—so; that's why

por favor—please

por fin—finally

por la buena (mala)—willingly (unwillingly)

por las buenas o las malas—by hook or crook

por lo pronto—for the time being

por lo menos—at least

Por nada.—You are welcome.

por si acaso—just in case

por supuesto—of course

por término medio—as an average

por todas partes—everywhere

prestar atención—to pay attention

¿Puedo servirle en algo?—May I help you?

quedar en (plus infinitive)—to agree upon

quedarse con—to keep; to retain

¿Qué día del mes tenemos?—What is the date?

¿Qué ha sido de . . .?—What has become of . . .?

¿Qué hora es?—What time is it?

¿Qué horas son?—What time is it?

¿Qué hubo?—What's up?

¿Qué le parece?—What do you think (of)?

Que le vaya bien.—Good luck.

Que lo pase bien.—Have a good day (night, etc.).

¿Qué pasó?—What happened?

¿Qué tal?—How are you?

Que vaya con Dios.—God be with you.

¿Qué sé yo?—What do I know?;
How should I know?
querer decir—to mean
¿Quién sabe?—Who knows?;
I don't know.
recibir noticias de—to hear from
respecto a—concerning; about
salir bien (mal)—to be successful
(to fail)
salirse con la suya—to have one's
way
se dice—it is said
sea lo que sea—be it what it may
seguro que sí—of course
sentar bien a—to fit well
ser (la) hora de—to be time (to eat,
to go, etc.)
Suelte Vd. la mano.—Relax your
hand.
tan a prisa—so hurriedly (fast)
tan de prisa—so hurriedly (fast)
tardar en—to be long in
tener . . . años—to be . . . years old
tener a la vista—to have in sight
tener calor—to be hot
tener cuidado—to be careful
tener dolor de . . .—to have a . . .
ache
tener en cuenta—to bear in mind
tener éxito—to be successful

tener frío—to be cold
tener ganas de—to feel like
tener gusto en—to be glad to
tener hambre—to be hungry
tener la culpa—to be to blame;
to be guilty
tener la palabra—to have the floor
tener lugar—to take place
tener miedo—to be afraid
tener por—to take for (a fool, etc.)
tener presente—to bear in mind
tener prisa—to be in a hurry
tener puesto—to wear; to have on
tener que (plus infinitive)—to have
tener razón—to be right
tener sed—to be thirsty
tener sueño—to be sleepy
tener vergüenza—to be shy; to be
ashamed
traer puesto—to wear; to have on
trastos de cocina—kitchen utensils
un poco de—a little bit of
valer la pena—to be worth while
¡Vaya!—Come now!; You don't say!
venga lo que venga—come what may
volver a (plus infinitive)—to do
again
volver corriendo—to hurry back
volver en sí—to regain consciousness
volverse loco—to go crazy

PRACTICE MATERIAL

Tengo las manos frías.
Él tiene los pies fríos.
Ella tiene los ojos azules.
¿Qué tiene Vd.?
¿Cuántos años tiene Vd.?
¿Qué edad tiene Vd.?
Habrá mucha gente aquí.
¿Está su papá? Sí, señor, pase Vd.

Mi reloj anda atrasado.
¿Qué tanto tiempo tiene Vd. aquí?
No caben muchos alumnos en este
cuarto.
Me duelen los ojos.
Él se puso a reparar el reloj.
Él no tardó en llegar.
Tengo gusto en conocerle.
Le presento al señor Jones.
Este es el señor Jones.

My hands are cold.
His feet are cold.
Her eyes are blue.
What is the matter with you?
How old are you?
How old are you?
There will be a lot of people here.
Is your papa at home? Yes, sir,
come in.
My watch is slow.
How long have you been here?
This room will not hold many
students.
My eyes hurt.
He set to work repairing the watch.
He was not long in arriving.
I am glad to know you.
This is Mr. Jones.
This is Mr. Jones.

Después supe que él era ciudadano de México	Then I found out that he was a citizen of Mexico.
Allá voy, señor.	I'm coming, sir.
Ya voy.	I'm going right now.
¿Qué tan lejos está?	How far is it?
¿Qué distancia hay de Juárez a El Paso?	How far is it from Juarez to El Paso?
¿Cuántas millas hay de Juárez a El Paso?	How many miles is it from Juarez to El Paso?
No tuve oportunidad de hacerlo.	I didn't have a chance to do it.
¿Qué tanto (cuánto) tiempo se quedó (pasó) Vd. allí?	How long did you stay there?
Él se puso a correr.	He began to run.
El carro se puso en marcha.	The car started.
Ella está bien de salud.	She is in good health.
Él pegó fuego a la casa.	He set the house on fire.
Ella se puso enojada.	She became angry.
Él se hizo rico.	He became rich.
Me puse el sombrero.	I put on my hat.
Póngase Vd. en pie.	Stand up.
Estamos muy atrasados porque mi esposo no tiene trabajo.	We are very much behind (set back) because my husband does not have work.
Pase Vd. por aquí.	Come this way.
Se prohibe estacionarse aquí.	Parking is prohibited here. No parking.
No hable tan aprisa.	Don't speak so fast.
¿En qué se ocupa Vd.?	What is your occupation?
¿Cuál es su nacionalidad?	What is your nationality?
¿De qué nacionalidad es Vd.?	What is your nationality?
¿De qué raza es Vd.?	What is your race?
Le voy a imponer una multa de $10.00.	I am going to fine you $10.00.
Me impusieron una multa de $5.00.	They fined me $5.00.
Le tengo por un buen hombre.	I consider him a good man.
Le vimos cruzar el río.	We saw him cross the river.
Subí a lo alto de la loma de arena.	I climbed to the top of the sand hill.
Yo entré en el automóvil hace poco.	I entered the car not long ago.
Tomamos un poco de agua.	We drank a little water.
Lo vendí en veinte pesos.	I sold it for twenty pesos.
El hombre acaba de entrar.	The man has just entered.
Eso está bien.	That is all right.
Creo que sí, pero él cree que no.	I think so, but he doesn't.
¿Llovió mucho ayer?	Did it rain much yesterday?
¡Ya lo creo!	I should say so!
Ella cumplió diez (años) ayer.	She was ten years old yesterday.
Dieron las tres hace rato.	It struck three (o'clock) a short time ago.
Mi casa da al norte.	My house faces the north.
Dimos un paseo en automóvil.	We took an automobile ride.
Lo hice de buena gana.	I did it gladly.
Su traje es muy de moda.	His suit is very stylish.

Él me dejó entrar.	He let me enter.
Ellos dejaron de venir.	They stopped coming.
Voy a escribirla en seguida.	I am going to write it at once.
Él trabajó todo el día.	He worked all day.
Iremos los dos a visitarla.	We shall both go visit her.
Vd. se equivoca.	You are mistaken.
Apresúrese Vd., se hace tarde.	Hurry, it is getting late.
Me parece que es culpa suya.	I think (it seems to me) that it is your fault.
Por malo que sea, es honesto.	However bad he is, he is honest.
Me quedan dos dólares.	I have two dollars left.
Seguimos escribiendo.	We continued writing.
Es la hora de comer.	It is time to eat.
¿No se siente Vd. bien?	Don't you feel well?
Yo me serví de su carro.	I used your car.
Tengo dolor de cabeza.	I have a headache.
Ahora me toca a mí decir algo.	Now it is my turn to say something.
Quiero decirle algo a Vd.	I want to tell you something.
La boda tuvo lugar ayer.	The marriage (wedding) took place yesterday.
Ella lo dijo en voz baja.	She said it in a whisper.
Él ya no fuma.	He no longer smokes.
No tenemos nada que vender.	We have nothing to sell.
Él salió de aquí muy de mañana.	He left here very early in the morning.

En la Sala de Espera

Acabamos de llegar a la estación. El tren de Chicago ha de llegar a las seis y ahora faltan diez para las seis. El tren no llega hasta las seis y media. Mucha gente baja del tren. Algunos van a quedarse en El Paso, y otros quieren algo que comer o beber antes de la salida del tren a las siete y cuarto. Todo el mundo está muy ocupado. Los porteros meten las maletas en los automóbiles. Un hombre viejo va al teléfono y llama un taxi. El viejo sube al carro y dice—Al Hotel Colón.—El chofer guía (maneja) el carro con cuidado porque no quiere chocar con otro carro. Hay muchos choques en las ciudades grandes.

Nos fijamos en (notamos a) un hombre que está sentado en la sala de espera leyendo un diario. Él está bien vestido. Lleva sombrero azul, traje gris, camisa blanca, corbata listada, y zapatos negros. Le saludamos y empezamos a platicar. Nos dice que es dueño de una mina en Toltec, México, y que ha venido a los Estados Unidos para comprar unos motores, y otra maquinaria. Su permiso es válido por tres semanas. El va a Denver para hacer las compras y entonces piensa regresar a México por el puerto de Nogales. Nos despedimos y hablamos con otros.

El Contrabandista

pasar de contrabando—to smuggle
la caída del sol—sunset
tener prisa—to be in a hurry
a verlo—let's see it

Un hombre nos había dicho que cierto contrabandista iba a pasar de contrabando a dos personas, a un hombre y a una mujer. Un poco después de la caída del sol, fuimos cosa de diez millas afuera de los límites de la ciudad y paramos nuestro carro en una curva. Colocamos un signo de carretera al lado de la carretera y pusimos una luz roja delante del signo.

No sabíamos en que clase de automóvil (coche) vendría el contrabandista, pero teníamos una buena descripción de él; por eso, tuvimos que detener cada carro. Como a las diez llegó un sedán negro. El carro caminó cincuenta pies más allá del signo antes de parar.

Dentro del carro había el chófer y una mujer en el asiento delantero (de enfrente). Dos maletas estaban en el asiento de atrás (trasero). El chófer parecía excitado y nervioso. Nos dijo que no paró el carro más pronto porque los frenos del carro necesitaban reparos. Dijo que tenía prisa porque su esposa—la señora a su lado—estaba enferma. Ella estaba envuelta en una cobija. Pronto reconocimos al contrabandista. El tenía una tarjeta de identificación de ciudadano. La mujer también tenía una tarjeta de ciudadana, pero al examinarla cuidadosamente notamos que el retrato en la tarjeta no era suyo. El contrabandista le había comprado la tarjeta a un muchacho en Juárez, el cual la había hallado en la calle.—¿Dónde está el esposo de esta mujer?—preguntó mi compañero.—¿Quién sabe? Venimos solos.—Vamos a ver el compartimiento de atrás.—No hay nada allí—dijo el hombre.—A verlo entonces.—Él abrió el compartimiento y allí estaba el esposo de la mujer.

—¡Qué mala suerte!—dijo ella.—¡Ojalá que no hubiéramos venido ilegalmente a los Estados Unidos!—

Animales Domésticos y Silvestres

En los ranchos de Texas hay muchos animales. De los animales domésticos, las vacas y los caballos son los más útiles. Los caballos y las mulas se usan para tirar arados, vagones, y para montar. Las vacas dan la leche de la cual se hace mantequilla, crema, queso, y otros alimentos. Comemos la carne del ganado y hacemos cuero de las pieles. Los burros se usan mucho por los mexicanos para llevar cargas de leña, legumbres (verduras), y otras cosas. Se trasquilan las cabras y los borregos dos veces al año. La lana se vende a los almacenes. La carne de estos animalitos es buena para comer. La carne de los marranos (puercos) es muy buena para comer también y de ella se hacen salchichas. Los gatos cogen ratas y ratones. Los perros son los compañeros del hombre.

Hay muchos animales silvestres en el monte. Mucha gente come la carne de los conejos y de las liebres. A muchas personas les gusta cazar venados. Es un deporte muy bueno e interesante. Se cazan venados en los meses de noviembre y diciembre.

Las gallinas ponen blanquillos (huevos) que se usan en muchos platos para la comida. Los pollos son buenos para comer. Nosotros comemos los guajalotes (cóconos) generalmente en el día de dar Gracias y en el día de Navidad. La gente del campo cría los animales y entonces se los vende a los comisionistas de las ciudades. También se cazan guajalotes, patos, palomas, codornices, y otras aves. Es muy deportivo tirar a estas aves volantes.

Las pieles de muchos animalitos tales como el coyote, el zorro, etc., valen mucho dinero y se usan para hacer abrigos, chaquetas, y toda clase de vestidos. Las pieles son mejores en el invierno. Sin los animales y sus productos sería muy difícil vivir.

SPANISH NAMES

Spanish and Spanish-American people usually use the surname of both parents. Neither is ever considered to be a middle name. In the case of an illegitimate child, usually the surname of the mother only is used.

The surname of the father precedes that of the mother, and the two surnames may or may not be joined by the conjunction "y" or by a hyphen. Example: **Juan Romero y Conde, Juan Romero-Conde. Juan** is the given name; **Romero,** the surname of the father, and **Conde,** the surname of the mother.

In addition, the following variations may be found:

Juan Conde Romero	**Juan Romero C.**
Juan C. Romero	**Juan Romero**
Juan Conde	

Legally a Spanish female retains her maiden name after marriage, but it is common practice to drop the surname of the mother and to add that of the husband joined by the preposition **"de."**

For example: **Luisa Romero-Conde** marries **Carlos Villa-Tovar** and is known as **Luisa Romero de Villa.**

Prior to her marriage she was known as:	**Luisa Romero-Conde,**
after marriage as:	**Luisa Romero de Villa,**
and, should her husband die, as:	**Luisa Romero Vda. de Villa.**
	(Vda., viuda—widow)

If the person gives only one surname, it will be necessary to question him further in order to obtain his full and correct name. After a Spanish-speaking person has resided in the United States for some time, he may anglicize his name. It must be remembered that a person's signature is not necessarily his full and correct name. This is particularly true of Spanish-speaking persons whose signatures **(firmas)** are often written with many flourishes **(rúbricas).** Whenever there is any doubt as to the correct spelling of a person's name, he should be asked to write it, as wrong names and incorrect spelling make it difficult and often impossible to verify previous records.

Spanish words are more phonetic than English words. However, due to similarity of the sounds of certain letters, differences in the spelling of proper names will be encountered. Examples of a few of these instances follow:

Letters	*Names*
s-c	Seballos—Ceballos
b-v	Baca—Vaca
c-z	Celaya—Zelaya
s-z	Sambrano—Zambrano
ll-y	Calletano—Cayetano
j-h	Jaro—Haro
i-e	Arriola—Arreola
g-j	Guantes—Juantes
rr-r	Arredondo—Aredondo
h	Any name with "h"
i-y	Ibarra—Ybarra

The prepositions **"de,"** with or without a definite article, **"el,"** etc., appear in a number of Spanish surnames. Formerly the preposition **"de"** was an indication of nobility, but today such a distinction does not exist, and the use of **"de"** is optional. However, it is retained by some families as a part of the surname. Examples: **De Haro, De Lora, Del Campo, Del Valle, De la Torre, De la Rosa, De la O.**

REGULAR VERBS

The Three Conjugations

FIRST CONJUGATION AR

Present participle	*Infinitive*	*Past participle*
habl ando	habl ar	habl ado

Indicative Mood

Present

yo habl o	I speak, am speaking, do speak
tú habl as	you speak, are speaking, do speak
él, ella, Vd. habl a	he, she, you speak, do speak, etc.
nosotros, as habl amos	we speak, are speaking, do speak
vosotros, as habl áis	you speak, are speaking, do speak
ellos, as, Vds. habl an	they (m-f), you speak, etc.

Imperfect

yo habl aba	I used to speak, was speaking
tú habl abas	you used to speak, were speaking
él, ella, Vd. habl aba	he, she, you used to speak, etc.
nosotros, as habl ábamos	we used to speak, were speaking
vosotros, as habl abais	you used to speak, were speaking
ellos, as, Vds. habl aban	they (m-f), you used to speak, etc.

Preterite

yo habl é	I spoke, did speak
tú habl aste	you spoke, did speak
él, ella, Vd. habl ó	he, she, you spoke, etc.
nosotros, as habl amos	we spoke, did speak
vosotros, as habl asteis	you spoke, did speak
ellos, as, Vds. habl aron	they (m-f), you spoke, etc.

Future

yo hablar é	I shall or will speak
tú hablar ás	you shall or will speak
él, ella, Vd. hablar á	he, she, you shall speak, etc.
nosotros, as hablar emos	we shall or will speak
vosotros, as hablar éis	you shall or will speak
ellos, as, Vds. hablar án	they (m-f), you shall speak, etc.

Conditional

yo hablar ía	I would speak
tú hablar ías	you would speak
él, ella, Vd. hablar ía	he, she, you would speak

nosotros, as hablar íamos	we would speak
vosotros, as hablar íais	you would speak
ellos, as, Vds. hablar ían	they (m-f), you would speak

SECOND CONJUGATION *ER*　　　THIRD CONJUGATION *IR*

Infinitive

| comer | recibir |

Present participle

| com iendo | recib iendo |

ast participle

| com ido | recib ido |

INDICATIVE MOOD

Present

com o	recib o
com es	recib es
com e	recib e
com emos	recib imos
com éis	recib ís
com en	recib en

Imperfect

com ía	recib ía
com ías	recib ías
com ía	recib ía
com íamos	recib íamos
com íais	recib íais
com ían	recib ían

Preterite

com í	recib í
com iste	recib iste
com ió	recib ió
com imos	recib imos
com isteis	recib isteis
com ieron	recib ieron

Future

comer é	recibir é
comer ás	recibir ás
comer á	recibir á
comer emos	recibir emos
comer éis	recibir éis
comer án	recibir án

Conditional

comer ía	recibir ía
comer ías	recibir ías
comer ía	recibir ía
comer íamos	recibir íamos
comer íais	recibir íais
comer ían	recibir ían

COMPOUND TENSES OF THE INDICATIVE MOOD

The compound tenses are formed by conjugating the auxiliary verb "haber" in the proper tense preceding the past participle of the main verb.

FIRST CONJUGATION AR

Infinitive

haber habl ado—to have spoken

Participle

habiendo habl ado—having spoken

INDICATIVE MOOD

Present perfect

yo he habl ado	I have spoken
tú has habl ado	you have spoken
él, ella, Vd. ha habl ado	he has, she has, you have spoken
nosotros, as hemos habl ado	we have spoken
vosotros, as habéis habl ado	you have spoken
ellos, as, Vds., han habl ado	they (m-f), you have spoken

Pluperfect (past perfect)[1]

yo había habl ado	I had spoken
tú habías habl ado	you had spoken
él, ella, Vd. había habl ado	he, she, you had spoken

---

[1] The preterite perfect has been omitted throughout this work and is, therefore, omitted in this treatment of verbs. The simple preterite may replace the preterite perfect at any time. Any time a past perfect is needed the pluperfect may be used.

nosotros, as habíamos habl ado   we had spoken
vosotros, as habíais habl ado   you had spoken
ellos, as, Vds., habían habl ado   they (m-f), you had spoken

Future perfect

yo habré habl ado   I shall or will have spoken
tú habrás habl ado   you shall or will have spoken
él, ella, Vd. habrá habl ado   he, she, you shall have spoken

nosotros, as habremos habl ado   we shall or will have spoken
vosotros, as habréis habl ado   you shall or will have spoken
ellos, as, Vds. habrán habl ado   they (m-f), you will have spoken

Conditional perfect

yo habría habl ado   I would have spoken
tú habrías habl ado   you would have spoken
él, ella, Vd. habría habl ado   he, she, you would have, etc.

nosotros, as habríamos habl ado   we would have spoken
vosotros, as habríais habl ado   you would have spoken
ellos, as, Vds. habrían habl ado   they (m-f), you would have, etc.

SECOND CONJUGATION *ER*   **THIRD CONJUGATION *IR***

Infinitive

haber com ido   **haber recib ido**

Participle

habiendo com ido   **habiendo recib ido**

INDICATIVE MOOD

Present perfect

he com ido	he recib ido
has com ido	has recib ido
ha com ido	ha recib ido
hemos com ido	hemos recib ido
habéis com ido	habéis recib ido
han com ido	han recib ido

Pluperfect (past perfect)

había com ido	había recib ido
habías com ido	habías recib ido
había com ido	había recib ido
habíamos com ido	habíamos recib ido
habíais com ido	habíais recib ido
habían com ido	habían recib ido

Future perfect

habré	com	ido		habré	recib	ido
habrás	com	ido		habrás	recib	ido
habrá	com	ido		habrá	recib	ido
habremos	com	ido		habremos	recib	ido
habréis	com	ido		habréis	recib	ido
habrán	com	ido		habrán	recib	ido

Conditional perfect

habría	com	ido		habría	recib	ido
habrías	com	ido		habrías	recib	ido
habría	com	ido		habría	recib	ido
habríamos	com	ido		habríamos	recib	ido
habríais	com	ido		habríais	recib	ido
habrían	com	ido		habrían	recib	ido

SUBJUNCTIVE MOOD

First Conjugation	Second Conjugation	Third Conjugation

Present

Hablar	*Comer*	*Recibir*
habl e	com a	recib a
habl es	com as	recib as
habl e	com a	recib a
habl emos	com amos	recib amos
habl éis	com áis	recib áis
habl en	com an	recib an

Imperfect "ra" form

habl ara	com iera	recib iera
habl aras	com ieras	recib ieras
habl ara	com iera	recib iera
habl áramos	com iéramos	recib iéramos
habl arais	com ierais	recib ierais
habl aran	com ieran	recib ieran

COMPOUND TENSES OF THE SUBJUNCTIVE MOOD

Present perfect

haya hablado	haya comido	haya recibido
hayas hablado	hayas comido	hayas recibido
haya hablado	haya comido	haya recibido
hayamos hablado	hayamos comido	hayamos recibido
hayáis hablado	hayáis comido	hayáis recibido
hayan hablado	hayan comido	hayan recibido

Pluperfect "ra"

hubiera hablado	hubiera comido	hubiera recibido
hubieras hablado	hubieras comido	hubieras recibido
hubiera hablado	hubiera comido	hubiera recibido
hubiéramos hablado	hubiéramos comido	hubiéramos recibido
hubierais hablado	hubierais comido	hubierais recibido
hubieran hablado	hubieran comido	hubieran recibido

IMPERATIVE MOOD[2]

habla tú	come tú	recibe tú
hablad vosotros	comed vosotros	recibid vosotros

SUBJUNCTIVE-IMPERATIVE[2]

hable Vd.	coma Vd.	reciba Vd.
hablen Vds.	coman Vds.	reciban Vds.

ORTHOGRAPHICAL CHANGING VERBS

In Spanish the sound of the final consonant of the stem of the infinitive is generally maintained throughout the conjugation of the verb. In order to do so, it is sometimes necessary to make certain changes in the spelling (orthography) of the stem before attaching the endings. Pronouncing the word will often help the beginner to identify the verb as orthographically changing rather than irregular. The following paragraphs list these changes. The orthographical changes are shown in capital letters in the examples following the rules.

RULES FOR MAKING ORTHOGRAPHICAL CHANGES IN VERBS

1. c of car changes to qu before e.
2. g of gar changes to gu before e.
3. gu of guar changes to gü before e.
4. g of ger and gir changes to j before a or o.
5. gu of guir drops the u before a or o.
6. qu of quir changes to c before a or o.
7. z of zar changes to c before e.
8. cer and cir preceded by a consonant change c to z before a or o.
9. ll and ñ followed by ie or ió drop the i.

---

[2] The imperative mood is used for the familiar command. The third person singular and plural of the subjunctive is used for the polite command. Some grammarians call this use of the subjunctive the "subjunctive-imperative" as so designated above.

10. i unaccented between two vowels changes to y.
11. cer and cir preceded by a vowel insert z before c before a or o.
12. uir unless u is silent, insert y before a, e, or o (strengthens).
13. Some verbs ending in iar and uar require the written accent mark (') over the i or u in the 1st, 2nd, and 3rd person singular, and 3rd person plural of the present indicative and present subjunctive and the singular imperative.

EXAMPLES

1. Buscar

Preterite indicative	Present subjunctive
busQUé	busQUe
buscaste	busQUes
buscó	busQUe
buscamos	busQUemos
buscasteis	busQUéis
buscaron	busQUen

2. Llegar

Preterite indicative	Present subjunctive
lleGUé	lleGUe
llegaste	lleGUes
llegó	lleGUe
llegamos	lleGUemos
llegasteis	lleGUéis
llegaron	lleGUen

3. Averiguar

Preterite indicative	Present subjunctive
averiGÜé	averiGÜe
averiguaste	averiGÜes
averiguó	averiGÜe
averiguamos	averiGÜemos
averiguasteis	averiGÜéis
averiguaron	averiGÜen

4. Coger

Present indicative	Present subjunctive
coJo	coJa
coges	coJas
coge	coJa
cogemos	coJamos
cogéis	coJáis
cogen	coJan

5. Distinguir

Present indicative	Present subjunctive
distinGo	distinGa
distingues	distinGas
distingue	distinGa
distinguimos	distinGamos
distinguís	distinGáis
distinguen	distinGan

6. Delinquir

Present indicative	Present subjunctive
delinCo	delinCa
delinques	delinCas
delinque	delinCa
delinquimos	delinCamos
delinquís	delinCáis
delinquen	delinCan

7. Empezar

Preterite indicative	Present subjunctive
empeCé	empieCe
empezaste	empieCes
empezó	empieCe
empezamos	empeCemos
empezasteis	empeCéis
empezaron	empieCen

8. Vencer

Present indicative	Present subjunctive
venZo	venZa
vences	venZas
vence	venZa
vencemos	venZamos
vencéis	venZáis
vencen	venZan

9. Bullir

Preterite indicative	Present participle
bullí	bull(i)endo
bulliste	
bull(i)ó	
bullimos	
bullisteis	
bull(i)eron	

10. Leer

Preterite indicative	Present participle
leí	leYendo
leíste	
leYó	
leímos	
leísteis	
leYeron	

11. Conocer

Present indicative	Present subjunctive
conoZco	conoZca
conoces	conoZcas
conoce	conoZca
conocemos	conoZcamos
conocen	conoZcan

12. Construir

Present indicative	Present subjunctive	Preterite indicative	Present participle	Imperative
construYo	construYa	construí	construYendo	construYe
construYes	construYas	construiste		
construYe	construYa	construYó		
construimos	construYamos	construimos		
construís	construYáis	construisteis		
construYen	construYan	construYeron		

13. Enviar

Present indicative	Present subjunctive	Imperative
envío	envíe	
envías	envíes	envía
envía	envíe	
enviamos	enviemos	
enviáis	enviéis	
envían	envíen	

IRREGULAR VERBS

Present ind.	Present subj.	Imp. ind.	Pret. ind.	Fut. ind.	Cond. ind.	Imp.
			andar			
caber	caber		caber	caber	caber	
caer	caer					
			conducir			
dar	dar		dar			
decir	decir		decir	decir	decir	decir

Present ind.	Present subj.	Imp. ind.	Pret. ind.	Fut. ind.	Cond. ind.	Imp.
estar	estar		estar			
haber	haber		haber	haber	haber	
hacer	hacer		hacer	hacer	hacer	hacer
ir	ir	ir	ir			ir
oír	oír					
			poder	poder	poder	
poner	poner		poner	poner	poner	poner
			querer	querer	querer	
saber	saber		saber	saber	saber	
salir	salir			salir	salir	salir
ser	ser	ser	ser			
tener	tener		tener	tener	tener	tener
traer	traer		traer			
valer	valer			valer	valer	valer
venir	venir		venir	venir	venir	venir
ver	ver	ver				

There are only twenty-two irregular verbs in common use in the Spanish language. Many of these verbs are irregular in several tenses, but none is irregular in all tenses.

In the present indicative tense eighteen are irregular. "Haber," "ir," and "ser" are completely irregular in this tense. "Estar" bears the written accent in the third person singular and plural. All others are irregular only in the first person singular, and with the exception of "dar" and "saber" the irregularity appears only in the stem of the verb. The endings are regular. "Decir," "tener," and "venir" follow the rule for radical changing verbs in the second and third persons singular and the third person plural.

The same eighteen verbs are also irregular in the present subjunctive tense. All others are regular in this tense. Only "haber," "ir," "saber," and "ser" are completely irregular. "Dar" and "estar" are regular except for the written accent. The remaining twelve verbs are conjugated in this tense by attaching the regular present subjunctive endings to the irregular stem of the first person singular of the present indicative.

In the imperfect indicative tense "ser," "ir" and "ver" are the only verbs that are irregular. "Ver" is irregular only in that it retains the "e" of the infinitive ending before attaching the regular endings.

There are seventeen verbs irregular in the preterite indicative tense. Fourteen of these have the same irregular endings that are attached to an irregular stem. "Ser" and "ir" are conjugated alike in this tense. "Dar" is irregular in that it is conjugated like a regular verb of the second or third conjugation.

There are twelve verbs that are irregular in the future indicative tense. The irregularity appears only in the stem of the verb.

The same twelve verbs are irregular in the conditional tense and to the same extent.

There are only eight verbs that are irregular in the imperative mood (familiar command). They are irregular in the singular. **"Valer"** has two familiar singular forms; **"val,"** irregular and **"vale,"** regular.

The imperfect subjunctive has not been listed as irregular as it may be conjugated by attaching the regular endings to the stem of the third person plural of the preterite indicative; however, the following two rules for orthographically changing verbs must be kept in mind:

(1) An unaccented "i" between two vowels is changed to "y."

Leer—leyera, leyeras, leyera, leyéramos, leyerais, leyeran
Caer—cayera, cayeras, cayera, cayéramos, cayerais, cayeran

(2) Those verbs whose stem ends in "j" drop the "i" of the imperfect subjunctive endings.

Traer—trajera, trajeras, trajera, trajéramos, trajerais, trajeran
Decir—dijera, dijeras, dijera, dijéramos, dijerais, dijeran

A simplified rule to follow in forming the imperfect subjunctive is: Drop the final "on" from the third person plural of the preterite indicative tense and to the remaining stem attach the following endings:

a, as, a, amos, ais, an

The verb **"reír"** (to laugh) is an orthographically changing verb, but because it undergoes so many changes it has been conjugated, but not listed as irregular, with this group of verbs.

The compounds of these verbs are irregular to the same extent as the "parent" verb; that is, **"obtener"** has the same irregularities as **"tener."**

In the following conjugations of the irregular verbs, regular tenses are not conjugated. However, if a verb is orthographically changing, it will be conjugated in such tense or tenses.

Verbs that have irregular past participles are not shown in the table of irregular verbs but are listed in the following conjugations.

Verbs that appear to be irregular in the present participle are either orthographically changing verbs or radically changing verbs of the third classification.

ANDAR

Preterite indicative	anduve, anduviste, anduvo, anduvimos, anduvisteis, anduvieron

CABER

Present indicative	quepo, cabes, cabe, cabemos, cabéis, caben
Present subjunctive	quepa, quepas, quepa, quepamos, quepáis, quepan
Preterite indicative	cupe, cupiste, cupo, cupimos, cupisteis, cupieron
Future indicative	cabré, cabrás, cabrá, cabremos, cabréis, cabrán
Conditional	cabría, cabrías, cabría, cabríamos, cabríais, cabrían

CONDUCIR

Present indicative	conduzco, conduces, conduce, conducimos, conducís, conducen
Present subjunctive	conduzca, conduzcas, conduzca, conduzcamos, conduzcáis, conduzcan
Preterite indicative	conduje, condujiste, condujo, condujimos, condujisteis, condujeron

DAR

Present indicative	doy, das, da, damos, dais, dan
Present subjunctive	dé, des, dé, demos, deis, den
Preterite indicative	dí, diste, dió, dimos, disteis, dieron

DECIR

Present indicative	digo, dices, dice, decimos, decís, dicen
Present subjunctive	diga, digas, diga, digamos, digáis, digan
Preterite indicative	dije, dijiste, dijo, dijimos, dijisteis, dijeron
Future indicative	diré, dirás, dirá, diremos, dirés, dirán
Conditional	diría, dirías, diría, diríamos, diríais, dirían
Imperative	di decid
Present participle	diciendo
Past participle	dicho

ESTAR

Present indicative	estoy, estás, está, estamos, estáis, están
Present subjunctive	esté, estés, esté, estemos, estéis, estén
Preterite indicative	estuve, estuviste, estuvo, estuvimos, estuvisteis, estu-vieron
Imperative	está estad [

HABER

Present indicative	he, has, ha, hemos, habéis, han
Present subjunctive	haya, hayas, haya, hayamos, hayáis, hayan
Preterite indicative	hube, hubiste, hubo, hubimos, hubisteis, hubieron
Future indicative	habré, habrás, habrá, habremos, habréis, habrán
Conditional	habría, habrías, habría, habríamos, habríais, habrían

HACER

Present indicative	hago, haces, hace, hacemos, hacéis, hacen
Present subjunctive	haga, hagas, haga, hagamos, hagáis, hagan
Preterite indicative	hice, hiciste, hizo, hicimos, hicisteis, hicieron
Future indicative	haré, harás, hará, haremos, haréis, harán
Conditional	haría, harías, haría, haríamos, haríais, harían
Imperative	haz haced
Past participle	hecho

IR

Present indicative	voy, vas, va, vamos, vais, van
Present subjunctive	vaya, vayas, vaya, vayamos, vayáis, vayan
Imperfect indicative	iba, ibas, iba, íbamos, ibais, iban
Preterite indicative	fuí, fuiste, fué, fuimos, fuisteis, fueron
Imperative	ve id
Present participle	yendo

OÍR

Present indicative	oigo, oyes, oye, oímos, oís, oyen
Present subjunctive	oiga, oigas, oiga, oigamos, oigáis, oigan
Preterite indicative	oí, oíste, oyó, oímos, oísteis, oyeron
Imperative	oye oíd
Present participle	oyendo
Past participle	oído

PODER

Preterite indicative	pude, pudiste, pudo, pudimos, pudisteis, pudieron
Future indicative	podré, podrás, podrá, podremos, podréis, podrán
Conditional	podría, podrías, podría, podríamos, podríais, podrían
Present participle	pudiendo

PONER

Present indicative	pongo, pones, pone, ponemos, ponéis, ponen
Present subjunctive	ponga, pongas, ponga, pongamos, pongáis, pongan
Preterite indicative	puse, pusiste, puso, pusimos, pusisteis, pusieron
Future indicative	pondré, pondrás, pondrá, pondremos, pondréis, pondrán
Conditional	pondría, pondrías, pondría, pondríamos, pondríais, pon-
Imperative	pon poned [drían
Past participle	puesto

QUERER

Preterite indicative	quise, quisiste, quiso, quisimos, quisisteis, quisieron
Future indicative	querré, querrás, querrá, querremos, querréis, querrán
Conditional	querría, querrías, querría, querríamos, querríais, que-.
	[rrían

REÍR

Present indicative	río, ríes, ríe, reímos, reís, ríen
Present subjunctive	ría, rías, ría, ríamos, ríais, rían
Preterite indicative	reí, reíste, rió, reímos, reísteis, rieron
Imperative	ríe reíd
Present participle	riendo
Past participle	reído

SABER

Present indicative	sé, sabes, sabe, sabemos, sabéis, saben
Present subjunctive	sepa, sepas, sepa, sepamos, sepáis, sepan
Preterite indicative	supe, supiste, supo, supimos, supisteis, supieron
Future indicative	sabré, sabrás, sabrá, sabremos, sabréis, sabrán
Conditional	sabría, sabrías, sabría, sabríamos, sabríais, sabrían

SALIR

Present indicative	salgo, sales, sale, salimos, salís, salen
Present subjunctive	salga, salgas, salga, salgamos, salgáis, salgan
Future indicative	saldré, saldrás, saldrá, saldremos, saldréis, saldrán
Conditional	saldría, saldrías, saldría, saldríamos, saldríais, saldrían
Imperative	sal salid

SER

Present indicative	soy, eres, es, somos, sois, son
Present subjunctive	sea, seas, sea, seamos, seáis, sean
Imperfect indicative	era, eras, era, éramos, erais, eran
Preterite indicative	fuí, fuiste, fué, fuimos, fuisteis, fueron
Imperative	sé sed

TENER

Present indicative	tengo, tienes, tiene, tenemos, tenéis, tienen
Present subjunctive	tenga, tengas, tenga, tengamos, tengáis, tengan
Preterite indicative	tuve, tuviste, tuvo, tuvimos, tuvisteis, tuvieron
Future indicative	tendré, tendrás, tendrá, tendremos, tendréis, tendrán
Conditional	tendría, tendrías, tendría, tendríamos, tendríais, ten-
Imperative	ten tened [drían

TRAER

Present indicative	traigo, traes, trae, traemos, traéis, traen
Present subjunctive	traiga, traigas, traiga, traigamos, traigáis, traigan
Preterite indicative	traje, trajiste, trajo, trajimos, trajisteis, trajeron
Present participle	trayendo
Past participle	traído

VALER

Present indicative	valgo, vales, vale, valemos, valéis, valen
Present subjunctive	valga, valgas, valga, valgamos, valgáis, valgan
Future indicative	valdré, valdrás, valdrá, valdremos, valdréis, valdrán
Conditional	valdría, valdrías, valdría, valdríamos, valdríais, val-
Imperative	val(e) valed [drían

VENIR

Present indicative	vengo, vienes, viene, venimos, venís, vienen
Present subjunctive	venga, vengas, venga, vengamos, vengáis, vengan
Preterite indicative	vine, viniste, vino, vinimos, vinisteis, vinieron
Future indicative	vendré, vendrás, vendrá, vendremos, vendréis, vendrán
Conditional	vendría, vendrías, vendría, vendríamos, vendríais, ven-
Imperative	ven venid [drían
Present participle	viniendo

VER

Present indicative	veo, ves, ve, vemos, veis, ven
Present subjunctive	vea, veas, vea, veamos, veáis, vean
Imperfect indicative	veía, veías, veía, veíamos, veíais, veían
Past participle	visto

RADICAL CHANGING VERBS

CERRAR

Present indicative	cierro, cierras, cierra, cerramos, cerráis, cierran
Present subjunctive	cierre, cierres, cierre, cerremos, cerréis, cierren

DORMIR

Present indicative	duermo, duermes, duerme, dormimos, dormís, duermen
Present subjunctive	duerma, duermas, duerma, durmamos, durmáis, duerman
Preterite	dormí, dormiste, durmió, dormimos, dormisteis, durmieron
Present participle	durmiendo

EMPEZAR

Present indicative	empiezo, empiezas, empieza, empezamos, empezáis, empiezan
Present subjunctive	empiece, empieces, empiece, empecemos, empecéis, empiecen

ENCONTRAR

Present indicative	encuentro, encuentras, encuentra, encontramos, encontráis, encuentran
Present subjunctive	encuentre, encuentres, encuentre, encontremos, encontréis, encuentren

ENTENDER

Present indicative	entiendo, entiendes, entiende, entendemos, entendéis, entienden
Present subjunctive	entienda, entiendas, entienda, entendamos, entendáis, entiendan

MENTIR

Present indicative	miento, mientes, miente, mentimos, mentís, mienten
Present subjunctive	mienta, mientas, mienta, mintamos, mintáis, mientan
Preterite	mentí, mentiste, mintió, mentimos, mentisteis, mintieron
Present participle	mintiendo

MORIR

Present indicative	muero, mueres, muere, morimos, morís, mueren
Present subjunctive	muera, mueras, muera, muramos, muráis, mueran
Preterite	morí, moriste, murió, morimos, moristeis, murieron
Present participle	muriendo

PEDIR

Present indicative	pido, pides, pide, pedimos, pedís, piden
Present subjunctive	pida, pidas, pida, pidamos, pidáis, pidan
Preterite	pedí, pediste, pidió, pedimos, pedisteis, pidieron
Present participle	pidiendo

PENSAR

Present indicative	pienso, piensas, piensa, pensamos, pensáis, piensan
Present subjunctive	piense, pienses, piense, pensemos, penséis, piensen

PERDER

Present indicative	pierdo, pierdes, pierde, perdemos, perdéis, pierden
Present subjunctive	pierda, pierdas, pierda, perdamos, perdáis, pierdan

REPETIR

Present indicative	repito, repites, repite, repetimos, repetís, repiten
Present subjunctive	repita, repitas, repita, repitamos, repitáis, repitan
Preterite	repetí, repetiste, repitió, repetimos, repetisteis, repitieron
Present participle	repitiendo

SEGUIR

Present indicative	sigo, sigues, sigue, seguimos, seguís, siguen
Present subjunctive	siga, sigas, siga, sigamos, sigáis, sigan
Preterite	seguí, seguiste, siguió, seguimos, seguisteis, siguieron
Present participle	siguiendo

SENTIR

Present indicative	siento, sientes, siente, sentimos, sentís, sienten
Present subjunctive	sienta, sientas, sienta, sintamos, sintáis, sientan
Preterite	sentí, sentiste, sintió, sentimos, sentisteis, sintieron
Present participle	sintiendo

ENGLISH-SPANISH VERB LIST

abandon—abandonar
accept—aceptar
accompany—acompañar
accuse—acusar
adjust—ajustar
admit—admitir
advise—avisar, aconsejar
affirm—alegar, afirmar
agree to—convenir en
aim—apuntar
allege—alegar
allow—dejar, permitir

answer—contestar, responder
appeal—apelar
appear—aparecer (se), parecer; (at a location or before a court)— presentarse
apply—aplicar, solicitar
appreciate—apreciar
apprehend—aprehender
approach—acercarse a
approve—aprobar (ue)
arrange—arreglar
arrest—arrestar

arrive—llegar a
ask (information)—preguntar
ask for—pedir (i)
ask questions—hacer preguntas
assault—asaltar, atacar
attack—atacar, asaltar
attend—asistir
authorize—autorizar

baptize—bautizar
bathe—bañar (se)
be—ser, estar
be able—poder (ue)
bear—aguantar (se)
beat up—golpear
be born—nacer
become—hacerse, ponerse, volverse
beg—rogar (ue)
begin—comenzar a (ie), empezar a (ie)
be guilty—ser culpable
be in charge—estar encargado de
believe—creer
be located—estar ubicado
belong—pertenecer
be situated—estar situado
be surprised—sorprenderse
bet—apostar (ue)
be worth—valer
bid farewell—despedirse (i)
bite—morder (ue)
blame—culpar
bless—bendecir
blink—parpadear
board—abordar
bore—cansar, aburrir
borrow—pedir (i) prestado
bother—molestar
break and enter—entrar por escalo
breakfast—almorzar (ue), desayunarse
bring—traer
build—construir
bundle—envolver (se)(ue)
burn—quemar
bury—enterrar (ie), sepultar
buy—comprar

call—llamar (se)
care—cuidar, importar
carry—llevar, cargar
castigate—castigar

catch—agarrar, coger
catch up—alcanzar
certify—afirmar, certificar
change—cambiar (se), mudarse
charge—cobrar
chat—charlar, platicar
check—revisar
choose—escoger
chop (cotton)—desahijar; limpiar
clean—limpiar (se)
climb—subir (se) a
close—cerrar (ie)
collide—chocar
comb—peinar (se)
come—venir
commit—cometer
complain—quejarse
complete—completar, cumplir
comply—cumplir con '
conduct—conducir
confess—confesar (ie)
confide—confiar
congeal—helar (ie)
conquer—conquistar, vencer
construct—construir
contact—comunicarse con
contain—caber, contener (ie)
continue—continuar, seguir (i)
contract—contratar
convict—condenar
convince—convencer
cook—cocinar, cocer (ue)
cost—costar (ue)
count—contar (ue)
cover—cubrir
crawl—arrastrarse, gatear
creep—arrastrarse
cross—cruzar, pasar
cry—llorar
curse—maldecir
cut—cortar

dance—bailar
dawn—amanecer
deceive—engañar
decide—decidir
defend—defender (ie), proteger
demonstrate—demostrar (ue)
deny—negar (ie)
depend—depender
deport—deportar
desire—desear, querer

detain—detener (se)
die—morir (se)(ue)
direct—dirigir (se)
discharge—despedir (i)
discover—descubrir
disembark—desembarcar (se)
dismiss—despedir (i)
dispatch—expedir (i)
dispense—dispensar
divorce—divorciar (se)
do—hacer
do again—volver (ue) a hacer
drag—arrastrar (se)
dream—soñar (ue)
dress—vestir (se)(i)
drink—tomar, beber
drive—manejar
drop—dejar caer
drown—ahogar (se)

earn—ganar
eat—comer
eat breakfast—desayunarse, almorzar (ue)
eat supper—cenar
eject—echar, expulsar
employ—emplear, contratar
endure—aguantar (se)
enjoy—gozar
enlist—enlistar (se), alistar (se) enganchar (se)
enter—entrar en, (a)
erase—borrar
err—errar
escape—escaparse
escort—llevar
examine—examinar, revisar
excuse—dispensar
expect—esperar
expel—echar, expulsar
explain—explicar
extinguish—apagar

fail—salir mal, fracasar
fall asleep—dormirse (ue)
fall—caer (se)
fall due—vencer
fear—temer
feel—sentir (se)(ie)
fight—pelear
file—archivar
file a complaint—poner una queja

fill—llenar
find—hallar, encontrar (ue)
find out—saber, averiguar
fine—multar
finish—terminar, acabar
fire—disparar
fish—pescar
fit—caber
fix—arreglar, componer, reparar
flee—huir, fugar
fly—volar (ue)
follow—seguir (i)
fool—engañar
force—forzar (ue)
forget—olvidar (se)
free—libertar
freeze—helar (ie)
frighten—asustar

gather—recoger, juntar
get—obtener, conseguir (i)
get angry—enojarse, enfadarse
get drunk—emborracharse
get in—meter (se)
get in (a vehicle)—subir (se) a
get lost—perderse (ie)
get married—casarse con
get ready—alistarse
get off—bajar (se) de
get out—salirse de
get out (of a vehicle)—apearse, bajarse
get out of the way—quitar (se)
get tired—cansarse
get together—juntarse
get up—levantarse
get wet—mojarse
give—dar
give up—rendirse (i), darse por vencido, ceder

glue—pegar
go—ir a
go ashore—desembarcar (se)
go away—irse
go thru—atravesar (ie)
grab—agarrar, coger
grant—ceder, conceder
grow—crecer
grow dark—anochecer, o(b)scurecer
guard—guardar
guide—guiar

hand over—entregar (ie)
hang—colgar (ue)
harvest—cosechar
hasten—apurarse
haul—cargar
have—haber (auxiliary)
have—tener (possession)
have just—acabar de
hear—oír
heed—hacer caso
help—ayudar
hide—esconder (se)
hire—ocupar, emplear, contratar
hit—pegar, golpear
hold—detener (se), guardar
hook—enganchar
hope—esperar
hunt—cazar
hurry up—apurarse, apresurarse
hurt—doler (ue), lastimar (se)

identify—identificar
impede—impedir (i)
import—importar
incarcerate—encarcelar
indict—enjuiciar
inform—informar, avisar
initial—firmar con iniciales
inquire—averiguar
iron—planchar
irrigate—regar (ie)
inspect—inspeccionar
investigate—investigar
invite—invitar
issue—expedir
join—reunir, unir, enlistarse, juntarse
jump—brincar, saltar

keep—guardar
kill—matar
knock—sonar (ue), tocar
know—conocer (familiarize, to become acquainted); saber (knowledge)

land (airplane)—aterrizar
lack—faltar
last—durar
laugh—reír (se)
lead—conducir
leap—saltar, brincar

learn—aprender
leave—salir de
leave (behind)—dejar
lend—prestar
let—dejar, permitir
liberate—libertar
lie—mentir (ie)
lie down—acostarse (ue)
lift—levantar, alzar
like—gustar
limp—cojear
listen—escuchar
live—vivir
locate—localizar
look at—mirar
look for—buscar
look like—parecerse
loosen—aflojar
lose—perder (ie)

mail—echar al correo, enviar
make—hacer
mark—marcar
matter—importar
mean—querer decir
measure—medir (i)
meet—encontrar (ue)
milk—(cow) ordeñar
miss—errar, faltar
mistreat—maltratar
molest—molestar
move—mover (se)(ue), cambiar (se), quitar (se), mudarse
name—nombrar
need—necesitar

obey—obedecer
obtain—obtener, conseguir (i)
occupy—ocupar
occur—ocurrir
offer—ofrecer
open—abrir
oppose—oponer (se)
order—mandar, ordenar
ought—deber
overtake—alcanzar
owe—deber

park—estacionar (se)
pass—pasar, cruzar
pay—pagar
permit—permitir, dejar

pick (harvest)—**pizcar**
pick out—**escoger**
pick up—**levantar, recoger**
place—**poner, colocar**
plant—**plantar**
play—**jugar (ue), tocar** (instrument)
plead guilty—**darse culpable**
please—**gustar**
plow—**arar**
point—**apuntar**
pray—**orar, rogar (ue)**
prepare—**preparar (se)**
present—**presentar**
press—**planchar, apretar (ie)**
prevent—**prevenir, impedir (i)**
promise—**prometer**
prosecute—**enjuiciar**
protect—**proteger**
prove—**probar (ue)**
provide—**proveer**
prune—**podar**
pull—**estirar, tirar**
punish—**castigar**
push—**empujar**
put—**poner**
put in—**meter**
put on—**ponerse**

quiet down—**callar (se)**

rain—**llover (ue)**
raise—**alzar, criar**
rap—**sonar (ue)**
reach—**alcanzar**
read—**leer**
reap—**cosechar**
rear—**criar**
receive—**recibir**
recognize—**reconocer**
refuse—**negar (ie)**
register—**registrar (se), matricular (se)**
rejoice—**gozar**
release—**soltar (ue)**
remain—**quedarse**
remember—**acordarse de (ue), recordar (ue)**
remove—**quitar (se)**
renew—**renovar**
rent—**rentar, alquilar**
repair—**componer, reparar**

repeat—**repetir (i)**
report—**reportar**
require—**requerir**
reside—**residir, radicar**
respect—**respetar**
rest—**descansar**
retain—**retener**
return—**regresar, volver (ue), devolver (ue) (articles)**
reveal—**revelar**
ring—**sonar (ue)**
rob—**robar**
run—**correr**

satisfy—**satisfacer**
save—**ahorrar** (money), **salvar**
say—**decir**
search—**esculcar, registrar**
secure—**conseguir (i), obtener**
see—**ver**
seek—**buscar**
seem—**parecer (se)**
select—**escoger**
sell—**vender**
send—**mandar, enviar**
sentence—**sentenciar, condenar**
separate—**separar**
serve—**servir (i)**
sew—**coser**
shave—**afeitar (se)**
shear—**trasquilar**
shoot—**tirar, disparar**
show—**enseñar, demostrar (ue), mostrar (ue)**
show gratitude—**agradecer**
shut up—**callar (se)**
sign—**firmar**
signify—**significar**
sit down—**sentarse (ie)**
sleep—**dormir (ue)**
smell—**oler (ue)**
smile—**sonreír (se)**
smoke—**fumar**
solicit—**solicitar**
sow—**sembrar (ie)**
speak—**hablar**
spell—**deletrear**
spend—**gastar** (money), **pasar** (time)
squat—**agacharse**
stand up—**pararse**

start—empezar a (ie), comenzar a (ie)
stay—quedarse
steal—robar
stoop—agacharse
stop—parar (se)
study—estudiar
stuff—llenar
stumble—tropezar (ie)
support—mantener, sostener
surprise—sorprender
surrender—rendirse
swear—(oath) jurar, hacer juramento
swim—nadar

take—llevar, tomar
take advantage of—aprovechar (se)
take a ride—pasear (se)
take a walk—pasear (se)
take away—quitar (se)
take care of—cuidar
take charge of—encargarse de
take notice—fijarse en
take off—quitar (se)
take out—sacar
talk—hablar, platicar, charlar
taste—probar (ue)
teach—enseñar
tear—romper
telephone—telefonear
tell—decir, contar (ue)
terminate—terminar, acabar
test—examinar, probar (ue)
testify—testificar, atestar
there to be—haber
thin (cotton)—desahijar
think—pensar (ie), creer
threaten—amenazar, hacer amenazas
throw—aventar, tirar

tie—amarrar, atar
tighten—apretar (ie)
tire—cansar (se)
top (beets)—descoronar
toss—echar
touch—tocar
transport—transportar, trasladar
travel—viajar, caminar
treat—tratar
trust—confiar
try—tratar
try—tratar de
turn loose—soltar (ue)
turn off—apagar

understand—entender (ie), comprender
unite—unir, reunir
use—usar

violate—violar
vote—votar
visit—visitar

wade—vadear, andar a pie por el agua
wait for—esperar
wake up—despertar (ie)
walk—andar, caminar
want—querer
warn—avisar, advertir
wash—lavar (se)
water—regar (ie)
weigh—pesar
whistle—chiflar, silbar
win—ganar
wish—desear, querer
withhold—retcner
work—trabajar
wrap—envolver (se)(ue)
write—escribir

SPANISH-ENGLISH VERB LIST

abandonar—to abandon
abordar—to board
abrir—to open
aburrir—to bore
acabar—to finish, terminate
acabar de—to have just
aceptar—to accept
acercarse a—to approach

acompañar—to accompany
aconsejar—to advise
acordarse de (ue)—to remember
acostarse (ue)—to lie down
acusar—to accuse
admitir—to admit
advertir (ie)—to warn
afeitar (se)—to shave

afirmar—to certify, affirm
aflojar—to loosen
agacharse—to stoop, squat
agarrar—to catch, grab
agradecer—to show gratitude
aguantar (se)—to bear, endure
ahogar (se)—to drown
ahorrar—to save (money)
ajustar—to adjust
alcanzar—to reach, overtake, catch up
alegar—to allege, affirm
alistar (se)—to get ready, enlist
almorzar (ue)—to breakfast
alquilar—to rent
alzar—to raise, lift
amanecer—to dawn
amarrar—to tie
amenazar—to threaten
andar—to walk
anochecer—to grow dark
apagar—to turn off, extinguish
aparecer (se)—to appear
apearse—to get out (of a vehicle)
apelar—to appeal
aplicar—to apply
apostar (ue)—to bet
apreciar—to appreciate
aprehender—to apprehend
aprender—to learn
apresurarse—to hurry up
apretar (ie)—to tighten, press
aprobar (ue)—to approve
aprovechar (se)—to take advantage of
apuntar—to aim, point
apurarse—to hurry up, hasten
archivar—to file
arrastrar—to drag
arrastrarse—to crawl, creep
arreglar—to fix, arrange
arrestar—to arrest
asaltar—to assault, attack
asistir—to attend
asustar—to frighten
atacar—to attack, assault
atar—to tie
atestar—to testify
atravesar (ie)—to go thru
autorizar—to authorize
aventar (ie)—to throw
averiguar—to find out, inquire

avisar—to advise, inform, warn
ayudar—to help

bailar—to dance
bajar (se) de—to get off or out
bañar (se)—to bathe
bautizar—to baptize
beber—to drink
bendecir—to bless
borrar—to erase
brincar—to jump, leap
buscar—to look for, seek

caber—to fit, contain
caer (se)—to fall
callar (se)—to quiet down, shut up
cambiar (se)—to change, move
caminar—to walk, travel
cansar—to bore, tire
cansarse—to get tired
cargar—to carry, haul, load
casarse con—to get married
castigar—to punish, castigate
cazar—to hunt
ceder—to give up, grant
cenar—to eat supper
cerrar (ie)—to close
certificar—to certify
charlar—to chat, talk
chiflar—to whistle
chocar—to collide
cobrar—to charge, collect
cocer (ue)—to cook
cocinar—to cook
coger—to catch, grab
cojear—to limp
colgar (ue)—to hang
colocar—to place
comenzar a (ie)—to begin
comer—to eat
cometer—to commit
completar—to complete
componer—to repair, fix
comprar—to buy
comprender—to understand
comunicarse con—to contact
conceder—to grant
condenar—to sentence, convict
conducir—to lead, conduct
confesar (ie)—to confess
confiar—to confide in, trust
conocer—to know (familiarize)

conquistar—to conquer
conseguir (i)—to obtain, secure, get
construir—to build, construct
contar (ue)—to count, tell
contener—to contain
contestar—to answer
continuar—to continue
contratar—to contract, hire, employ
convencer—to convince
convenir en—to agree to
correr—to run
cortar—to cut
cosechar—to harvest, reap
coser—to sew
costar (ue)—to cost
crecer—to grow
creer—to believe, think
criar—to raise, rear
cruzar—to cross, pass
cubrir—to cover
cuidar—to take care of, care for
culpar—to blame
cumplir—to complete
cumplir con—to comply

dar—to give
·darse culpable—to plead guilty
darse por vencido—to give up
deber—to owe, ought
decidir—to decide
decir—to tell, say
defender (ie)—to defend
dejar—to let, allow, permit, leave (behind)
dejar caer—to drop
deletrear—to spell
demostrar (ue)—to demonstrate, show
depender—to depend
deportar—to deport
desahijar—to thin (cotton)
desayunarse—to breakfast
descansar—to rest
descoronar—to top (beets)
descubrir—to discover
desear—to wish, desire
desembarcar (se)—to disembark, go ashore
despedir (i)—to dismiss, discharge
despedirse (i)—to bid farewell
despertar (ie)—to wake up
detener (se)—to detain, hold

devolver (ue)—to return (articles)
dirigir (se)—to direct
disparar—to shoot, fire
dispensar—to excuse, dispense
divorciar (se)—to divorce
doler (ue)—to hurt
dormir (ue)—to sleep
dormirse—to fall asleep
durar—to last

echar—to eject, expel, toss
echar al correo—to mail
emborracharse—to get drunk
empezar a (ie)—to begin, start
emplear—to hire, employ
empujar—to push
encarcelar—to incarcerate
encargarse de—to take charge of
encontrar (ue)—to meet, find
enfadarse—to get angry
enganchar—to hook
enganchar (se)—to enlist
engañar—to deceive, fool
enjuiciar—to indict, prosecute
enlistar (se)—to join, enlist
enojarse—to get angry
enseñar—to teach, show
entender (ie)—to understand
enterrar (ie)—to bury
entrar en, (a)—to enter
entrar por escalo—to break and enter
entregar (ie)—to hand over
enviar—to mail, send
envolver (se)(ue)—to wrap, bundle
errar—to err, miss
escaparse—to escape
escoger—to choose, select, pick out
esconder (se)—to hide
escribir—to write
escuchar—to listen
esculcar—to search (person)
esperar—to wait for, expect, hope
estacionar (se)—to park
estar—to be
estar encargado de—to be in charge
estar situado—to be situated
estar ubicado—to be located
estirar—to pull
estudiar—to study
examinar—to examine, test
expedir (i)—to issue, dispatch

explicar—to explain
expulsar—to expel, eject

faltar—to lack, miss
fijarse en—to take notice
firmar—to sign
firmar con iniciales—to initial
forzar (ue)—to force
fracasar—to fail
fugar—to flee
fumar—to smoke

ganar—to earn, win
gastar—to spend (money)
gatear—to crawl
golpear—to beat up, hit
gozar—to enjoy, rejoice
guardar—to guard, keep, hold
guiar—to guide
gustar—to like, please

haber—to have (auxiliary)
hablar—to talk, speak
hacer—to do, make
hacer amenazas—to threaten
hacer caso—to heed, pay attention
hacer preguntas—to ask questions
hacerse—to become
hallar—to find
helar (ie)—to freeze, congeal
huir—to flee

identificar—to identify
informar—to inform
impedir (i)—to prevent, impede
importar—to import, care, matter
inspeccionar—to inspect
investigar—to investigate
invitar—to invite
ir a—to go
irse—to go away

jugar (ue)—to play
juntar—to gather
juntarse—to get together, to join
jurar—to swear (oath)

lastimar (se)—to hurt
lavar (se)—to wash
leer—to read
levantar—to pick up, lift
levantarse—to get up

libertar—to free, liberate
limpiar (se)—to clean
localizar—to locate
llamar (se)—to call, to be named
llegar a—to arrive
llenar—to fill, stuff
llevar—to take, carry, escort, wear
llorar—to cry
llover (ue)—to rain

maldecir—to curse
maltratar—to mistreat
mandar—to send, order
manejar—to drive
mantener—to support
marcar—to mark
matar—to kill
matricular (se)—to register
medir (i)—to measure
mentir (ie)—to lie
meter—to put in
meter (se)—to get in
mirar—to look at
mojarse—to get wet
molestar—to molest, bother
morder (ue)—to bite
morir (se)(ue)—to die
mostrar (ue)—to show
mover (se) (ue)—to move
mudarse—to change, move
multar—to fine

nacer—to be born
nadar—to swim
necesitar—to need
negar (ie)—to deny, refuse
nombrar—to name

obedecer—to obey
obtener—to obtain, get, secure
o(b)scurecer—to grow dark
ocupar—to occupy, hire
ocurrir—to occur
ofrecer—to offer
oír—to hear
oler (ue)—to smell
olvidar (se)—to forget
oponer (se)—to oppose
orar—to pray
ordenar—to order

pagar—to pay

parar (se)—to stop
pararse—to stand up, stop
parecer (se)—to seem, appear
parpadear—to blink
pasar—to pass, cross, spend (time)
pasear (se)—to take a walk, ride
pedir (i)—to ask for
pedir (i) prestado—to borrow
pegar—to hit, glue
peinar (se)—to comb
pelear—to fight
pensar (ie)—to think
perder (ie)—to lose
perderse (ie)—to get lost
permitir—to permit, let, allow
pertenecer—to belong
pesar—to weigh
pescar—to fish, catch
pizcar—to pick (harvest)
planchar—to iron, press
plantar—to plant
platicar—to talk, chat
podar—to prune
poder (ue)—to be able
poner—to put, place
ponerse—to put on, become
poner una queja—to file a complaint
preguntar—to ask (information)
preparar (se)—to prepare
presentar—to present, introduce
presentarse—to appear (at a location or before a court)
prestar—to lend
prevenir—to prevent
probar (ue)—to prove, taste, test
prometer—to promise
proteger—to protect, defend
proveer—to provide

quebrar—to break
quedarse—to stay, remain
quejarse (de)—to complain (about), (of)
quemar—to burn
querer—to want, wish, desire
querer decir—to mean
quitar (se)—to remove, take off, take away, get out of the way

radicar—to reside
recibir—to receive

reconocer—to recognize
recoger—to gather, pick up
recordar (ue)—to remember
regar (ie)—to irrigate, water
registrar (se)—to register, search
regresar—to return
reír (se)—to laugh
rendir (se)(i)—to surrender, give up
renovar (ue)—to renew
rentar—to rent
reparar—to repair, fix
repetir (i)—to repeat
requerir—to require
residir—to reside
responder—to answer, respond
reportar—to report
respetar—to respect
retener—to retain, withhold
reunir—to unite, join
revelar—to reveal
revisar—to examine, check
robar—to rob, steal
rogar (ue)—to beg, pray
romper—to tear
saber—to know (knowledge), find out
sacar—to take out
salir de—to leave
salirse de—to get out
salir mal—to fail
saltar—to leap, jump
salvar—to save
satisfacer—to satisfy
seguir (i)—to follow, continue
sembrar (ie)—to sow
sentarse (ie)—to sit down
sentenciar—to sentence
sentir (se)(ie)—to feel
separar—to separate
sepultar—to bury
ser—to be
ser culpable—to be guilty
servir (i)—to serve
significar—to signify
silbar—to whistle
solicitar—to apply, solicit
soltar (ue)—to turn loose, release
sonar (ue)—to knock, rap, ring
sonreír (se)—to smile
soñar (ue)—to dream

sorprender—to surprise
sorprenderse—to be surprised
sostener—to support
subir (se) a—to climb, get in (on)
telefonear—to telephone
temer—to fear
tener—to have (possession)
terminar—to terminate, finish
testificar—to testify
tirar—to throw, shoot, pull
tocar—to play (instrument), knock, touch
tomar—to take, drink
trabajar—to work
traer—to bring
transportar—to transport
trasladar—to transport
trasquilar—to shear
tratar—to try, treat
tratar de—to try, attempt

tropezar (ie)—to stumble, meet by accident
unir—to unite, join
usar—to use
vadear—to wade
valer—to be worth
vencer—to conquer, fall due
vender—to sell
venir—to come
ver—to see
vestir (se)(i)—to dress
viajar—to travel
violar—to violate
visitar—to visit
vivir—to live
volar (ue)—to fly
volver (ue)—to return
volver a (ue) hacer—to do again
volverse (ue)—to become
votar—to vote

ENGLISH-SPANISH VOCABULARY

a—un, una
abode—domicilio, m; residencia, f
about—acerca de, tocante a, de, como
above—arriba
absence—ausencia, f
absent—ausente
accent—acento, m
accord—acuerdo, m
according to—según
ache—dolor, m
acquaintance—conocido, -a
acre—acre, m
addict—adicto, -a
address—dirección, f
admission—admisión, f
advice—aviso, m; consejo, m
a few—unos, unos cuantos, unos pocos
affair—asunto, m; negocio, m
affidavit—declaración, f
afoot—a pie
after—después (de), después (de) que, detrás (de)
afternoon—tarde, f
afterwards—después
again—otra vez, de nuevo
against—en contra de, contra

age—edad, f
agent—agente, m
ago—hace
a great deal of—mucho, -a
agreement—acuerdo, m; pacto, m
ahead—adelante, delante
air—aire, m
airplane—avión, m
airport—aeropuerto, m
alien—extranjero, -a
all—todo
alley—callejón, m
all right—está bien, bueno
almost—ya mero, casi
alone—solo, -a
along—a lo largo de
a lot of—mucho, -a
already—ya
also—también
although—aunque
always—siempre
America—América, f
American—americano, -a
ammunition—munición(es), f; parque, m
among—entre
an—un una
and—y

angry—enojado, -a
animal—animal, m
announcement—anuncio, m
another—otro, -a
answer—contestación, f; respuesta, f
any—algún(o), -a; cualquier(a)
anybody—alguien, cualquiera, nadie
anyhow—de cualquier modo, de todos modos
anyone—nadie, alguien, cualquier(a)
any place—cualquier lugar, algún lugar, ningún lugar
anything—algo, nada
anyway—de cualquier modo, de todos modos
anywhere—cualquier lugar, algún lugar, ningún lugar
apartment—apartamiento, m
apple—manzana, f
application—aplicación, f; solicitud, f
appointment—cita, f; compromiso, m
April—abril
archive—archivo, m
are there?—¿hay?
argument—disgusto, m
arm—brazo, m
army—ejército, m
around—alrededor
arrangement—arreglo, m
arrival—llegada, f
artist—artista, m-f
as—como, de, tan
as far as—en cuanto, hasta
as many—tantos, -as
as much—tanto, -a
assistant—ayudante, m
as soon as—luego que, tan pronto como
as soon as possible—lo más pronto posible
at—en, a
at dawn—al amanecer, a la madrugada
at dusk—al anochecer
at first—al principio
at home—en casa
at last—al fin
at least—a lo menos, por lo menos, al menos

at once—en seguida, al instante
at present—actualmente
at sun down—a la caída del sol, a la caída de la tarde
at the beginning—al principio
at the end of—al fin de
at times—a veces
August—agosto
aunt—tía, f
authority—autoridad, f
automobile—automóvil, m; carro, m; coche, m
autumn—otoño, m
avenue—avenida, f
axe—hacha, f (el)
Aztec—azteca

B

baby—niño, -a; bebé; nene, m; nena, f; infante, m
bachelor—soltero, m
back—detrás (de), atrás (de), espalda, f
back door—puerta de atrás, f; puerta trasera, f
back seat—asiento de atrás, m; asiento trasero, m
bacon—tocino, m
bad—mal(o), -a
badge—placa, f
badly—mal
bag—bolsa, f
baggage—equipaje, m
baggage check—contraseña, f
bail—fianza, f
baker—panadero, m
bakery—panadería, f
bald—pelón, -a (slang); calvo, -a
banana—banana, f; plátano, m
bandit—bandido, m
bank—banco, m; orilla, f
banker—banquero, m
banner—bandera, f
banquet—banquete, m
baptismal certificate—fe de bautismo, f
baptismal name—nombre de pila, m
bar—cantina, f
barbecue—barbacoa, f
barber—peluquero, m; barbero, m

barber shop—peluquería, f; barbería, f

barely—apenas

barge—barco, m; lancha, f

barmaid—cantinera, f

barrack—barraca, f

barrel—barril, m

bartender—cantinero, m

base—base, f

bastard—bastardo, -a

bath—baño, m

bathroom—cuarto de baño, m

battery—batería f; pila, f; acumulador, m

beach—playa, f

bean—frijol, m

bear—oso, -a

beard—barba, f

beautiful—bello, -a; hermoso, -a

because—porque

because of—a causa de; por

bed—cama, f

bedroll—mochila, f

bedroom—recámara, f

beef—res, f

beefsteak—bistec, m

beer—cerveza, f

beet—betabel, m

before (front of)—delante de

before (time)—antes de

beggar—mendigo, m

behind—detrás (de), atrás (de)

bell—campana, f

belly—panza, f

below—debajo (de), abajo (de)

belt—cinto, m; cinturón, m; faja, f

belt maker—talabartero, m

bench—banco, m; banca, f

beneath—debajo (de)

beside—al lado (de); cerca (de)

besides—además (de)

best—mejor

better—mejor

between—entre

B-girl—fichera, f (slang)

big—grande

bigamist—bígamo, m

bigamy—bigamia

big belly—panzón, -a

bill—billete, m; cuenta, f

billiard room—billar, m

billfold—billetera, f; cartera, f

binoculars—gemelos, m; lentes de larga distancia, m

biology—biología, f

bird—pájaro, m; ave, f (el)

birth—nacimiento, m

birth certificate—certificado de nacimiento, m; acta de nacimiento, f (el)

birthday—cumpleaños, m

birthmark—estigma, f; marca de nacimiento, f

biscuit—bollo, m; bizcocho, m

black—negro, -a

blackboard—pizarra, f; pizarrón, m

blacksmith—herrero, m; forjador, m

blame—culpa, f; falta, f

blanket—cobija, f; frazada, f

blind—ciego, -a

block (city)—cuadra, f; manzana, f

blond—rubio, -a; huero, -a

blood—sangre, f

blouse—blusa, f

blue—azul

boat—bote, m; barco, m; lancha, f

body—cuerpo, m

bond—fianza, f

bone—hueso, m

bookkeeper—tenedor de libros, m

boot—bota, f

border—frontera, f; orilla, f

Border Patrol—Patrulla de la Frontera, f; migra, f (slang)

boss—patrón, m; jefe, m

both—ambos, -as; los (las) dos

bottle—botella, f

bottom—fondo, m

bow-legged—patizambo, -a

box—caja, f; cajón, m

boxcar—furgón, m

boy—muchacho, m; chamaco, m (slang), chavalo, m (slang), niño

bracelet—pulsera, f; brazalete, m

brake—freno, m

branch—ramo, m; rama, f

brave—valiente, bravo, -a

brawl—barullo, m; disputa, f

bread—pan, m

breakfast—desayuno, m; almuerzo, m

breast—pecho, m

brewery—cervecería, f
brick—ladrillo, m
brickmason (layer)—albañil, m
bridge—puente, m
bridle—freno, m
broad—ancho, -a
broken—roto, -a; quebrado, -a
brood—cría, f
broom—escoba, f
broomcorn—millo de escoba, m
brother—hermano, m
brother-in-law—cuñado, m
brown—café
brunette—moreno, -a; trigueño, -a
brush—chaparral, m; monte, m; matorral, m
bucket—cubeta, f; balde, m; bote, m
building—edificio, m
bull—toro, m
bullet—bala, f; balazo, m
bulletin—boletín, m
bundle—bulto, m; chiva, f (slang)
burn—quemada, f
burn scar—quemada, f
bus—autobús, m; camión, m; ómnibus, m
bus boy—mozo, m
business—negocio, m
busy—ocupado, -a
but—pero, sino, mas
butcher—carnicero, m
butter—mantequilla, f
button—botón, m
by—por, para
by (near)—cerca de
by day—de día
by means of—por medio de
by night—de noche

C

cabbage—repollo, m; col, m
cafe—café, m
cake—bollo, m; pastel, m
calendar—calendario, m; cromo, m
calf—becerro, -a
camp—campo, m
can—bote, m; lata, f
candy—dulce, m
canoe—canoa, f; chalupa, f
cap—cachucha, f; gorra, f

capital—capital, f
car—carro, m; auto, m; coche, m
card—tarjeta, f
care—cuidado, m
careful—cuidado; cuidadoso, -a
carefully—cuidadosamente
carpenter—carpintero, m
carpenter shop—carpintería, f
carrot—zanahoria, f
cash—al contado
cashier—cajero, m; contador, m
cat—gato, -a
cattle—ganado, m
cattleguard—guardavacas, m
cattleman—ganadero, m
cause—causa, f
cave—cueva, f
ceiling—cielo, m
cemetery—cementerio, m; panteón, m
cent—centavo, m
century—siglo, m
certain—seguro, -a; cierto, -a
certainly—ciertamente; ¿cómo no?
certificate—certificado, m
chair—silla, f
chalk—tiza, f
chance—oportunidad, f
change—cambio, m
charming—simpático, -a
chauffer—chofer, m
cheap—barato, -a
check (commercial)—cheque, m
cheek—mejilla, f
cheese—queso, m
cherry—cereza, f
chest—pecho, m; baúl, m
chicken—pollo, m; gallina, f
chief—jefe, m; patrón, m
child—niño, -a
child's nurse—nana, f
chin—barba, f
Christian name—nombre de pila; m; primer nombre, m
Christmas—Navidad, f
Christmas Eve—Nochebuena, f
church—iglesia, f
cigar—puro, m; cigarro, m
cigarette—cigarrillo, m; cigarro, m
citizen—ciudadano, -a
citizenship—ciudadanía, f

city—ciudad, f
civil—civil
class—clase, f
clay—barro, m
clean—limpio, -a
clear—claro, -a
clearly—claramente
clerk—dependiente, m-f
clock—reloj, m
close—cerca (de)
clothes—ropa, f
clothing—ropa, f
cloud—nube, f
coach—coche, m
coat—saco, m; abrigo, m
cobbler—zapatero, m
cock—gallo, m
coffee—café, m
cold—frío, -a; frío, m
collar—cuello, m
collision—choque, m
colony—colonia, f
color—color, m
commission merchant—comisionista, m-f
communist—comunista, m-f
companion—compañero, -a
company—compañía, f
compartment—compartimiento, m
complaint—queja, f
complete—completo, -a
complexion—tez, f
concerning—acerca de, tocante a, de
constable—alguacil, m
consul—cónsul, m
consulate—consulado, m
content(ed)—contento, -a
contents—contenidos, m
contract laborer—bracero, m
contractor—contratista, m
convict—convicto, m
cook—cocinero, -a
cool—fresco, -a
cop—chota, f (slang)
copper—cobre, m
cord—cordón, m; cuerda, f
corn (dry)—maíz, m
corn (fresh)—elote, m
corner—esquina, f; rincón, m
cornfield—milpa, f
corral—corral, m

correct—correcto, -a
cotton—algodón, m
cotton picking—pizca, f
cottonwood—álamo, m
counsel—consejo, m; aviso, m
country—país, m; campo, m
country house—villa, f
countryman—campesino, m
countryman (fellow)—paisano, m
county—condado, m
court—corte, f
courthouse—casacorte, f
cousin—primo, -a
cow—vaca, f
cowboy—vaquero, m
coyote—coyote, m
crate box—cajón, m
crazy—loco, -a
cream—crema, f
credit (on)—al fiado; crédito, m
creek—arroyo, m; riachuelo, m
crew (ship)—tripulación, f
crewman—tripulante, m
crime—crimen, m; delito, m
criminal—criminal, m; reo, m
cripple—rengo, -a; cojo, -a
cross—cruz, f
crude—crudo, -a
crutch—muleta, f
cry—grito, m
crybaby—llorón, -a
cucumber—pepino, m
cup—taza, f
curve—curva, f
custom—costumbre, f; moda, f
customs—aduana, f
customs officer—aduanero, m
cut—cortada, f
cute—bonito, -a; lindo, -a
cut scar—cortada, f

D

dad—papá, m
daily—diario, -a
daily newspaper—diario, m
dairy—lechería, f
damage—daño, m
dance—baile, m
dancer—bailarín, -a
danger—peligro, m

dangerous—peligroso, -a
dark—o(b)scuro, -a
date—fecha, f; cita, f
daughter—hija, f
daughter-in-law—nuera, f
day—día, m
day after tomorrow—pasado mañana
day before yesterday—anteayer
day laborer—jornalero, m
day off—día de descanso, m
dead—muerto, -a
deaf—sordo, -a
dear (affection)—querido, -a
dear (costly)—caro
death—muerte, f
debt—deuda, f
December—diciembre
deed—hecho, m; acto, m
deep—hondo, -a
deer—venado, -a
defect—defecto, m
delicious—delicioso, -a
dentist—dentista, m-f
departure—salida, f
dependent—dependiente, m-f
deportation—deportación, f
description—descripción, f
desert—desierto, m
destination—destinación, f
detail—detalle, m
detective—detectivo, m; detective, m
detention camp—corralón, m (slang)
devil—diablo, m
difference—diferencia, f
different—diferente
difficult—difícil, duro, -a (slang)
difficulty—dificultad, f
dinner—cena, f; comida, f
direction—dirección, f; rumbo, m
director—director, m
dirt—polvo, m; tierra, f
dirty—sucio, -a; mugroso, -a (slang)
dispute—disgusto, m; mitote, m
distance—distancia, f
distant—distante
district—distrito, m
ditch—zanja, f; acequia, f; canal, m
divisional—divisorio, -a
divorce—divorcio, m
doctor—doctor, -a; médico, m

document—documento, m
dog—perro, -a
doll—muñeca, f
dollar—dólar, m
domestic—doméstico, -a
domicile—domicilio, m
donkey—burro, -a
door—puerta, f
double—doble
doubt—duda, f
dough—masa, f
dove—paloma, f
down—abajo
dozen—docena, f
drag—rastra, f
drag trail—sendero rastreado, m
drawer—cajón, m
dress—vestido, m; traje, m
dressmaker—costurera, f; modista, f
driver—chofer, m
drug—droga, f
druggist—droguero, m; boticario, m
drug store—botica, f; farmacia, f; droguería, f
drunk—borracho, ebrio, tomado
drunkard—borrachón, m
drunkenness—borracher(í)a, f; borrachez, f
dry—seco, -a
duck—pato, -a
during—durante
dusk—anochecer, m
dust—polvo, m
duty—obligación, f; deber, m
duties (customs)—derechos, m; impuestos, m

E

each—cada
eagle—águila, f (el)
ear (inner)—oído, m
ear (outer)—oreja, f
early—temprano
earring—arete, m
earth—tierra, f
easily—fácilmente
east—este, m; oriente, m
eastern—oriental
easy—fácil
ebony—ébano, m

echo—**eco, m**
education—**educación. f**
egg—**huevo, m; blanquillo, m**
eight—**ocho**
eighth—**octavo, -a**
either—**o**
elbow—**codo, m**
election—**elección, f**
electric—**eléctrico, -a**
electricity—**electricidad, f**
elegant—**elegante**
embassy—**embajada, f**
emigrant—**emigrante, m**
employee—**empleado, -a; trabajador, -a**
employment—**empleo, m; trabajo, m; chamba, f** (slang)
empty—**vacío, -a**
enemy—**enemigo, -a**
engine—**locomotora, f; máquina, f**
engineer—**ingeniero, m; maquinista, m**
English—**inglés, -a**
English (language)—**inglés, m**
enough—**bastante, suficiente, basta**
entire—**entero, -a**
entrance—**entrada, f**
entrance gate—**garita, f** (slang)
entry—**entrada, f**
envelope—**sobre, m**
equal—**igual**
eraser—**borrador, m**
errand—**mandado, m; recado, m**
error—**error, m; falta, f**
especial—**especial**
even—**llano, -a; liso, -a**
evening—**tarde, f; noche, f**
ever—**alguna vez**
every—**cada; todos los——; todas las——**
everybody—**todos, todo el mundo**
everywhere—**por todas partes, por donde quiera**
evidence—**evidencia, f**
ewe—**oveja, f**
exact—**exacto, -a; mero, -a** (slang)
exactly—**exactamente, mero** (slang)
examination—**examen, m**
example—**ejemplo, m**
excellent—**excelente**

except—**menos**
exclusion—**exclusión, f**
excuse—**excusa, f**
exercise—**ejercicio, m**
expenses—**gastos, m**
expensive—**caro, -a**
express—**expreso, m; exprés, m**
extension—**extensión, f**
extra—**extra**
eye—**ojo, m**
eyebrow—**ceja, f**
eyeglasses—**anteojos, m; lentes, m**
eyelash—**pestaña, f**
eyelid—**párpado, m**

F

face—**cara, f**
fact—**hecho, m**
factory—**fábrica, f**
fair—**claro, -a**
faith—**fe, f**
fall—**otoño, m**
false—**falso, -a**
falsehood—**falsedad, f; mentira, f**
family—**familia, f**
far—**lejos**
fare—**pasaje, m**
farm—**rancho, m; hacienda, f**
farmer—**hacendado, m; ranchero, m; campesino, m**
farm laborer—**labrador, m; cultivador, m; sembrador, m**
farther—**más lejos**
fashion—**moda, f; manera, f**
fast—**rápido, -a**
fat—**gordo, -a**
father—**padre, m; papá, m**
father-in-law—**suegro, m**
fault—**culpa, f**
February—**febrero**
federal—**federal**
fee—**derecho, m**
fellow countryman—**paisano, m**
female—**hembra, f**
fence—**cerca, f; cerco, m**
fence jumper—**alambrista, m-f** (slang)
few—**pocos, -as; unos, -as**
fewer—**menos**
field—**campo, m; labor, f**

fifteen—quince
fifth—quinto, -a
fifty—cincuenta
fight—pelea, f; pleito, m
file—archivo, m; lima, f
film—película, f
final—final, último, -a
finally—al fin, por fin
fine—multa, f
finger—dedo, m
fingernail—uña, f
fingerprints—huellas digitales, f; huellas de los dedos, f
fire—lumbre, f; fuego, m
fireman—bombero, m; fogonero, m
firewood—leña, f
first—primer(o), -a
fish—pez, m; pescado, m
fisherman—pescador, -a
fishing—pesca, f
five—cinco
five hundred—quinientos, -as
flag—bandera, f
flame—llama, f
flashlight—luz de mano, f (slang); foco de mano, m
flat (tire)—llanta pinchada, f
flat-nosed—chato, -a
flight—vuelo, m
flood—inundación, f; diluvio, m
floor—piso, m; suelo, m
flour—harina, f
flower—flor, f
fly—mosca, f
following—siguiente
food—alimento, m; comida, f
fool—tonto, -a
foot—pie, m
foot bridge—puente de a pie, m
footpath—senda, f; sendero, m; vereda, f
for—por, para
forearm—canilla, f
forehead—frente, f
foreign—extranjero, -a
foreman—mayordomo, -a
forest—selva, f; bosque, m
forgery—falsificación, f
fork—tenedor, m; horca, f
form—forma, f
former—anterior

formerly—anteriormente, antes
for that reason—por eso, así que
fortnight—quincena, f
forty—cuarenta
forward—adelante
four—cuatro
fourteen—catorce
fourth—cuarto, -a
fowl—ave, f (el)
fox—zorro, -a
frank—franco, -a
frankness—franqueza, f
free—libre
freedom—libertad, f
freight—carga, f
freight train—tren de carga, m
French—francés, -a
frequently—frecuentemente, a menudo
fresh—fresco, -a
friar—fraile, m
Friday—viernes, m
friend—amigo, -a
from—de, desde
from time to time—de vez en cuando
front of—delante de
front seat—asiento de enfrente, m
fruit—fruta, f
fryer (chicken)—pollo, m
frying pan—sartén, f
full—lleno, -a
furniture—muebles, m
furniture store—mueblería, f
future—futuro, m; porvenir, m

G

gain—ganancia, f
gambler—tahur, m
garage—garage, m
garlic—ajo, m
generally—generalmente
gentleman—caballero, m
German—alemán, -a
gift—regalo, m
girdle—faja, f; cinto, m
girl—muchacha, f; niña, f
glance—mirada, f; ojeada, f
glass—vidrio, m
glass (drinking)—vaso, m
glove—guante, m

goat—cabra, f; chivo, -a

goatherd—pastor, m; chivero, m; borreguero, m; cabrero, m

God—Dios

goddaughter—ahijada, f

godfather—padrino, m

God grant—ojalá

godmother—madrina, f

godson—ahijado, m

gold—oro, m

good—bueno, -a

goodbye—adiós

governess—nana, f

government—gobierno, m

grain combine—segadora de combinación, f

grandchild—nieto, -a

grandfather—abuelo, m

grandmother—abuela, f

grape—uva, f

grapefruit—toronja, f

grass—sacate, m; yerba, f

graveyard—panteón, m; cementerio, m

gray—gris; (hair) pelo canoso, m

great—grande, famoso, -a

green—verde

grocer—abacero, m

groceries—abarrotes, m

ground—suelo, m; tierra, f

group—grupo, m

guarantee—garantía, f

guard—guardia, m-f

guest—huésped, -a

guide—guía, m-f

guilt—culpa, f

guilty—culpable

gulf—golfo, m

gun—fusil, m; (shotgun—escopeta, f)

gunshot—tiro, m; disparo, m; balazo, m

H

hair—pelo, m; cabello, m

hairy—peludo, -a; velludo, -a

half—medio, -a; mitad, f

half-brother—medio hermano, m

half-sister—media hermana, f

hand—mano, f

handcuffs—esposas, f; manillas, f

handkerchief—pañuelo, m

handsome—guapo, -a

hangover—cruda, f

happy—feliz, alegre, contento,- a

harbor—puerto, m

hard—duro, -a; difícil

harm—daño, m

harvest—cosecha, f

harvester—cosechero, m; segadora, f

harvest season—pizca, f

hat—sombrero, m

hate—odio, m

hawk—gavilán, m

hay—heno, m; sacate, m

head—cabeza, f

health—salud, f

hearing—audiencia, f

heart—corazón, m

heat—calor, m

heater—calorífero, m

heavy—pesado, -a

heel—talón, m

helicopter—helicóptero, m

hell—infierno, m

hello—hola, bueno

help—ayuda, f

hen—gallina, f

herb—hierba, f; yerba, f

herd—ganado, m; rebaño, m

here—aquí, acá

hide—piel, f

hidden—escondido, -a

high—alto, -a

high priced—caro, -a; costoso, -a

highway—carretera, f; calzada, f

hill—loma, f; cerro, m

hip—cadera, f

history—historia, f

hoe—azadón, m

hog—marrano, -a; puerco, -a

hole—agujero, m; pozo, m; hoyo, m

holiday—día de fiesta, m

holster—funda, f

home—casa, f; hogar, m; domicilio, m

home (at)—en casa

homeland—patria, f; tierra, f

homework—tarea, f

honest—honesto, -a

hope—esperanza, f

horse—caballo, m
horn (auto)—bocina, f; pito, m
horn (animal)—cuerno, m
horseshoe—herradura, f
horse stable—caballeriza, f
hose—media, f
hose (garden)—manguera, f
hospital—hospital, m
host—huésped, m
hostess—huéspeda, f; fichera (B-girl), f (slang)
hot—caliente
hotel—hotel, m
hour—hora, f
house—casa, f
household goods—muebles, m; menaje de casa, m
housekeeper—ama de llaves, f; doméstica, f
housemaid—sirvienta, f; criada, f
house trailer—casa de remolque, f
housewife—ama de casa, f (el)
how—como
however—sin embargo
how long—cuanto tiempo
how many—cuantos, -as
how much—cuanto, -a
hundred—cien(to)
hunger—hambre, f (el)
hungover—crudo, -a (slang)
hurricane—huracán, m
hurry!—¡ándele!; ¡apresúrese!
husband—esposo, m; marido, m

I

ice—hielo, m
ice cream—helado, m; nieve, f
idea—idea, f
identical—idéntico, -a
identification—identificación, f
idiot—idiota, m-f
if—si
if (that is) so—si es así
ill—enfermo, -a; malo, -a
illegal—ilegal
illegally—ilegalmente
illegitimate child—hijo, -a natural; hijo, -a ilegítimo, -a
illiterate—analfabeto, -a
illness—enfermedad, f

immediately—en seguida, inmediatamente
immigrant—inmigrante, m-f
immigrant inspector—inspector de inmigración, m
immigration—inmigración, f
immoral—inmoral
importance—importancia, f
important—importante
impossible—imposible
impression—impresión, f
in—en
inch—pulgada, f
incident—incidente, m
independence—independencia, f
independent—independiente
Indian—indio, -a
indolence—desidia, f; indolencia, f
industry—industria, f
in front—en frente, delante
inhabitant—habitante, m
ink—tinta, f
innocent—inocente
in order (to)—para
in order that—de manera que, para que
insane—loco, -a
insecticide—insecticida, f
inside—dentro (de)
inspector—inspector, m
in spite of—a pesar de
instead of—en vez de
intelligent—inteligente
intention—intención, f
interest—interés, m
interior—interior, m
international—internacional
intestine—tripa, f; intestino, m
intimate—íntimo, -a
investigation—investigación, f
iron—hierro, m; fierro, m
iron (clothes)—plancha, f
irrigation ditch—acequia, f
island—isla, f
is there?—¿hay?
Italian—italiano, -a
Italy—Italia

J

jack (auto)—gato, m; yaque, m (slang)

jacket—chaqueta, f
jack rabbit—liebre, f
jail—cárcel, f
janitor—portero, m; conserje, m
January—enero
jaw—quijada, f; mandíbula, f
jewel—joya, f
jeweler—joyero, m
jewelry—alhajas, f; joyas, f
jewelery shop—joyería, f
job—trabajo, m; chamba, f (slang)
journey—viaje, m
judge—juez, m
juice—jugo, m
July—julio
June—junio
jury—jurado, m
just—no más, nada más, justo, -a
justice—justicia, f
justice of peace—juez de paz, m

K

key—llave, f
khaki—kaki, caqui
kid—cabrito, m; chavalo, -a (slang);
  chamaco, -a (slang)
kidnaper—secuestrador, m
kidnaping—secuestro, m
kidney—riñon, m
kilogram—kilogramo, m
kilometer—kilómetro, m
kind—clase, f; bondadoso, -a
kiss—beso, m
kitchen—cocina, f
kitchen utensils—trastos de cocina,
  m
kite—papalote, m
knapsack—mochila, f
knee—rodilla, f
knife—navaja, f; cuchillo, m
knife (large)—machete, m
knowledge—sabiduría, f; conocimiento, m

L

labor—labor, f; trabajo, m
laborer—trabajador, m; jornalero,
  m
lack—falta, f

lad—mozo, m; joven, m
lady—señora, f; señorita, f
lake—lago, m; laguna, f
lamb—borrego, -a; cordero
lame—rengo, -a; cojo, -a
land—tierra, f; terreno, m
landing (airplane)—aterrizaje
landlord—patrón, m
language—idioma, m; lengua, f
lard—manteca, f
large—grande
large-bellied—panzón, -a
lariat—lazo, m
lasso—lazo, m
last—último, -a
last month—el mes pasado
last name—apellido, m
last night—anoche
last week—la semana pasada
last year—el año pasado
late—tarde
lately—últimamente
later—después, más tarde
launch—lancha, f; chalupa, f
laundress—lavandera, f
laundry—lavandería, f
law—ley, f
lawyer—abogado, -a; licenciado, -a
laziness—desidia, f; pereza, f
lazy—perezoso, -a; flojo, -a (slang)
lead—plomo, m
leader—líder, m; jefe, m
leaf—hoja, f
lean—delgado, -a; flaco, -a
least (at)—a lo menos, por lo menos
leather—cuero, m; baqueta, f
leatherworker—talabartero, m
left—izquierdo, -a
leg—pierna, f
legal—legal
legally—legalmente
lemon—limón, m
length—longitud, m; largo, m
less—menos
lesson—lección, f
let's see—vamos a ver
letter—carta, f; letra, f
level ground—llano, m; plano, m
liberty—libertad, f
license—licencia, f
license plate—placa, f

lie—mentira, f
life—vida, f
light—luz, f
light (weight)—ligero, -a
light (color)—claro
light (electric)—luz eléctrica, f
light (bulb)—foco, m
lighter (cigarette)—encendedor, m
like—como
like—semejante
like that—así
like this—así
likewise—también
lime—lima, f
limit—límite, m
line—línea, f
lip—labio, m
list—lista, f
little—poco, -a (quantity); pequeño, -a (size)
livestock—ganado, m
living—vida, f; subsistencia, f
living room—sala, f
load—carga, f
lobster—langosta, f
local—local
location—lugar, m; sitio, m
long—largo, -a
look out!—¡cuidado!
loose—flojo, -a; suelto, -a
love—amor, m
low—bajo, -a
luck—suerte, f
lunch—merienda, f; lonche, m (slang)
lunch counter—lonchería, f (slang)
lung—pulmón, m

M

machine—máquina, f
machinery—maquinaria, f
machinist—maquinista, m-f
mad—loco, -a; enojado, -a
magazine—revista, f
maid—criada, f
mail—correo, m
mailman—cartero, m
maimed—mocho, -a
main boss—mero gallo, m (slang)
maize—maíz, m

maize field—milpa, f
mamma—mamá, f
man—hombre, m; señor, m
manager—gerente, m; director, m
mandate—orden, f
manner—manera, f; modo, m
many—muchos, -as
map—mapa, m
March—marzo
mare—yegua, f
margin—margen, m; orilla, f
marijuana—marijuana, f
mark—marca, f; seña, f; signo, m
market—mercado, m
market place—mercado, m
marriage—casamiento, m; matrimonio, m
marriage certificate—certificado de matrimonio, m
married—casado, -a
mason—albañil, m
mass—misa, f (church); conjunto, m (people)
matches—cerillos, m; fósforos, m
matter—asunto, m
May—mayo
maybe—quizá, quizás, tal vez
mayor—presidente municipal, m; alcalde, m
meal—comida, f
mean—malo, -a
meanwhile—mientras tanto, entre tanto
meat—carne, f
meat market—carnicería, f
mechanic—mecánico, m
medallion—medalla, f
medicine—medicina, f
meeting—junta, f
member—miembro, -a
menu—carta, f; lista, f; menú, m
merchant—comerciante, m
metal—metal, m
method—método, m; modo, m
Mexican—mexicano, -a
Mexican dollar—peso, m
mid-day—mediodía, m
middle—medio
midnight—medianoche, f
midwife—partera, f
mile—milla, f

milk—leche,
milkman—lechero, m
mill—molino, m
miller—molinero, m
mine—mina, f
miner—minero, m
mineral—mineral, m
minor—menor (de edad)
minus—menos
minute—minuto, m
miracle—milagro, m
Miss—señorita, f
mistake—falta, f; error, m
mistress—mujer de pie, f; querida, f
mode—modo, -a; manera, f
mold—moho, m
mole—lunar, m
Mom—mamá, f
moment—momento, m
Monday—lunes, m
money—dinero, m; moneda, f
month—mes, m
moon—luna, f
more—más
morning—mañana, f
mosquito—zancudo, m; mosquito, m
moss—moho, m
mother—madre, f; mamá, f
mother-in-law—suegra, f; madre política, f
motive—motivo, m
motor—motor, m
mountain—montaña, f; monte, m
mouse—ratón, m
mouth—boca, f
movie (theatre)—cine, m
Mr.—señor, m
Mrs.—señora, f
much—mucho, -a
mud—lodo, m
mule—mula, f
municipality—municipio, m
murder—asesinato, m; homicidio, m
murderer—asesino, -a
music—música, f
musician—músico, m
mustache—bigote, m
mustard—mostaza, f
mutilated—mocho, -a

N

name—nombre, m
namesake—tocayo, -a
narcotic—narcótico, m
narrow—angosto, -a; estrecho, -a
nation—nación, f
national—nacional
nationality—nacionalidad, f
native—nativo, -a
native country—tierra, f; patria, f
naturalization—naturalización, f
near—cerca (de)
nearly—casi
necessary—necesario, -a
neck—cuello, m; pescuezo, m
neighbor—vecino, -a
neighborhood—barrio, m; vecindad, f
neither—ni, tampoco
neither . . . nor—ni . . . ni
nephew—sobrino, m
nervous—nervioso, -a
never—nunca, jamás
nevertheless—sin embargo
new—nuevo, -a
news—noticia(s), f
newspaper—periódico, m; diario, m
New Year—año nuevo, m
next—después, siguiente, luego, próximo, -a
next month—el mes que viene, el mes que entra
next week—la semana que viene, la semana que entra
next year—el año que viene, el año que entra
nickname—sobrenombre, m; apodo, m
niece—sobrina, f
night—noche, f
night before last—anteanoche
nightfall—anochecer, m
nine—nueve
ninth—noveno, -a
no—no
nobody—nadie
noise—ruido, m
no longer—ya no
no more—ya no
none—ninguno, -a

nook—rincón, m
noon—mediodía, m
no one—nadie
nor—ni
north—norte, m
nose—nariz, f
not—no
not any—ningún (o), -a
not anymore—ya no
nothing—nada
not yet—todavía no
November—noviembre
novice—novicio, -a
now—ahora
nowadays—hoy día
number—número, m
nurse—enfermera, f
nurse (for children)—niñera, f
nut—nuez, f

O

oak—roble, m
oath—juramento, m
oats—avena, f
occupation—ocupación, f
occupied—ocupado, -a
October—octubre
of—de
of course—claro, por supuesto, seguro que sí
off duty—franco, -a
offense—ofensa, f
offer—oferta, f
office—oficina, f
officer—oficial, m
official—oficial, m
offspring—cría, f
often—a menudo
oil—aceite, m
okay—está bien
old—viejo, -a; anciano, -a
older—mayor
oldest—mayor
on—en, sobre
once—una vez
(at) once—en seguida
one—un(o), -a
one-eyed—tuerto, -a
one hundred—cien (to)
on foot—a pie

onion—cebolla, f
only—nada más, no más, sino, solo, único, -a
on the outside—por fuera
on time—a tiempo
open—abierto, -a
opium—opio, m
opportunity—oportunidad, f
opposite—opuesto, -a
or—o, u
orange—naranja, f
orange tree—naranjo, m
order—orden, f-m
orphan—huérfano, -a
organization—organización, f
orient—oriente, m; este, m
oriental—oriental
origin—origen, m
original—original
other—otro, -a
otherwise—de otra manera, de otro modo
our—nuestro, -a, etc.
ours—el nuestro, etc.
out—afuera, fuera
outside—afuera, fuera
over—sobre, encima
overalls—pantalón de pechera
overcoat—abrigo, m; sobretodo, m
over there—allá
owner—dueño, -a; amo, -a (el)
oyster—ostión, m

P

package—paquete, m
packing shed—bodega, f
page—página, f
pain—dolor, m
painter—pintor, -a
pair—par, m
pants—pantalones, m
paper—papel, m
papa—papá, m
pardon—perdón, m
parents—padres, m
park—parque, m
part—parte, f
party—fiesta, f
pass—paso, m
passage—pasaje, m

passenger—pasajero, -a
past—pasado, -a; último, -a
pasture—potrero, m; pasto, m
path—vereda, f; senda, f; sendero, m
patrol—patrulla, f; migra, f (slang)
patrol inspector—patrullero, m
paved—pavimentado, -a
paw—pata, f
pay day—día de pago, m
peach—durazno, m
peace officer—alguacil, m
pear—pera, f
pen (writing) pluma, f
pen (stock)—corral, m
pencil—lápiz, m
penitentiary—penitenciaría, f; casa de corrección, f
penknife—navaja, f
penny—centavo, m
pepper—chile, m; pimiento, m; pimienta, f
people—gente, f
perhaps—quizá, quizás, tal vez
perjury—perjurio, m
permanent—permanente
permission—permiso, m
permit—permiso, m
person—persona, f
pharmacy—farmacia, f; botica, f
photograph—fotografía, f; foto, f
pick(axe)—pico, m
picker—pizcador, -a
picking season—pizca, f
picture—retrato, m; foto, f
picture show—cine, m; vistas, f (slang)
picture film—película, f
piece—pedazo, m; pieza, f
pig—marrano, -a; puerco, -a
pillow—almohada, f
pillow case—funda de almohada, f
pilot—piloto, m; aviador, m
pimp—alcahuete, m
pin—alfiler, m; broche, m
pineapple—piña, f
pistol—pistola, f
pity—lástima
place—lugar, m; sitio, m
plant—planta, f
planter—plantador, m; sembrador,

plate—plato, m; placa, f
plaza—plaza, f
please—por favor
plow—arado, m
plumber—plomero, m
pocket—bolsa, f; bolsillo, m
pocket-book—bolsa, f; portamonedas, m
pocketknife—navaja, f
poison—veneno, m
point—punto, m; punta, f
pole—palo, m; vara, f
police force—policía, f
policeman—policía, m
pool—charco, m; billares, m
pool hall—billar, m; salón de billares, m
poor—pobre
Pope—Papa, m
poplar—álamo, m
pork—puerco, m
port—puerto, m
porter—portero, m
port of entry—puerto de entrada, m; garita, f (slang)
portrait—retrato, m
possible—posible
post—poste, m; palo, m
postman—cartero, m
postmaster—administrador de correos, m
post office—correo, m; estafeta, f
potato—papa, f; (sweet) camote, m
pound—libra, f
power—poder, m; fuerza, f
prayer—oración, f
preceding—anterior
precise—preciso, -a
presence—presencia, f
present—presente, regalo, m
president—presidente, m
pretty—bonito, -a; lindo, -a
price—precio, m
priest—cura, m; sacerdote, m; padre, m
print—huella, f; impresión, f
prison—prisión, f; cárcel, f
prisoner—prisionero, -a; preso, -a
problem—problema, m
proceedings—procedimientos, m; actas, f

process—proceso, m
product—producto, m
professor—profesor, -a
promise—promesa, f
promoter—promotor, m; empresario,
m
proof—prueba, f
property—propiedad, f
prostitute—prostituta, f
prostitution—prostitución, f
provided (that)—con tal que, siempre que
puddle—charco, m
pug-nosed—chato, -a
pulse—pulso, m
pump—bomba, f
punctual—puntual
pupil—alumno, -a; pupila, f (eye)
pure—puro, -a
purpose—propósito, m
purse—bolsa, f; bolsillo, m

Q

quail—codorniz, f
quarrel—disgusto, m; riña, f
quart—cuarto, m
quarter—peseta, f (coin); cuarto, m
(measure)
question—pregunta, f
quick—pronto, -a
quickly—pronto
quota—cuota, f

R

rabbit—conejo, -a
race—raza, f
radish—rábano, m
radio—radio, m-f (instrument, m;
transmission, f)
raft—balsa, f
rag—trapo, m
railroad—ferrocarril, m
railroad track—traque de——, m;
vía, f
rain—lluvia, f
rake—rastrillo, m
ram—carnero, m
ranch—rancho, m
rancher—ranchero, m

ranch foreman—caporal, m
rape—rapto, m; estupro, m
rapid—rápido, -a
rare—raro, -a
rarely—muy raro (coll); casi nunca
(coll)
rascal—pícaro, m
rat—rata, f
rattle snake—víbora de cascabel, f
ravine—arroyo, m; cañada, f
raw—crudo, -a
ready—listo, -a
real—real, mero, -a (slang)
really—de veras
reason—razón, f; causa, f
receipt—recibo, m
recent—reciente
recently—recientemente
record—récord, m; transcripción, f;
disco, m (phono)
red—rojo, -a; colorado, -a
relative—pariente, -a
rendezvous—cita, f
rent—renta, f
report—reporte, m
republic—república, f
requirement—requisito, m
residence—residencia, f; domicilio,
m
resources—bienes, m; riquezas, f
restaurant—restaurante, m
rest room—servicio, m; cuarto de
baño, m; excusado, m
retail—al por menor
reunion—reunión, f
review—repaso, m
revolver—revólver, m
rib—costilla, f
rice—arroz, m
rich—rico, -a
rifle—rifle, m; fusil, m
right?—¿verdad?
right—derecho, -a; derecho, m
right away—pronto, prontito, en seguida, inmediatamente
right now—ahorita, ahora mismo
ring—anillo, m
river—río, m
road—camino, m
robber—ladrón, m; ratero, m
robbery—robo, m

rock—piedra, f; roca, f; peñasco, m
rod—vara, f
rogue—pícaro, m
roof—techo, m
room—cuarto, m
rooster—gallo, m
rope—soga, f; reata, f
rose—rosa, f
rough—áspero, -a
round—redondo, -a
round trip fare—pasaje de ida y vuelta, m; pasaje redondo, m
route—rumbo, m; vía, f; ruta, f
row boat—bote de remos, m
rubber—hule, m; goma, f
rule—regla, f
ruler—regla, f (measure); gobernador, m (person)
ruralman—campesino, m
rust—moho, m

S

sabotage—sabotaje, m
sack—costal, m (cloth); bolsa, f (paper)
sad—triste
safe—seguro, -a
sailor—marinero, m
saint—santo, -a; san
salary—sueldo, m; salario, m
sale—venta, f
saloon—cantina, f; salón, m
salt—sal, f
same—igual, mismo, -a
sample—muestra, f
sand—arena, f
sandal—sandalia, f; huarache, m
sandwich—sandwich, m (slang); emparedado, m
Saturday—sábado, m
sausage—chorizo, m; salchicha, f
scale—balanza, f; báscula, f; escala, f
scar—cicatriz, f
scarcely—apenas
school—escuela, f
sea—mar, m
season—estación, f
seat—asiento, m
second—segundo, m; segundo, -a

secretary—secretario, -a
seed—semilla, f
sentence—sentencia, f; oración, f
sentry box—garita, f
September—septiembre
servant—sirviente, -ta
service—servicio, m
seven—siete
seventeen—diez y siete
seventh—séptimo, -a
several—varios, -as
sex—sexo, m
shame—vergüenza, f; lástima, f
sharecropper—mediero, m
sharp—filoso, -a; en punto (time)
sheep—borrego, m; carnero, m; oveja, f
sheriff—jerife, m; sherife, m (slang)
shin—canilla, f
ship—barco, m; buque, m; vapor, m
shirt—camisa, f
shoe—zapato, m
shoe shop—zapatería, f
shop—taller, m
shore—costa, f; playa, f; orilla, f (bank of a stream)
short—bajo, -a; corto, -a; chaparro, -a; chapo, -a (slang)
shorts—calzoncillos, m
short time—rato
shot—tiro, m; disparo, m; balazo, m
shot gun—escopeta, f
shoulder—hombro, m
shovel—pala, f
shrimp—camarón, m
sick—enfermo, -a; malo, -a
side—lado, m
sidewalk—banqueta, f; acera, f
sight—vista, f
sign—seña, f; marca, f; signo, m; rótulo, m; letrero, m
signature—firma, f
silk—seda, f
silver—plata, f
since—desde
single—soltero, -a
sir—señor, m
sister—hermana, f
sister-in-law—cuñada, f
site—sitio, m; lugar, m

six—seis
sixteen—diez y seis; dieciséis
sixth—sexto, -a
sixty—sesenta
size—tamaño, m
skin—cutis, m; piel, f
skinny—flaco, -a
skirt—falda, f
skunk—zorillo, -a
sky—cielo, m
slender—delgado, -a; flaco, -a
sling—honda, f
slip—fondo, m
slipper—chancla, f; sandalia, f
slow—despacio; lento
slowly—despacio, lentamente
small—pequeño, -a; chico, -a
smoke—humo, m
smooth—suave, liso, -a; llano, -a
smuggled goods—contrabando, m
smuggler—contrabandista, m-f
snake—víbora, f; culebra, f
snow—nieve, f
so—así que, conque, tan, por eso
soap—jabón, m
social security card—tarjeta de seguro social, f
sock—calcetín, m
soft—suave, blando, -a
soil—tierra, f; suelo, m
soldier—soldado, m
so many—tantos, -as
some—algún(o), -a; unos, -as
somebody—alguien; alguna persona
someone—alguien, alguna persona
some place—algún lugar
something—alguna cosa, algo
sometimes—a veces
so much—tanto, -a
son—hijo, m
son-in-law—yerno, m
soon—pronto
sort—clase, f; modo, m
soul—alma, f (el)
soup—caldo, m; sopa, f
south—sur, m
Spain—España
Spaniard—español, -a
Spanish—español (language), m; español, -a

special—especial
spectacles—anteojos, m; lentes, m
speed—velocidad, f
spider—araña, f
spinach—espinaca, f
spoon—cuchara, f
spoon (tea)—cucharilla, f
sport—deporte, m
sporting—deportivo, -a
spring—primavera, f; ojo de agua, m
spy—espía, m-f
squall—chubasco, m
square—plaza, f; cuadrado, -a
squash—calabaza, f
stair—escalón, m
stall—puesto, m
stamp—timbre, m; estampilla, f; sello, m
stand—puesto, m
star—estrella, f
state—estado, m
statement—declaración, f
station—estación (de), f
stationwagon—camioneta, f
status—estado, m
steam—vapor, m
steer—novillo, m; rez, f
step—paso, m; escalón (stairs), m
stepchild—hijastro, -a
stepfather—padrastro, m
stepmother—madrastra, f
stick—palo, m; vara, f
still—todavía, aun
stocking—media, f; calcetín, m
stomach—estómago, m
stone—piedra, f
stop—alto, basta, parada, f
store—tienda, f
storeroom—bodega, f; almacén, m
storm—tormenta, f; chubasco, m
story—cuento, m; historia, f
story (floor)—piso
stove—estufa, f
stowaway—polizón, m
straight—derecho, -a; recto, -a
stranger—extranjero, -a; desconocido, -a
statue—estatua, f
straw—paja, f
street—calle, f

streetcar—tranvía, m
strength—fuerza, f; poder, m
strike—huelga, f (work stoppage)
string—cordón, m; hilo, m; cuerda, f
striped—listado, -a
strong—fuerte; poderoso, -a
stub (ticket)—talón, m
student—estudiante, m-f; alumno, -a
study—estudio, m
subject—sujeto, m
suburb—barrio, m
such—tal
suddenly—de repente
sufficient—suficiente
sugar—azúcar, m
suit—traje, m
suit (law)—queja, f; pleito, m
suitcase—maleta, f; veliz, m
sum—suma, f
summer—verano, m
sun—sol, m
Sunday—domingo, m
supper—cena, f
sure—seguro que sí, seguro, -a
surname—apellido, m
suspicion—sospecha, f
suspicious—sospechoso, -a
swarthy—trigueño, -a; moreno, -a
sweater—suéter, m; chamarra, f
sweet—dulce
sweetheart—novio, -a
swimsuit—traje de baño, m

T

table—mesa, f
tail—cola, f; rabo, m
tailor—sastre, m
tailor shop—sastrería, f
tall—alto, -a
tangerine—mandarina, f; tangerina, f
tank—tanque, m
target—blanco, m
task—tarea, f
tatoo—tatuaje, m; tatú, m
taxi—taxi, m; carro de sitio, m
tea—té, m
teacher—maestro, -a
teeth—dientes, m

telegram—telegrama, m
telephone—teléfono, m
television—televisión, f
television set—televisor, m
ten—diez
tenth—décimo, -a
tequila—tequila, m
terrible—terrible
territory—territorio, m; terreno, m
test—prueba, f; examen, m
testimony—testimonio, m
Texas—Texas (Tejas)
than—que
thanks—gracias, f
that—ese, -a; aquel, -lla; eso, que
that's why—por eso, así que
that which—lo que
the—el, la, los, las
theater—cine, m; teatro, m
then—entonces, luego, después
there—allí, allá, ahí
there are—hay
therefore—por eso, así que
there is—hay
there was—había
there were—había
these—estos, -as
thick—grueso, -a; espeso, -a; denso, -a
thief—ladrón, m; ratero, m
thin—delgado, -a; flaco, -a
thing—cosa, f
third—tercero, -a
thirteen—trece
thirty—treinta
this—este, esta, esto
those—esos, -as; aquellos, -as
though—aunque
thousand—mil
thread—hilo, m
threat—amenaza, f
three—tres
through—por
thumb—pulgar, m
Thursday—jueves, m
thus—así
ticket—boleto, m; billete, m
tie—corbata, f
time—tiempo, m; vez, f; hora, f
tin—lata, f; hojalata, f; estaño, m
tire—llanta, f

tired—cansado, -a
title—título, m
to—a, para
tobacco—tabaco, m
today—hoy
toe—dedo (del pie), m
toenail—uña, f
together—junto(s), -a(s)
toilet—servicio, m; excusado, m
tomato—tomate, m
tomorrow—mañana
tongue—lengua, f
tonight—esta noche, a la noche
too—también
tools—herramienta(s), f
too many—muchos, -as; demasiados, -as
too much—mucho, -a; demasiado, -a
tooth—diente, m
top—cima, f; cumbre, f
tourist—turista, m-f
toward—hacia
town—pueblo, m
tracks—huellas, f
track (railroad)—vía, f; riel, m; traque, m (slang)
tractor—tractor, m
tractor driver—tractorista, m-f
trail—pisada, f; huellas, f; vereda, f; sendero, m
train—tren, m
trainee—novicio, m
traitor—traidor, -a
traveler—viajero, -a
tree—árbol, m
trial—juicio, m
trip—viaje, m
trousers—pantalones, m
truck—camión, m; troque, m (slang); troca, f (slang)
truck driver—troquero, m (slang)
true—verdad, cierto
trunk—baúl, m; petaca, f
trunk (car)—cajuela, f
truth—verdad, f
Tuesday—martes, m
turkey—guajalote, m; cócono, m (coll)
twelve—doce
twenty—veinte
twig—vara, f

twin—gemelo, m; cuate, m
two—dos

U

ugly—feo, -a
uncle—tío, m
under—debajo (de), bajo, abajo
under oath—bajo juramento
undershirt—camiseta, f
underwear—ropa interior, f
uniform—uniforme, m
United States—Estados Unidos, m
university—universidad, f
unjust—injusto, -a
unknown—desconocido, -a
unless—a menos que
until—hasta, hasta que
up—arriba
upon—sobre, al
upright—justo, -a
upstairs—arriba
up to—hasta
useful—útil
usually—generalmente, usualmente

V

vacation—vacación(es), f
vaccination—vacuna, f
valid—válido, -a
valise—veliz, m
valley—valle, m
value—valor, m; precio, m
various—varios, -as
vegetable—legumbre, f; verdura, f
verb—verbo, m
very—muy
vest—chaleco, m
view—vista, f
village—aldea, f; villa, f; población, f
vinegar—vinagre, m
violation—violación, f
violence—violencia, f
visa—visa, f
visible—visible
visit—visita, f
visitor—visitante, m
voice—voz, f
voluntarily—voluntariamente

voluntary—voluntario, -a
volunteer—voluntario, -a
vote—voto, m

W

wages—sueldo, m
wagon—vagón, m
waist—cintura, f
waiter—mesero, -a
waiting room—sala de espera, f
walking cane—bastón, m
wall—pared, f
war—guerra, f
warehouse—bodega, f; almacén, m
warm—tibio, -a; caliente
warning—aviso, m
warrant (of arrest)—orden de arresto, f; fallo de arresto, m
wart—verruga, f
was there?—¿había?
watch—reloj, m
watchmaker—relojero, m
watch out!—¡cuidado!
water—agua, f (el)
waterhole—tanque, m; charco, m
wave—ola, f; onda, f
wax—cera, f
way—rumbo, m; camino, f; vía, f
weak—débil
weapon—arma, f (el)
weather—tiempo, m
wedding—boda, f; casamiento, m
Wednesday—miércoles, m
weed—hierba, f; yerba, f
week—semana, f
weight—peso, m
well—noria, f; pozo, m; pues, bien
were there?—¿había?
west—oeste, m; poniente, m; occidente, m
wet—mojado, -a
wetback—mojado, -a (slang)
what—lo que
what?—¿qué?
what color—de que color
whatever—cualquier (a)
what for—para que
wheat—trigo, m
wheel—rueda, f
when—cuando

where—donde
whether—si
which—cual, que
while—mientras
white—blanco, -a
who?—¿quién?; ¿quiénes?
who—quien, -es; que
whole—entero, -a
wholesale—al por mayor
wholesale house—almacén, m
whom—quien, -es
whose—de quien, -es, cuyo
why—por que
wide—ancho, -a
widow—viuda, f
widower—viudo, m
width—anchura, f; ancho, m
wiener—salchicha, f
wife—esposa, f
wig—peluca, f
wild—salvaje, silvestre
willing—dispuesto, -a
wind—viento, m
windmill—papalote, m; molino de viento, m
windshield—parabrisa, m
window—ventana, f
wine—vino, m
winter—invierno, m
wire—alambre, m
wise—sabio, -a; erudito, -a
with—con
within—dentro (de)
without—sin
witness—testigo, -a
wolf—lobo, -a
woman—mujer, f; señora, f
wood—madera, f
wood (fire)—leña, f
wood chopper—leñador, m
woods—monte, m; bosque, m
wool—lana, f
word—palabra, f
work—trabajo, m; empleo, m; labor, f; chamba, f (slang)
worker—trabajador, -a; obrero, -a
workshop—taller, m
world—mundo, m
world war—guerra mundial, f
worse—peor
wreck—choque, m

wrinkle—arruga, f
wrist—pulso, m; muñeca, f

Y

yard—yarda, f
year—año, m
yellow—amarillo, -a
yes—sí

yesterday—ayer
yet—todavía, aún
yonder—allá
young—joven, m-f
young lady—señorita, f
young lad—mozo, m
young goat—cabrito. m
youngster—chamaco, -a (slang);
  chaval, -a

SPANISH-ENGLISH VOCABULARY

A

a—to, at
abajo—under, below, down
abierto, -a—open
abogado, m—lawyer
abrigo, m—coat, overcoat
abril—April
abuela, f—grandmother
abuelo, m—grandfather
acá—here
acento, m—accent
acequia, f—(irrigation) ditch
acera, f—sidewalk
acerca de—about, concerning
acre, m—acre
acta de nacimiento, f (el)—birth
  certificate
acumulador, m—battery (storage)
además (de)—besides
adicto, -a—addict
adiós—good-bye
admisión, f—admission
aduana, f—customs
aduanero, m—customs agent
aeropuerto, m—airport
afuera—outside, out
agosto—August
agua, f (el)—water
agujero, m—hole
ahijado, -a—godchild
ahora—now
ahora mismo—right now
ahorita—right now
aire, m—air
a la caída de la tarde—at sun down
a la caída del sol—at sun down
a la madrugada—at dawn
al amanecer—at dawn
alambre, m—wire

alambrista, m-f—fence jumper
  (slang)
álamo, m—cottonwood, poplar
a la noche—tonight
al anochecer—at dusk
albañil, m—bricklayer, mason
alcahuete, m—pimp
aldea, f—village
alemán, -a—German
al fin—finally, at last
al fin de—at the end of
algo—something, anything
algodón, m—cotton
alguacil, m—constable, peace officer
alguien—someone, somebody,
  anyone, anybody
alguna cosa—something, anything
alguna vez—ever
algún lugar—anywhere, some place,
  any place, somewhere
algún(o), -a—some, any
alhajas, f—jewelry
alimento, m—food
al lado (de)—beside
alma, f (el)—soul
almacén, m—wholesale house, warehouse
almohada, f—pillow
al principio—at first, at the beginning
alrededor—around
alto—stop
alto, -a—tall, high
alumno, -a—pupil, student
allá—over there, yonder, there
allí—there
ama de casa, f (el)—housewife
amanecer, m—dawn, daybreak
amarillo, -a—yellow
amenaza, f—threat

a menos (de)—unless
americano, -a—American
amigo, -a—friend
amo, m—owner
analfabeto, -a—illiterate
anciano, -a—old
anillo, m—ring
anoche—last night
anochecer, m—nightfall, dusk
anteanoche—night before last
anteayer—day before yesterday
anteojos, m—eyeglasses
anterior—preceding, former
anteriormente—formerly
antes (de)—before, formerly
anuncio, m—announcement
año, m—year
año nuevo, m—new year
apellido, m—last name, surname
apenas—scarcely, barely
a pesar de—in spite of
a pie—on foot
aquel—that (at a distance)
aquella—that (at a distance)
aquellos, -as—those (at a distance)
aquí—here
arado, m—plow
araña, f—spider
árbol, m—tree
archivo, m—file, archive
arena, f—sand
arete, m—earring
arma, f (el)—weapon (arm)
arreglo, m—arrangement
arriba—above, up
arroz, m—rice
artista, m-f—artist
asesinato, m—murder
asesino, m—murderer
así—thus, like this, like that
asiento, m—seat
asiento de atrás, m—back seat
asiento de enfrente, m—front seat
así que—therefore, for that reason, so
asunto, m—matter
a tiempo—on time
atrás (de)—behind, back
audiencia, f—hearing
aun—yet, still
aunque—although, though
auto, m—auto, car

autobús, m—bus
automóvil, m—automobile
autoridad, f—authority
ave, f (el)—fowl, bird
a veces—at times, sometimes
avenida, f—avenue
aviador, m—pilot
avión, m—airplane
aviso, m—warning, advice
ayer—yesterday
ayer por la mañana—yesterday morning
ayuda, f—help
azteca—Aztec
azúcar, m—sugar
azul—blue

B

bailarín, -a—dancer
baile, m—dance
bajo—low, short, under
bajo juramento—under oath
balsa, f—raft
banco, m—bank
banco, -a—bench
bandera, f—flag, banner
bandido, m—bandit
banquero, m—banker
banqueta, f—sidewalk
baño, m—bath
baqueta, f—leather
barato, -a—cheap
barba, f—chin, beard
barbacoa, f—barbecue
barbería, f—barber shop
barbero, m—barber
barco, m—boat, barge, ship
barraca, f—barrack
barril, m—barrel
barrio, m—neighborhood, suburb
barro, m—clay
base, f—base
basta—enough, stop
bastante—enough
bastardo, -a—bastard, born out of wedlock
bastón, m—walking cane
batería, f—battery
baúl, m—trunk, chest
becerro, -a—calf
bello, -a—beautiful

beso, m—kiss
betabel, m—beet
bien—well
bigote, m—mustache
billar, m—billiard room, pool hall
billete, m—bill
billetera, f—billfold
biología, f—biology
bistec, m—beefsteak
bizcocho, m—biscuit
blanco, m—target
blanco, -a—white
blusa, f—blouse
boca, f—mouth
boda, f—wedding
bodega, f—storeroom, warehouse
bola, f—ball
boletín, m—bulletin
boleto, m—ticket
bolsa, f—purse, pocket, bag, sack
bolsillo, m—purse, pocket
bollo, m—biscuit (small), cake
bomba, f—pump
bonito, -a—pretty, cute
borrador, m—eraser
borrego, -a—lamb
bota, f—boot
bote, m—boat, can, jail (slang)
bote de remos, m—rowboat
botella, f—bottle
botón, m—button
bracero, m—contract laborer,
    manual laborer
brazalete, m—bracelet
brazo, m—arm
bueno—hello, all right
bueno, -a—good
bulto, m—bundle
burro, m—donkey
buque, m—ship

C

caballeriza, f—stable
caballero, m—gentleman
caballo, m—horse
cabello, m—hair
cabeza, f—head
cabra, f—goat
cabrito, m—young goat, kid
cachucha, f—cap
cada—each, every

cadera, f—hip
café, m—coffee, brown
caja, f—box
cajón, m—crate box, drawer
cajuela, f—car trunk
calcetín, m—sock
calendario, m—calendar
caliente—warm, hot
calvo, -a—bald
calzón, m—white pants
calzoncillos, m—shorts
calle, f—street
callejón, m—alley
cama, f—bed
cambio, m—change
camino, m—road, way
camión, m—truck, bus
camioneta, f—stationwagon
camisa, f—shirt
camiseta, f—undershirt
campana, f—bell
campesino, m—ruralman, farmer
campo, m—field, camp, country
canilla, f—forearm, shin
canoa, f—canoe
cantina, f—bar
cantinera, f—barmaid
cantinero, m—bartender
cansado, -a—tired
caporal, m—ranch foreman
cara, f—face
cárcel, f—jail
carga, f—load, freight, cargo
carne, f—meat
carnero, m—sheep, ram
carnicero, m—butcher
caro, -a—expensive
carpintero, m—carpenter
carretera, f—highway
carro, m—car, automobile
carta, f—letter
cartera, f—billfold
cartero, m—mailman, postman
casa, f—house, home
casacorte, f—courthouse
casa de remolque, f—house trailer
casado, -a—married
casi—almost, nearly
casi nunca (coll)—rarely
causa, f—cause
ceja, f—eyebrow
cena, f—dinner, supper

centavo, m—cent
cerca, f—fence
cerca (de)—near, close, about, beside
certificado, m—certificate
certificado de nacimiento, m—birth certificate
cerveza, f—beer
cicatriz, f—scar
ciego, -a—blind
cielo, m—sky, ceiling
cien(to)—one hundred
cierto, -a—certain, true
cigarrillo, m—cigarette
cigarro, m—cigar, cigarette
cinco—five
cine, m—theater, movie
cinto, m—belt, girdle
cintura, f—waist
cinturón, m—belt
cita, f—date, rendezvous, appointment
ciudad, f—city
ciudadanía, f—citizenship
ciudadano, -a—citizen
claramente—clearly
claro, -a—clear
claro—of course
clase, f—class, kind, type
cobija, f—blanket
cocinero, -a—cook
cócono, m—turkey
coche, m—car, coach
codo, m—elbow, stingy (slang)
codorniz, f—quail
cojo, -a—cripple, lame
color, m—color
colorado, -a—red
comadre, f—close friend
comerciante, m—merchant
comida, f—dinner, food
comisionista, m-f—commission merchant
como—as, like, about, how
compadre, m—close friend
compañero, -a—companion
compañía, f—company
compartimiento, m—compartment
completo, -a—complete
con—with
condado, m—county
conejo, -a—rabbit

conmigo—with me
conocido, -a—acquaintance
conocimiento, m—knowledge
conque—so
consigo—with you
cónsul, m—consul
consulado, m—consulate
con tal que—provided
contento, -a—content(ed)
contestación, f—answer
contigo—with you (familiar)
contra—against
contrabandista, m-f—smuggler
contrabando, m—smuggled goods
contraseña, f—baggage check
corazón, m—heart
corbata, f—tie
cordón, m—cord, string
corral, m—corral
corralón, m (slang)—detention camp
correcto, -a—correct
correo, m—post office, mail
cortada, f—cut, cut scar
corte, f—court
corto, -a—short
cosa, f—thing
cosecha, f—harvest
costal, m—sack
costilla, f—rib
costumbre, f—custom
coyote, m—coyote
crema, f—cream
cría, f—brood, offspring, suckling
criada, f—maid
crimen, m—crime
cromo, m—calendar
crudo, -a—raw, crude, hungover
cruz, f—cross
cuadra, f—block
cual—which
cualquier, -a—any, anyone, anybody
cualquier lugar—anywhere, anyplace
cuando—when
cuanto, -a—how much
cuantos, -as—how many
cuanto tiempo—how long
cuarenta—forty
cuarto, m—room
cuarto, -a—fourth
cuatro—four
cuchillo, m—knife
cuello, m—neck, collar

cuenta, f—bill
cuero, m—leather
cuerpo, m—body
cueva, f—cave
cuidado, m—care, careful, watch out, look out
cuidadosamente—carefully
cuidadoso, -a—careful, cautious
culpa, f—guilt, fault, blame
culpable—guilty
cumpleaños, m—birthday
cuñada, f—sister-in-law
cuñado, m—brother-in-law
cuota, f—quota
cura, m—priest
curva, f—curve

CH

chaleco, m—vest
chalupa, f—launch, small vessel, boat, canoe
chamaco, m (slang)—youngster, boy, kid
chamarra, f—sweater
chamba, f (slang)—work, job
chancla, f—old shoe, slipper
chaparral, m—low brush
chaparro, -a—short
chapo (slang)—short
chaqueta, f—jacket
charco, m—pool, puddle, waterhole
chato, -a—flat-nosed, pug-nosed
chaval, -a, m-f—youngster
chico, -a—small
chiva, f (slang)—bundle, personal item
chivo, -a—goat
chofer, m—chauffeur, driver
choque, m—wreck
chorizo, m—sausage
chubasco, m—squall, storm

D

de—of, from, about, as
debajo (de)—under, beneath, below
décimo, -a—tenth
declaración, f—statement
de cualquier modo—any way
de día—by day

dedo, m—finger
delante (de)—in front, before, ahead
delgado, -a—thin, slender, lean
delito, m—crime, offense
de manera que—in order that
demasiado, -a—too much
demasiados, -as—too many
de noche—by night, at night
dentista, m-f—dentist
dentro (de)—within, inside
de nuevo—again
de otra manera—otherwise, (in) another way
de otro modo—otherwise, (in) another way
dependiente, m-f—clerk
deporte, m—sport
deportivo—sporting
de que color—what color
de quien, -es—whose
derecho, -a—right, straight
desconocido, -a—stranger, unknown
descripción, f—description
desde—since, from
desierto, m—desert
despacio—slow, slowly
después (de)—after, later, next, then
detalle, m—detail
de todos modos—anyhow, anyway
detrás (de)—behind, after, back
¡de veras!—really!
de vez en cuando—from time to time
día, m—day
diablo, m—devil
día de descanso, m—day off, day of rest
día de fiesta, m—holiday
diario, m—daily newspaper
diario, -a—daily
diciembre—December
diente, m—tooth
diez—ten
difícil—difficult, hard
dificultad, f—difficulty, trouble
dinero, m—money
dirección, f—direction, address
disgusto, m—argument, disagreement
dispuesto, -a—willing
distrito, m—district
doble—double

doctor, -a—doctor
documento, m—document
dólar, m—dollar
dolor, m—pain, ache
doméstico, -a—domestic
domicilio, m—domicile, abode, home
domingo, m—Sunday
donde—where
droga, f—drug
dueño, -a—owner
dulce, m—candy, sweet
durante—during
duro, -a—hard, difficult (slang)

E

ébano, m—ebony
eco, m—echo
edad, f—age
edificio, m—building
educación, f—education
ejemplo, m—example
ejercicio, m—exercise
ejército, m—army
el—the
el año pasado—last year
el año que viene—next year
elección, f—election
el mes pasado—last month
el mes que viene—next month
elote, m—corn (fresh)
embajada, f—embassy
empleado, -a—employee
empleo, m—employment, work
en—in, on, at
en contra de—against
en cuanto—as far as
enemigo, -a—enemy
enero—January
enfermera, f—nurse
enfermo, -a—sick, ill
en frente—in front
enojado, -a—angry, mad
en punto—sharp (on the dot)
en seguida—immediately
entero, -a—whole
entonces—then
entrada, f—entry, entrance
entre—between, among
en vez de—instead of
equipaje, m—baggage
esa—that

escopeta, f—shotgun
escuela, f—school
ese—that
eso—that (neuter)
esos, -as—those
espalda, f—back (of body)
español, m—Spanish (language)
español, -a—Spanish, Spaniard
esperanza, f—hope
espía, m-f—spy
espinaca, f—spinach
esposa, f—wife
esposo, m—husband
esquina, f—corner
esta—this
está bien—okay, all right
estación, f—season
estación de, f—. . . . station
estado, m—state, status
Estados Unidos, m—United States
estafeta, f—post office
esta noche—tonight
este—this
este, m—east, orient
estómago, m—stomach
esto—this (neuter)
estos, -as—these
estudiante, m—student
evidencia, f—evidence
examen, m—test, examination
excitado, -a—excited
excusado, m—restroom, toilet
extranjero, -a—stranger, alien,
    foreigner

F

fábrica, f—factory
fácil—easy
facilmente—easily
faja, f—belt, girdle
falda, f—skirt
falso, -a—false
familia, f—family
farmacia, f—pharmacy
fe, f—faith
febrero—February
fecha, f—date
fe de bautismo, f—baptismal certifi-
    cate
federal—federal
feliz—happy

feo, -a—ugly
ferrocarril, m—railroad
fianza, f—bail, bond
fichera, f—B-girl, hostess (slang)
fiesta, f—fiesta, party
filoso, -a—sharp
flaco, -a—skinny, thin, lean, slender
flojo, -a—loose, lazy (slang)
fondo, m—bottom, slip
forma, f—form
francés, -a—French
franco, -a—frank, off duty
frazada, f—blanket
freno, m—brake, bridle
frente, f—forehead
frijol, m—bean
frío, m—cold
frío, -a—cold
frontera, f—border
fuego, m—fire
fuera—out, outside
funda, f—holster, pillow case
furgón, m—boxcar
fusil, m—rifle

G

gallina, f—hen, chicken
gallo, m—rooster, cock
ganado, m—cattle, herd, livestock
ganancia, f—gain, earning
garage, m—garage
garita, f—sentry box, entrance gate,
  port of entry (slang)
garantía, f—guarantee
gastos, m—expenses
gato, -a—cat
gavilán, m—hawk
generalmente—generally, usually
gente, f—people
gobierno, m—government
gorra, f—cap
grande—large, big
granero, m—granary
gris—gray
grupo, m—group
guajalote, m—turkey
guante, m—glove
guapo, -a—handsome
guardavacas, m—cattleguard
guerra, f—war
guerra mundial, f—world war

H

había—there was, there were
¿había?—was there?, were there?
hace—ago
hacendado, m—farmer
hacia—toward
hacienda, f—farm
hacha, f (el)—axe
hambre, f (el)—hunger
hasta—until, as far as, up to, to
hay—there is, there are
¿hay?—is there?, are there?
hermana, f—sister
hermano, m—brother
hermoso, -a—beautiful
herradura, f—horseshoe
herramienta(s), f—tools
herrero, m—blacksmith
hierba, f—weed, herb
hija, f—daughter
hijastro, -a—stepchild
hijo, m—son
hijo, -a ilegítimo, -a—illegitimate
  child
hijo, -a natural—illegitimate child
hilo, m—thread, string
hogar, m—home
hola—hello
hombre, m—man
hombro, m—shoulder
honda, f—sling, wave
hondo, -a—deep
honesto, -a—honest
hora, f—hour, time
hotel, m—hotel
hoy—today
hoy día—nowadays
hoyo, m—hole
huarache, m—sandal
huelga, f—strike
huella, f—track, print, impression
huellas de los dedos, f—fingerprints
huellas digitales, f—fingerprints
huero, -a—blonde
hueso, m—bone
huésped, m—guest, host
huéspeda, f—guest, hostess
huevo, m—egg
hule, m—rubber
huracán, m—hurricane

I

idéntico, -a—identical
identificación, f—identification
iglesia, f—church
igual—same
ilegal—illegal
ilegalmente—illegally
importante—important
imposible—impossible
impresión, f—impression
incidente, m—incident
inglés, m—English, Englishman
inglés, -a—English
injusto, -a—unjust
inmigración, f—immigration
inocente—innocent
inspector, m—inspector
inteligente—intelligent
internacional—international
intestino, m—intestine
íntimo, -a—intimate
investigación, f—investigation
invierno, m—winter
izquierdo, -a—left

J

jamás—never
jamón, m—ham
jefe, m—chief, boss, leader
jornalero, m—day-laborer, manual
  laborer
joven, m-f—young person
joven—young
joyas, f—jewels, jewelry
joyería, f—jewelry shop
joyero, m—jeweler
jueves, m—Thursday
juez, m—judge
juicio, m—trial
julio—July
junio—June
junta, f—meeting
junto(s), -a(s)—together
jurado, m—jury
juramento, m—oath
justicia, f—justice
justo, -a—just, upright

L

la, -s—the
labio, m—lip

labor, f—field, work
lado, m—side
ladrillo, m—brick
ladrón, m—thief, robber
lana, f—wool
lancha, f—launch, boat, barge
lápiz, m—pencil
largo, -a—long
la semana pasada—last week
la semana que viene—next week
lástima—shame, pity
lavandera, f—laundress, washerwoman
lazo, m—lasso, lariat
leche, f—milk
lechería, f—dairy, dairy farm
lechero, m—milkman
legal—legal
legalmente—legally
legumbre, f—vegetable
lejos—far
lengua, f—tongue
lentes, m—eyeglasses
leña, f—firewood
ley, f—law
libertad, f—freedom, liberty
libra, f—pound
libre—free
licencia, f—license
líder, m—leader
liebre, f—jackrabbit
lima, f—lime, file
límite, m—limit
limón, m—lemon
limpio, -a—clean
lindo, -a—pretty, cute
línea, f—line
listo, -a—ready
local—local
loco, -a—mad, crazy
lodo, m—mud
loma, f—hill
lo más pronto posible—as soon as
  possible
lo que—that which, what
luego—then, next
luego que—as soon as
lugar, m—place, location
lumbre, f—fire
luna, f—moon
lunar, m—mole
lunes, m—Monday

luz, f—light
luz de mano, f—flashlight

LL

llama, f—flame
llano, m—level ground
llanta, f—tire
llave, f—key
llegada, f—arrival
lleno, -a—full
llorón, -a—crybaby
lluvia, f—rain

M

madrastra, f—stepmother
madre, f—mother
madrina, f—godmother
madrugada, f—dawn, wee hours of
  the morning, early morning
maestro, -a—teacher
maíz, m—corn (dry), maize
mal—badly
maleta, f—suitcase
malo, -a—bad, sick, ill, mean
mamá, f—mamma, mom, mother
manera, f—manner, fashion, way
mano, f—hand
mantequilla, f—butter
manzana, f—apple, block (city)
mañana—tomorrow
mañana, f—morning
mapa, m—map
máquina, f—machine
maquinaria, f—machinery
maquinista, m-f—machinist
mar, m—sea
marca, f—mark, sign
margen, m—margin
marido, m—husband
marijuana, f—marijuana
marinero, m—sailor
marrano, -a—hog, pig
martes, m—Tuesday
marzo—March
más—more
mas—but
masa, f—dough
más tarde—later
mayo—May
mayor, m—older, oldest

mayordomo, m—foreman
mecánico, m—mechanic
medalla, f—medal, medallion
media, f—hose, stocking
medianoche, f—midnight
médico, m—doctor
medio, -a—half
mediodía, m—noon, midday
mejilla, f—cheek
mejor—better, best
mendigo, m—beggar
menos—less, minus, except
mentira, f—lie
mercado, m—market, market place
mero, -a (slang)—real
mes, m—month
mesa, f—table
metal, m—metal
método, m—method
mexicano, -a—Mexican
miembro, -a—member
mientras—while
miércoles, m—Wednesday
migra (slang), f—Border Patrol
milagro, m—miracle
milpa, f—cornfield, maize field
milla, f—mile
mina, f—mine
minero, m—miner
minuto, m—minute
mirada, f—glance
misa, f—mass (church)
mismo, -a—same
mochila, f—knapsack, bedroll
mocho, -a—maimed, mutilated
moda, f—fashion, mode, custom
modo, m—method, manner
moho, m—rust, moss, mold
mojado, -a—wet, wetback (slang)
molino de viento, m—windmill
moneda, f—money
montaña, f—mountain
monte, m—high brush, mountain
moreno, -a—brunette, swarthy, dark
mosca, f—fly
mosquito, m—mosquito
mostaza, f—mustard
motivo, m—motive
motor, m—motor
mozo, m—bus boy, young chap, lad
muchacha, f—girl
muchacho, m—boy

mucho, -a—much, a great deal of, a lot of, too much
muchos, -as—many, too many
muebles, m—furniture
muerte, f—death
muerto, -a—dead
muestra, f—sample
mujer, f—woman
mujer de pie, f—mistress
mula, f—mule
muleta, f—crutch
munición(es), f—ammunition
municipio, m—municipality
mundo, m—world
muñeca, f—wrist, doll
música, f—music
músico, m—musician
muy—very

N

nacimiento, m—birth
nación, f—nation
nacional—national
nacionalidad, f—nationality
nada—nothing, anything
nada más—just, only
nadie—nobody, no one, anyone, anybody
nana, f—governess, child's nurse
naranja, f—orange
naranjo, m—orange tree
narcótico, m—narcotic
nariz, f—nose
nativo, -a—native
navaja, f—knife, penknife, pocket-knife
Navidad, f—Christmas
necesario, -a—necessary
negocio, m—business
negro, -a—black
nervioso, -a—nervous
ni—neither, nor
nieto, -a—grandchild
nieve, f—snow
ningún(o)-a—none, not any
niño, -a—child
no—no, not
noche, f—night
Nochebuena, f—Christmas Eve
no más—just, only
nombre, m—name
nombre de pila, m—Christian name

noria, f—well
norte, m—north
noticia(s), f—news, notice
noveno, -a—ninth
novicio, -a—novice, trainee
noviembre—November
novio, -a—sweetheart
nuera, f—daughter-in-law
nueve—nine
nuevo, -a—new
número, m—number
nunca—never, not ever

O

obrero, m—worker
o(b)scuro, -a—dark
octavo, -a—eighth
octubre—October
ocupación, f—occupation
ocupado, -a—occupied, busy
ocho—eight
odio, m—hate
oeste, m—west
ofensa, f—offense
oferta, f—offer
oficial, m—officer, official
oficina, f—office
oído, m—(inner) ear
ojalá—God grant
ojo, m—eye
ola, f—wave
ómnibus, m—bus
opio, m—opium
oportunidad, f—opportunity
opuesto, -a—opposite, opposed
oración, f—sentence, prayer
orden, f—order, mandate
oreja, f—(outer) ear
organización, f—organization
oriental—oriental, eastern
oriente, m—orient, east
origen, m—origin
original—original
orilla, f—border, margin, shore, bank
oro, m—gold
oso, -a—bear
otoño, m—autumn, fall
otra vez—again
otro, -a—another, other
oveja, f—sheep, ewe

P

padrastro, m—stepfather
padre, m—father, priest
padrino, m—godfather
página, f—page
país, m—country
paisano, m—fellow countryman
paja, f—straw
pájaro, m—bird
palabra, f—word
paloma, f—dove
pan, m—bread
panadería, f—bakery
panadero, m—baker
pantalones, m—trousers, pants
panza, f—belly
panzón, -a—large bellied, big belly
pañuelo, m—handkerchief
Papa, m—Pope
papá, m—dad, father
papa, f—potato
papalote, m—windmill, kite
papel, m—paper
paquete, m—package
para—in order (to), for, by, to
para que—what for
pared, f—wall
pariente, -ta—relative
párpado, m—eyelid
parque, m—ammunition, park
partera, f—midwife
pasado mañana—day after tomorrow
pasaje, m—passage, fare
pasaje de ida y vuelta, m—round
　trip fare
pasaje redondo, m—round trip fare
pasaporte, m—passport
paso, m—step, pass
pastel, m—cake
patituerto, -a—deformed (leg)
patizambo, -a—bow-legged
pato, -a—duck
patria, f—homeland
patrón, -a—boss, chief
patrullero, m—patrol inspector
pecho, m—chest
pelea, f—fight
película, f—film (movie)
peligro, m—danger
peligroso, -a—dangerous
pelo, m—hair

pelota, f—ball
peluca, f—wig
peluquería, f—barber shop
peluquero, m—barber
peor—worse
pequeño, -a—small, little
pera, f—pear
perezoso, -a—lazy
periódico, m—newspaper
permanente—permanent
permiso, m—permit, permission
pero—but
perro, -a—dog
persona, f—person
pesado, -a—heavy
pesca, f—fishing
pescado, m—fish
pescador, m—fisherman
pescuezo, m—neck
peseta, f—quarter (coin)
peso, m—Mexican dollar
pestaña, f—eyelash
petaca, f—trunk
pez, m—fish
pícaro, -a—rascal, rogue
pie, m—foot
piel, f—skin, hide
pierna, f—leg
pila, f—battery, holy-water basin
piloto, m—pilot
pintor, -a—painter
piso, m—floor
pista, f—trail
pistola, f—pistol
pizarra, f—blackboard
pizarrón, m—blackboard
pizca, f—harvest season, picking
　season
pizcador, m—picker
placa, f—badge, license plate
planta, f—plant
plata, f—silver
plato, m—plate
plaza, f—plaza, square
pleito, m—fist fight
plomero, m—plumber
plomo, m—lead
pluma, f—pen
pobre—poor
poco, -a—little (amount)
pocos, -as—few
policía, m—policeman

policía, f—police force
pollo, m—fryer (chicken)
poniente, m—west
por—for, through, by
por dondequiera—everywhere
por eso—for that reason, therefore, that's why, so
por favor—please
por fin—finally, at last
por fuera—on the outside
porque—because
por que—why
por supuesto—of course
portamonedas, m—billfold
portero, m—porter
por todas partes—everywhere
posible—possible
potrero, m—pasture, meadow
pozo, m—hole, well
precio, m—price
preciso, -a—precise, necessary
pregunta, f—question
presa, f—dam
presencia, f—presence
presente—present
preso, -a—prisoner
primavera, f—spring
primer nombre, m—first name, given name
primer(o), -a—first
primo, -a—cousin
prisión, f—prison
prisionero, -a—prisoner
problema, m—problem
proceso, m—process
producto, m—product
profesor, -a—professor
promesa, f—promise
prontito—quickly, right away
pronto—quick, soon, right away
propiedad, f—property
propósito, m—purpose
prostitución, f—prostitution
prostituta, f—prostitute
próximo, -a—next
prueba, f—proof, test
pueblo, m—town
puente, m—bridge
puerco, m—pork, pig
puerta, f—door
puerto, m—port, harbor

puerto de entrada, m—port of entry (sea)
pues—well
puesto, m—stand, stall
pulgada, f—inch
pulgar, m—thumb
pulmón, m—lung
pulsera, f—bracelet
pulso, m—pulse, wrist
puntual—punctual
puro, -a—pure
puro, m—cigar

Q

que—that, who, than
¿qué?—what?
queja, f—complaint
quemada, f—burn, burn scar
queso, m—cheese
querida, f—mistress
quien, -es—who, whom
quijada, f—jaw
quincena, f—fortnight
quinto, -a—fifth
quizá(s)—maybe, perhaps

R

rábano, m—radish
radio, m-f—radio
ranchero, m—rancher, farmer
rancho, m—farm, ranch
rápido, -a—rapid, fast
raro, -a—rare
rata, f—rat
ratero, -a—thief, robber
ratito, m—very short time (slang)
rato, m—short time
ratón, m—mouse
raza, f—race
razón, f—reason
real—real
reata, f—rope, riata, lariat
recámara, f—bedroom
recibo, m—receipt
record, m—record
regalo, m—present, gift
reloj, m—clock, watch
relojero, m—watchmaker
remo, m—oar
rengo, -a—cripple, lame

renta, f—rent
repaso, m—review
repollo, m—cabbage
reporte, m—report
res, f—beef, steer
respeto, m—respect
respuesta, f—answer, response
restaurante, m—restaurant
retrato, m—picture
reunión, f—reunion
revista, f—magazine
revólver, m—revolver
rico, -a—rich
rifle, m—rifle
río, m—river
rincón, m—corner, nook
riñón, m—kidney
rodilla, f—knee
rojo, -a—red
ropa, f—clothes, clothing
ropa interior, f—underwear
rosa, f—rose
rótulo, m—sign
rubio, -a—blonde
ruido, m—noise
rumbo, m—way, direction, route

S

sábado, m—Saturday
sabiduría, f—knowledge
sabotaje, m—sabotage
sacerdote, m—priest
saco, m—coat
sal, f—salt
sala, f—living room
sala de espera, f—waiting room
salario, m—salary
salchicha, f—wiener, sausage
salida, f—departure, exit
salud, f—health
salvaje—wild
san, m—saint
sandalia, f—slipper, sandal
santo, -a—saint
sartén, f—frying pan
sastre, m—tailor
seco, -a—dry
secretario, -a—secretary
seda, f—silk
según—according to
segundo, -a—second

seguro, -a—sure, certain, safe
seguro que sí—sure, of course
seis—six
semana, f—week
senda, f—path, footpath
sendero, m—path, trail
sentencia, f—sentence
seña, f—sign, mark
señor, m—Mr., sir, man
señora, f—Mrs., woman, lady
señorita, f—Miss, lady (unmarried)
septiembre—September
séptimo, -a—seventh
servicio, m—service, restroom, toilet
sexto, -a—sixth
sí—yes
si—if
siempre—always
siempre que—provided (that)
si es así—if so, if that is so
siete—seven
siglo, m—century
signo, m—sign, mark
siguiente—following, next
silvestre—wild
silla, f—chair
sin—without
sin embargo—nevertheless
sino—but, only
sirvienta, f—servant, housemaid
sitio, m—place, location, site
sobre, m—envelope
sobre—on, upon
sobrenombre, m—nickname, alias
sobretodo, m—overcoat
sobrina, f—niece
sobrino, m—nephew
soga, f—rope, riata, lariat
sol, m—sun
soldado, m—soldier
solo—alone
sólo—only
soltero, -a—single
sombrero, m—hat
sordo, -a—deaf
sospechoso, -a—suspicious
suave—soft
sucio, -a—dirty
suegra, f—mother-in-law
suegro, m—father-in-law
sujeto, m—subject

sueldo, m—salary, wages
suelo, m—floor, ground
suerte, f—luck
suéter, m—sweater
suficiente—sufficient, enough
sur, m—south

T

tabaco, m—tobacco
tahur, m—gambler
tal—such
talabartero, m—leather worker,
  beltmaker
talón, m—stub, heel
tal vez—perhaps
taller, m—shop
tamaño, m—size
también—also, too, likewise, as well
tampoco—either, neither
tan—as, so
tan pronto como—as soon as
tanque, m—tank, waterhole
tanto, -a—as much, so much
tantos, -as—as many, so much
tarde, f—afternoon, evening
tarde—late
tarea, f—homework, task
tarjeta, f—card
taxi, m—taxi
taza, f—cup
té, m—tea
teatro, m—theater
techo, m—roof
teléfono, m—telephone
televisión, f—television
televisor, m—television set
temprano—early
tenedor de libros, m—bookkeeper
tequila, m—tequila
tercer(o), -a—third
territorio, m—territory
terreno, m—territory, land
terrible—terrible
testigo, -a—witness
testimonio, m—testimony
tez, f—complexion
tía, f—aunt
tibio, -a—warm
tiempo, m—time, weather
tienda, f—store
tierra, f—earth, native country,
  land, soil

tinta, f—ink
tío, m—uncle
tiro, m—shot
título, m—title
tiza, f—chalk
tobillo, m—ankle
tocante a—about, concerning
tocayo, -a—namesake
tocino, m—bacon
todavía—still, yet
todavía no—not yet
todo, -a—all, everything
todo el mundo—everybody
todos, -as—everybody, all
tomate, m—tomato
tormenta, f—storm
toro, m—bull
trabajador, -a—worker, employee
trabajo, m—work, employment, job
tractor, m—tractor
tractorista, m—tractor driver
traidor, -a—traitor
traje, m—suit
traje de baño, m—swimsuit
tranvía, m—street car, trolley
tren, m—train
tren de carga, m—freight train
tres—three
trigo, m—wheat
trigueño, -a—swarthy, dark
tripa, f—gut, intestine
trique, m (slang)—personal belonging, personal item
triste—sad
troca, f (slang)—truck
troque, m (slang)—truck
troquero, m (slang)—truck driver
tuerto, -a—one-eyed
turista, m-f—tourist

U

últimamente—lately
último, -a—last
un, -a—a, an, one
único, -a—only
uniforme, m—uniform
universidad, f—university
unos, -as—few, some
unos, -as cuantos, -as—a few
unos, -as pocos, -as—a few
uña, f—fingernail, toenail

útil—useful
uva, f—grape

V

vaca, f—cow
vacaciones, f—vacation
vagón, m—wagon
válido, -a—valid
valiente—brave
vamos a ver—let's see
vapor, m—ship, steam
vaquero, m—cowboy
vara, f—twig, pole, rod
varios, -as—several, various
vaso, m—(drinking) glass, tumbler
vecindad, f—neighborhood
vecino, -a—neighbor
veliz, m—valise, suitcase
venado, m—deer
ventana, f—window
verano, m—summer
verdad, f—truth, true
¿verdad?—right?
verde—green
verdura, f—vegetable
vereda, f—trail, path
vestido, m—dress
vez, f—time
vía, f—way, route, railroad track
viaje, m—trip, journey
vida, f—life
vidrio, m—glass
viejo, -a—old

viento, m—wind
viernes, m—Friday
villa, f—village, country house
vino, m—wine
violencia, f—violence
visa, f—visa
visible—visible
visita, f—visit
vista, f—sight, view
viuda, f—widow
viudo, m—widower
voluntariamente—voluntarily
voluntario, -a—volunteer, voluntary

Y

y—and
ya—already
ya mero—almost
ya no—no more, not anymore,
   no longer
yarda, f—yard
yegua, f—mare
yerba, f—weed, herb
yerno, m—son-in-law

Z

zancudo, m—mosquito
zapatería, f—shoe shop
zapatero, m—cobbler
zapato, m—shoe
zorillo, -a—skunk
zorro, -a—fox